Making Change

Making Change

YOUTH SOCIAL ENTREPRENEURSHIP AS AN APPROACH TO POSITIVE YOUTH AND COMMUNITY DEVELOPMENT

Tina P. Kruse

MACALESTER COLLEGE
ST. PAUL, MINNESOTA
USA

OXFORD
UNIVERSITY PRESS

Oxford University Press is a department of the University of Oxford. It furthers
the University's objective of excellence in research, scholarship, and education
by publishing worldwide. Oxford is a registered trade mark of Oxford University
Press in the UK and certain other countries.

Published in the United States of America by Oxford University Press
198 Madison Avenue, New York, NY 10016, United States of America.

Library of Congress Cataloging-in-Publication Data
Names: Kruse, Tina (Tina P.), 1972– author.
Title: Making change : youth social entrepreneurship as an approach to
positive youth and community development / Tina P. Kruse.
Description: New York, NY : Oxford University Press, [2019] |
Series: Social justice and youth community practice series |
Includes bibliographical references and index.
Identifiers: LCCN 2018037358 (print) | LCCN 2018053037 (ebook) |
ISBN 9780190849801 (updf) | ISBN 9780190849818 (epub) |
ISBN 9780190849825 (Online Component) | ISBN 9780190849795 (paperback)
Subjects: LCSH: Social entrepreneurship–United States. | Youth with social
disabilities–Employment–United States. | Young adult–owned business
enterprises–United States. | Community development–United States.
Classification: LCC HD60.5.U5 (ebook) | LCC HD60.5.U5 K78 2019 (print) |
DDC 362.7068/4–dc23
LC record available at https://lccn.loc.gov/2018037358

9 8 7 6 5 4 3 2 1

Printed by WebCom, Inc., Canada

Dedicated to Sister Jean Thuerauf (1931–2016) and all who have a vision
for the potential of youth and community where others only see problems.

If I were to wish for anything,
I should not wish for wealth and power,
but for the passionate sense of the potential,
for the eye which, ever young and ardent,
sees the possible.

—Søren Kierkegaard

CONTENTS

SECTION I **The Context for Youth Social Entrepreneurship**

SECTION II **Youth Social Entrepreneurship's Potential for All Youth**

SECTION III **Youth Social Entrepreneurship's Role in Social Justice**

SECTION IV **Entrepreneurship, Employment, and Youth Social Entrepreneurship**

SECTION V **Addressing the Larger Social Good**

ACKNOWLEDGMENTS

With immeasurable gratitude, I would like to acknowledge here the many people who helped transform this book from possibility to reality. First and foremost, Dr. Melvin Delgado whose inspiring 2004 text on this topic set the wheels of my mind turning and instilled a deep desire to help carry the story of youth social entrepreneurship evermore forward. His guidance, insight, and persistent enthusiasm for this book is reflected in every page. I hope the words within will do justice to the generous mentorship he has provided. Much thankfulness, as well, to Dana Bliss, and all the staff at Oxford University Press who shepherded this project to its completion with thoughtfulness and encouragement.

Central to this book are the stories and lives of the youth and the youth workers who engage every day in efforts to better their communities, their lives, and our society. My singular goal has been to amplify their wisdom by connecting it to research, theory, and policy and projecting it to a broader audience. For this reason, very special thanks goes to Marit Michels and the Cookie Cart staff; Yasameen Sajady, Khadra Fiqi, Zikriyat Adem, Ashley Taylor, and the Sisterhood Boutique staff; Caitlin Gibb and Tanisha Wakumi Douglas of SOUL Sisters Leadership Collective; Roberto Rivera; and Jeneen Hartley; and special thanks to Peg Thomas and Nancy Jacobs of Sundance Family Foundation for supporting youth social entrepreneurship and countless youth.

As a lifelong learner who has the privilege of teaching what I learn, I also thank my many students who have contributed to this book in a variety of ways. Of particular note, I'd like to acknowledge Leah Krieble, my former student and continuing friend, who willingly explored youth social entrepreneurship ideas with me at the start, middle, and last moments of this book, as well as whose energetic commitment to youth became a pilot social enterprise featured herein. Gratitude as well goes to former student Omar Leal who puts the youth development ideas into practice at every turn, tells it like it is with and about the youth, and has taught me as much about identity development as any "expert." Also, let me include a special acknowledgment to former student Cecilia Martinez-Miranda, who came to me to inquire about this "youth social entrepreneurship" model she couldn't quite find enough scholarship on. Without your query, this book wouldn't be. Curiosity pays dividends.

And with all my heart, thanks to my family and friends who have been supportive and enthusiastic during this endeavor. To my children—Maddie, Ethan, and Chloe—who patiently permitted me "writing time," and my husband Bill who always sees possibilities in me, even when I don't: thank you.

INTRODUCTION

> We decided that instead of waiting for someone to give us an opportunity, we'd make one ourselves.
>
> —15-YEAR-OLD WHO HELPED START "SISTERHOOD BOUTIQUE," A
> CONSIGNMENT SHOP IN MINNEAPOLIS RUN BY YOUNG WOMEN OF
> EAST AFRICAN DESCENT

In 2014, a small group of adolescent females opened a store to sell second-hand clothing. They had seen how some teen boys who lived in the same neighborhood had successfully begun a coffee shop in recent years. "We felt like there were not a lot of activities for girls in the community," remembers one of the store's founders, "So we had a meeting of girls to talk about what we wanted to do. There's a strength in girls and we wanted to do something for our community to create more opportunity" (Wallsjasper, 2014, p. 2). They partnered with a local college whose students helped them write a business plan and gain funding. Their community center provided leadership training and helped secure a storefront. Neighbors gained a place to sell and purchase clothing that is near to their homes and sensitive to the environment in their reuse. They called the project "the Sisterhood of the Traveling Scarf" (a reference to the young-adult novel and film "The Sisterhood of the Traveling Pants") as a nod to the traditional Muslim clothing items they sold, such as head scarves. Their store manager sums it up: "This project really is young people taking the initiative by responding to what the community needs" (Wallsjasper, 2014, p. 3). Four years later, the project continues to thrive: the store now known as "Sisterhood Boutique" is open and sustainable, the young women continue to have employment experiences there, and the community continues to benefit by their presence.

There are many paths these youth and this neighborhood could have taken to elicit similar outcomes *other than* the one they chose. The distinct fields of youth development, community development, and entrepreneurship offer some typical possibilities. They might have gained leadership skills as summer camp counselors. Perhaps they might have learned to write a business plan in a school-based entrepreneurship class. They might have affected the vibrancy of their neighborhood by serving on an advisory council as youth representatives. Many other types of more traditional, commonplace youth development applications would have been possible. However, none of these paths would likely, individually or in combination, result in the dynamic outcome of a functioning social enterprise led by youth themselves with their community in mind. One expects that the effects on the youth themselves and the surrounding community members exceed those of the single-variable paths. Furthermore, because this example involves youth in an economically and politically marginalized community—recent immigrant and refugee populations—the potential of the approach is of particular importance. When well-implemented, it strives to disrupt the patterns of powerlessness by giving youth a sense of agency over outcomes. The persistent, deleterious gap in opportunity for marginalized youth is weakened, if only by a degree.

Just as the effects are complex, so is conceptualizing the model undertaken by the Sisterhood Boutique, as well as studying it, measuring it, or replicating it. Instead, this example, which has come to be known as "youth social entrepreneurship," sits at the intersection of multiple areas of research and practice, drawing from the established fields of positive youth development, social entrepreneurship, and community engagement. The scholarship on this highly specific niche is minimal, and the practical documentation is slim. Yet there are rich resources coming from each of the contributing, foundational fields that undergird the youth social entrepreneurship model. Therefore, a necessary step toward shaping and growing youth social entrepreneurship as an approach to socially just youth development is to gather all the threads from their various disciplinary sources and weave them together into a cohesive fabric—one that potentially can support future aims of programmatic evaluation, analysis, scaling, and adoption, one that allows the participants to pull themselves into new environments and experiences of their choosing. This books aims to do just that.

To begin, I offer a working conceptualization that blends aspects of positive youth development, community development, and social entrepreneurship (Figure I.1). While these factors are salient to varying degrees in the diverse practices of youth social entrepreneurship, each must exist in order for any program to be using this model. The ambiguous blending that entails is explored in Chapter 3 of this volume.

The establishment of youth social entrepreneurship as an independent approach is aptly timed in recent history. Over the past half-century the field of youth development has successfully altered perceptions about how the social sector should engage youth in a number of key ways. First, the movement toward positive approaches has shaped a belief in the high potential of each and every youth, as well as an assumption that effective engagement must begin "where the youth is," in their development not where the youth worker believes they should be (Hamilton & Hamilton, 2004). This outlook further asserts that risk behaviors are linked to a lack of protective factors, many of which can be bolstered through community resources and experiences offered to the youth. The asset-focus offered by positive youth development ultimately places the attention on the strengths of the youth, not their perceived or demonstrated deficiencies (Lerner et al., 2009).

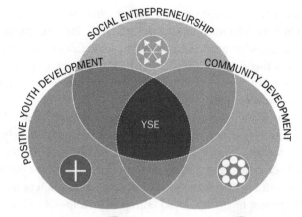

Positive Youth Development

Intentional efforts to engage youth in building developmental assets. Focus is on positive programmatic activities, social emotional skill development, and intergenerational relationships to promote well-being.

Social Entrepreneurship

An approach by individuals and groups creating new economic enterprise opportunities with an emphasis on social good as one of the most important value propositions.

Community Development

A process in which community members take collective action and generate solutions to common problems.

FIGURE I.1 Interdisciplinary Foundations of Youth Social Entrepreneurship (YSE).

Reproduced with the permission of the Sundance Family Foundation

Culture is included in this strength-based perspective, thus resulting in more culturally relevant and responsive models of youth work.

Next, researchers and practitioners in the field have shifted the locus of responsibility for youth development to a broad collection of participants. Now, not only are parents, teachers, and social professionals seen as critical in the healthy development of a community's youth, but the larger community itself, including the business sector, community institutions, and neighbors (Benson, 1997). Third, a significant change that has altered the course of youth development work is the importance of authentic youth engagement. Effective youth approaches must incorporate youth leadership and authentically meaningful contribution (Pittman, 1999; 2016).

The next wave of change in positive youth development must include attention to the broader systems in which disparity for youth well-being exists. Increased understanding of the "opportunity gap" is needed to explain and address the imperative of educational equity, in contrast to the outcome-oriented "achievement gap" (Carter, Welner, & Ladson-Billings, 2013). The gap in opportunities is extensive, and decades of research now exists to document both its types and effects, all of which are related to socioeconomic disparity. Furthermore, since the trends of unemployment rates are disproportionately higher for all individuals of color in the United States (Economic Policy Institute, 2015), the orientation must be to intervene with approaches particularly useful to youth from communities of need. The work of asset theorists suggests further that empowering approaches garner uniquely heightened positive effects, particularly for members of impoverished communities (Sherraden, 1992).

Simultaneous to these paradigm shifts in the field of youth development are recent movements in the work of community changemakers. Namely, the rise of "social entrepreneurship" as a concept has unleashed numerous efforts to recognize the capacity of individuals or small groups of citizens to drive social change in ways top-down, institutional models have not. The intersection of these spaces—positive youth development and social entrepreneurship—presents a conceptually potent antidote to some of the opportunity gaps most hindering youth whose lives have disadvantaged them to reaching their own personal potential. While the scholarship on this unique interconnection is in its infancy, the practice has been well under way and many positive results are identified by stakeholders.

This book draws on examples from the field to illuminate the theoretical framework throughout. The goal is to provide the reader with both a solid conceptual foundation on which to situate youth social entrepreneurship in the landscape of social change, fed by fields of youth development and social entrepreneurship, and with a rich menu of examples to illustrate the concepts and enable action for those who hope to pursue the path.

Put simply, youth social entrepreneurship is an application of principles from three main disciplines: youth work (youth development), social change (community development), and social entrepreneurship. This book explores that intersection, clarifying the key overlaps as spaces for powerful, positive youth and community change and asserts steps and structures to support its practice. Though youth social entrepreneurship sits at the intersection of multiple disciplines, practice demonstrates that it exists as an independent approach, deserving of the empirical, practical, and financial support afforded other youth initiatives. Given the conditions of economic and educational systems in the United States, the practice of youth social entrepreneurship holds particular promise for positive outcomes for youth in disenfranchised communities. In this way, the evolution of youth social entrepreneurship is a matter of social justice. It is hoped that the current abundant interest and energy around youth social entrepreneurship will be aided by the context, terminology, and framework offered in this volume.

Who Should Read This Book?

While I hope this book will be read widely by a general audience who are drawn to learn more about youth development and social justice and to put ideas into action, the likely readers will have more targeted purposes.

First, readers with an academic purpose are likely to gain from this book. Namely, graduate students and advanced undergraduates in studies of youth development, community development, and/or social work will find this text to offer a review of concepts melded with out-of-field theory that expands their thinking. The illustrative examples provide images of practice grounded in established theory and emerging research. As a supplement to coursework or an engine for one's independent scholarship, I hope this book serves as source of learning, connecting, and inspiring multidisciplinary ideas about youth development and the nature of social justice.

Second, this book will, I hope, be useful to professionals engaged in the work of youth and community development. Truly, I prepared this book with youth workers in mind, especially those interested in dipping a toe into youth social entrepreneurship endeavors and seeking some guidance to help them begin and, perhaps, sustain. As practitioners are the heart of the youth development field—and scholars are then the takers of the pulse—my intent is that the theory and research herein is meaningful and accessible to professionals at all levels of youth work, to community members, and to the young people engaged in the social enterprises that will improve our world.

Furthermore, researchers, funders, and/or policymakers interested in advancing social justice through youth development and social entrepreneurship will find value in the range of topics included in this book. Intentionally, there is ample coverage of the foundational ideas across the resident disciplines such that a novice to any will find the information accessible. In this way, I hope, this set of readers will grow their comfort in advocating for youth via connections to multiple fields of scholarship.

Regardless of the background of the reader, I hope the book will inspire all to embrace the complexities of effective youth practice, to be comfortable with the "messy" frameworks that yield robust outcomes by acknowledging the multifaceted contexts and parameters of human development in our world today. It is also my hope that this book's attempt at holding still such complexities, even for brief moments, to study and name them will result in a meaningful container into which the practices known as "youth social entrepreneurship" can reside, at least for a time.

This Book's Organization

Through an exploration of key theoretical foundations and numerous, illustrative case examples, this book leads the reader to consider the complex reality of contemporary American youth within their complicated American context and then imagine how the described model of youth social entrepreneurship might interface with those lived experiences, contexts, and communities. The journey includes a wide array of disciplinary twists and turns, offering foundational ideas to the newcomer as well as deepening connections to the well-versed reader. My hope is that each reader will gain new perspectives in the material, whether those are disciplinary, such as a sociologist considering the developmental psychological principles within, or topical, such as an expert in entrepreneurship experiencing ideas from critical pedagogy. The timing for this perspective is ripe: there is a burgeoning willingness among many scholars to reach outside of their spheres of expertise to learn the tools and language of other fields in order to more fully represent knowledge about human development. To wit, noted sociologists McEwen and McEwen (2017) recently published a sociological-biological model to account for intergenerational poverty, asserting that "sociologists have much to gain from learning some of the language and research of biology, developmental psychology, and neuroscience. By doing so, sociologists will not lose their focus on social structures and processes but will instead find their understanding of the mechanisms through which they work significantly enhanced" (p. 471).

Perhaps even more importantly, my hope is that the reader will connect with the text in ways that are not only intellectual but also practical, whether this be a social worker considering youth program design or academic researchers inspired to include a new interdisciplinary perspective, seeking a more well-rounded representation of their subjects. To this end, the book is organized via sections that present building blocks of the described multidisciplinary understanding.

First, Section I reviews a concise summary of the history and working definitions of both social entrepreneurship and youth development. Furthermore, the chapters of Section I outline current problems that I've identified about youth social entrepreneurship as a field of practice and inquiry, coupled with a summary of its potential. Potential is considered via related practices and research areas that can inform our understanding of youth social entrepreneurship. The hope is that this section will bring new questions and open the reader's imagination about the youth social entrepreneurship model, built on some combination of their own previous knowledge and experience or simply on the background content offered in the first chapters.

Next, Section II delves more deeply into the relevant theories within youth development that undergird youth social entrepreneurship in order to describe how this practice can have potency for the healthy development of all youth. The chapters in this section primarily draw from fields of developmental psychology, education, and neuroscience. Drawing on a more "universal" approach to youth development, this second section acknowledges the myriad ways youth social entrepreneurship grows the individual assets of every young person, with little regard to their social identities, position within society, or socioeconomic status. In this way, the theories address youth social entrepreneurship's potential for *all* youth.

Because a decontextualized account of youth development offers an incomplete view, Section III considers youth social entrepreneurship's targeted impact for marginalized and minoritized youth. These chapters address the many systemic injustices affecting youth of color and/or of low socioeconomic status in the United States at this time in history. To depict this reality, I aim to weave together complex, interdisciplinary theories in the hopes of representing most fully the complex experiences of youth and communities. The chapters of this section primarily draw on the fields of social work, sociology, political science, economics, and cultural studies to achieve a multidimensional understanding of the opportunity and expectation gaps facing so many young people and their deep wells of resilience and creativity that they bring to the table when permitted. Given the disparities in power and privilege that exist, this chapter concludes that youth social entrepreneurship may be even more potent for marginalized youth by connecting them to expanded networks of social and economic capital and by facilitating self-empowering practices.

Section IV enables the reader to explore the constituent parts of youth social entrepreneurship as a model; namely, a rudimentary review of the field and practices of entrepreneurship education and youth employment. The chapters in this section focus on the economic elements of youth social entrepreneurship, addressing the similarities and differences between business entrepreneurship and social entrepreneurship as they pertain to youth participation. Basic consideration of social enterprises and the phases of their creation is included, as well as "scaling up" as a concern of many youth social enterprises and the practical concerns of training, assessment, scale, and model fidelity. In addition to clarifying concepts and tracing practical steps, chapters in this section tackle head-on the concerns about capitalism and commerce within youth development to offer some reconciliation of values.

Finally, Section V addresses the many "bigger pictures" of youth social entrepreneurship, such as community development, youth agency and activism, and the global context. These chapters include community-building concepts such as asset mapping, civic capacity, and sustainability, as well as practical examples of community change. This section also reviews how youth social entrepreneurship as a model plays out in places other than the United States, in both developed and developing countries. Also included are emerging trends of research and programmatic developments in the youth social entrepreneurship field. The final chapter includes a focus on advocacy opportunities, such as funding, policy, and education.

A Word About Words

Both because language can be powerful and because language on this topic can be slippery and amorphous, this book commits to carefully defining the important words used in the interdisciplinary facets of youth social entrepreneurship. Thus, the reader will notice details about the terminology, for example, of *achievement* versus *opportunity gaps, social businesses* versus *social enterprises*, and *opportunity youth* versus *disconnected youth*. Furthermore, because terminology is constantly changing and evolving, an attempt is made to place each term within the context of its socio-historic timing.

In particular, the word "youth" is not easily defined. There is not a simple, universally agreed upon definition in any of the fields of scholarship or practice reviewed within this book. Some developmental theorists choose to define the age limits for "youth" as "the second decade of life," meaning ages 10–20 years (Hamilton & Hamilton, 2004). Others select an older subset of youth as 18–30 years, particularly in developing countries. Each of the youth-oriented programs featured herein offer their own widely ranging age-based definitions such as 12–18, 15–18, or 16–24 years. Navigating this amorphous designation of age and identity is challenging. I reconcile this difficulty by including age parameters as they are known, and I encourage the reader to be aware of these distinctions.

The sources of information that inform this book are diverse, some may even say "eclectic." I have purposefully included high-level, peer-reviewed scholarship; private-sector reporting; easy-access periodicals; and popular press readings to represent the inclusive vantage point of the work at hand. To the point, since the very nature of youth development, community development, and social entrepreneurship is egalitarian, the material reflected here is as well! Everyone can and should understand it, contribute to it, and act on it. I hope the readers will find this a useful frame for informing their understanding of the field, which itself includes the esoteric and the banal, the intellectual and the earthy. Just as Jane Addams, considered the founder of the social work profession in America, is said to have asserted: an effective social worker should "have one foot in the library and one foot in the street." Similarly the "knowledge" represented in this volume comes both from the "library" and "the street."

Furthermore, it may be noted that the language used within this book tends to regularly shift from scholarly to simple and straightforward and back again. This vacillation is purposeful as it mirrors the dual nature of the field and as the book aims to be accessible to a diverse audience. That is to say, the shift in "voice" is intentional, not accidental, and I ask readers to be generous in their evaluation of this shift, recognizing the ways in which it may be beneficial to others' perspectives and needs.

A Word About Perspective: Positionality Statement

On the topic of perspectives, availing readers of my perspective and positionality aims to reduce the effects of scholar bias, despite never being able to eliminate it completely. Scholarship and teaching in any field, but especially in the social sciences, can never be value-free (Carr, 2005, p. 347). In particular, qualitative research is subject to a researcher's implicit biases and perspectives on the world via lived experiences.

Qualitative researchers are urged, then, to "actively monitor their role in the production of knowledge, and attempt not to let their views overshadow the participants' perspectives" (Underwood, Satterthwait, & Bartlett, 2010, p. 1586). The act of examining one's scholarship in relation to one's positionality involves reflexivity, a self-conscious awareness of the relationship between the researcher and the objects of the research (i.e., the "other").

Positionality in a textual account, like this one, of the theoretical and lived experiences of youth begs the author to examine herself within the social context of the concepts being described, with the goal of inching closer to "objectivity"; that is, minimizing bias and acknowledging privileged perspectives where they are:

> To achieve a pure objectivism is a naïve quest, and we can never truly divorce ourselves of subjectivity. We can strive to remain objective, but must be ever mindful of our subjectivities. Such is positionality. We have to acknowledge who we are as individuals, and as members of groups, and as resting in and moving within social positions. (Bourke, 2014, p. 7)

Applying reflexive consideration to my own positionality reveals several relevant findings, which the reader might want to know upfront. As a white, heterosexual, cisgender woman, I am afforded many of the advantages the current American society offers. I wield privileges of a middle-class socioeconomic status, advanced education, relatively stable employment, health, and extensive social and cultural capital. I live in the Upper Midwest of the Unites States, but have also resided in the Southeast and Mid-Atlantic East Coast; therefore, my perspectives of region are informed by residence as well as travel. My scholarly views have been heavily influenced by the progressive policies and practices of my home cities, and, professionally and personally, I hold a high value for contextualized, asset-focused approaches to community and individual development. This is a preconception that I admit to carrying into my writing.

Furthermore, my family of origin was working-class and second-generation immigrant, but successful entrepreneurship and good fortune resulted in intragenerational upward mobility for my parents during my childhood. I was the first generation in my family to complete college and then graduate school. In many ways, my lens differs from that of the youth in many of the programs I study. My bias toward education and entrepreneurship as sources of success within society is woven into my story; nonetheless, I strive for as much objectivity as possible in the selection and analysis of material in this book.

Lastly, I acknowledge my concern about the risk of co-opting the stories of youth and practitioners who are acting for social justice in their lives and communities. This is a central fear of engaging in writing this book, an account outside of my own lived experience. I resolve such misgivings in two main ways: (1) by being as transparent as possible about the limits of my perspective and not claiming expertise on the challenges, toil, and successes of others in the field, both to the reader and to the stakeholders of this work; and (2) by outweighing my fear of co-opting with another, greater fear of not leveraging my position to project as loudly as possible the viewpoints and actions of so many socially committed people and programs. So it is with those fears at my side that I weave the following chapters of multidisciplinary research and multisetting case examples with a central goal of advancing the brave and needed progress of youth development and social justice.

A Word About Case Examples

Each section includes narrative about two focal case examples to illustrate the ideas described within. The conceptual groundwork of each chapter will come alive when adjoined to the lived experiences of two distinct programs engaged in youth social entrepreneurship. These appear at the end of each section and contain primary interview data with representatives from the organizations. The overall story of the examples comes, then, in installments that explicitly connect practical experiences with the background concepts of that section. In this way, the focal cases read out as episodes of a story, asking the readers to continue their growing familiarity with the case just as their conceptual mastery has deepened. The purpose is threefold: first, to provide the reader with a field-based, practical application to connect to the overarching topics of each section; second, to explore two different types of youth social entrepreneurship programming, yet observe their similarities; and third, to hold up examples for other youth social entrepreneurs to consider if and how they might follow these leaders. Background information as an introduction to the two cases is provided here, in the Introduction to the book.

Woven throughout the book are shorter case examples meant to explicate a specific point each time. Descriptions of these cases are derived primarily from publicly available sources, such as program websites, reports, and news coverage. These practical examples represent a wide array of youth social entrepreneurship types and locales with the intent of giving readers a sense, too, of the mosaic that is youth social entrepreneurship in the United States. A listing of these programs appears at the end of the book.

Focal Case 1: SOUL Sisters Leadership Collaborative

BACKGROUND AND OVERVIEW

Based in both New York City and Miami, the SOUL (Sisters Organizing for Understanding & Leadership) Sisters Leadership Collaborative (SSLC) is a youth program devoted to interrupting cycles of poverty and injustice. Focal participants are young women of color most affected by disparities in the current economic and justice systems in the United States. They range in age from middle school to high school. The program model stands on four pillars: Leadership Development, Cultural & Social Justice Education, Arts Education, and Personal Healing. SSLC engages "systems-involved girls and femmes of color—black, brown, and indigenous—to interrupt cycles of state violence, poverty, and oppression . . . to support young women who have lived and breathed social inequality to become agents of personal and community transformation" (https://www. soulsistersleadership.org/mission—vision). They also work on a macro level, aiming to disrupt patterns of criminalization and violence by mobilizing all SSLC participants to undertake Social Action Projects and through professional development for staff in schools and community-based organizations, focusing on restorative justice and trauma-informed practices. They are driven by this philosophy:

> As we move towards the alleviation of violence and poverty, it is crucial that we develop female community leaders who have the social awareness to change how vulnerable communities interact with systems. When provided with opportunities and support, these women will help lead community transformation. First, they must be afforded the right to heal. (https://www. soulsistersleadership.org/our-philosophy)

Co-founders Caitlin Gibb and Wakumi Douglas met while working together in Brooklyn, New York, in an alternative-to-incarceration program. Both with advanced social work degrees from Columbia University, they designed SSLC to be a two-city venture that simultaneously practices equity-focused positive youth development and community development in their two regions of the United States. In both Miami and New York City, they partner with a number of agencies to offer the SSLC programs to young women who would benefit most; their partners include juvenile justice organizations, homeless shelters, community centers, and schools.

The programming follows two phases: after the young women are identified through the site partner to participate and form a cohort, they begin Phase One of SSLC, "Leadership." At this point, they learn the "foundations of SOUL Sisters: trust, political education, social justice, healing" (C. Gibbs & W. Douglas, personal communication, 2017). The cohort sizes vary by site, ranging from only 3 to as many as 15 participants. In the second phase, they create and implement a social action project that is issue-focused and engages their leadership skills and social change perspectives. Topics vary, but always include social justice concerns, such as how to break patterns of youth incarceration, also known as the "school-to-prison pipeline."

In 2016, an SSLC social action project piloted a social enterprise—creating and selling their own line of merchandise to reflect their program focus on healing and love. They integrated three separate program groups to contribute to a central, retail enterprise. Their "Youth Leaders Board" helped manage every aspect of the project through monthly meetings, phone calls, and email consultation. The first product of the project were t-shirts designed by the youth and a bag designed with an adult partner from the New York City fashion industry.

Focal Case 2: "Cookie Cart"

BACKGROUND AND OVERVIEW

Cookie Cart has provided thousands of teens with hundreds of thousands of hours of bakery training and employment through a structured program focused on four key areas of youth development: (1) connectedness to new communities, (2) goal orientation, (3) interpersonal and life skills, and (4) critical thinking.

Cookie Cart is aptly named because it started as just that: cookies on an actual rolling cart, baked by neighborhood kids in North Minneapolis. This small, home-grown project was started in the 1980s by a Catholic nun, Sister Jean Thuerauf, who invited disconnected neighborhood youth into her home after school for help with their homework and to bake some cookies. At the time, the surrounding community was plagued by crime, violence, and gang activity. Sister Jean's vision was simple yet powerful: to provide a safe and engaging place for the local youth to be, in their own neighborhood, and to learn some new skills while they were at it. "Kids were just drawn to her," says Cookie Cart's director of development some 40 years later. Many of the first teens to bake with Sister Jean recall their time with her with great fondness: "if she was there, Sister Jean was opening the door [for us] and without fear" (Xiong, 2016).

In 1988, Sister Jean's vision for a safe, secure, creative, and engaging space for North Minneapolis's youth became more formal and was registered as a 501(c) (3) nonprofit named Cookie Cart. Since then, it has grown substantially in the number of youth involved and in the places the program reaches. The first cart Sister Jean gave to kids to sell cookies in is now honored in the current Cookie Cart's building.

Today, Cookie Cart's programming begins with employment as local teens (aged 15–17) apply for a job in the bakery. Once accepted, they progress through an organized system of preparation for their Cookie Cart involvement. The curriculum engages the youth through individual and group learning strategies that complement and enhance their work experience and lead them toward mastery of skills needed to be successful on the job, in their lives outside of Cookie Cart, and in securing, maintaining, and thriving in future employment (Cookie Cart Community Report, 2016). The first part of the training is experiential learning in "The Bakery Program." Through hands-on job training, they gain all the basic job readiness skills for baking in the bakery. Next, they learn the concepts and skills required to provide exceptional customer service, including an extensive exploration of interpersonal communication. Teens who complete this part of the training then begin practicing their new skills at Cookie Cart's front counter, as well as at community events.

The curriculum includes three key phases: Foundations, which sets youth employees up for success in the workplace; Leadership, in which youth discover and practice their individual leadership style; and Bright Futures, which provides the youth with the tools they need for their next jobs. In addition, all Cookie Cart youth complete courses in financial literacy and customer service training.

Focal Cases Summary

Both focal cases illustrate programs with humble beginnings and powerful intentions. While SOUL Sisters aims to mobilize young, often low-income women of color into leadership for social change, Cookie Cart more generally aims to engage low-income youth of color in employment and personal growth. For SOUL Sisters, social entrepreneurship is only one aspect of their overall programming. For Cookie Cart, the program itself is a social enterprise. The young people are central to the leadership of social entrepreneurship at SOUL Sisters, while youth leadership is progressive at Cookie Cart; they gain opportunities for leadership within the enterprise over their time in the program. These case studies embody two different ways that social entrepreneurship blends with intentional youth development practices to effect community change. Their similarities and differences are magnified here to demonstrate the range of models that can be seen as "youth social entrepreneurship."

Making Change

SECTION I

The Context for Youth Social Entrepreneurship

1

Social Entrepreneurship

AN OVERVIEW

> Social entrepreneurs are not content just to give a fish or teach how
> to fish.
> They will not rest until they have revolutionized the fishing industry.
> —BILL DRAYTON, *FOUNDER OF ASHOKA:*
> *INNOVATORS FOR THE PUBLIC*

Introduction

This chapter offers the reader a short history of social entrepreneurship from
which the following discussions of youth-centered social entrepreneurship will
proceed. The intention is to explore the basic concepts and foundational elements
of social entrepreneurship as a whole before differentiating it with youth social
entrepreneurship. The reader who is new to the field of social entrepreneurship
will find appropriate introduction, while readers who are more experienced in this
area will find it to be a review that shapes the explorations of youth social entrepreneurship to come.

What Is Social Entrepreneurship?

Although many definitions of social entrepreneurship exist, a feature common to
all is the disruption of a current condition. Social entrepreneurs innovate to improve the status quo from many different directions and with diverse approaches
but share this feature: they are "building platforms that unleash human potential"
(Bornstein & Davis, 2010, p. xix).

In recent decades, social entrepreneurs have developed innovative business models that blend traditional capitalism with solutions that address the
long-term needs of people and the planet. They tackle chronic social problems,
ranging from healthcare delivery in sub-Saharan Africa to agricultural transformation in East Asia and public school funding in the United States. Social
entrepreneurs are working in close collaboration with local communities,

incubating groundbreaking (and often life-saving) innovations; modeling synergistic partnerships with governments, companies, and traditional charities; and building business models that deploy technology and enable networking to create wins for investors and clients alike. "Social entrepreneurs are mad scientists in the lab," says Pamela Hartigan, director of the Skoll Centre for Social Entrepreneurship at Oxford University. "They're harbingers of new ways of doing business" (Murphy & Sachs, 2013).

Social entrepreneurship is seen as "well-suited for our times" (Dees, 1998) because three key forces are at play: first, government and social institutions are widely viewed by the public as inefficient and ineffective; second, the characteristics of a stereotypical entrepreneur are highly valued in this society—innovative, disciplined, bold; third, the economic gap grows and the residual inequality goes unresolved, causing the attention of the populus to be on solutions and social consciousness. Thus, the rise of social entrepreneurship at this particular moment of human history is not surprising. The allure of making social change is powerful, and successful ventures are well-known and well-celebrated.

Some suggest that the blending of for-profit and not-for-profit strategies constitute a fourth sector of society, one coming after the first sector (public organizations, government), the second sector (for-profit businesses), and the third sector (volunteerism, charities) (Sabeti, 2011). This fourth sector is a space for all social entrepreneurship that results in new enterprises bent on creating a profit, but that in turn benefit a social cause.

The Recent History of Social Entrepreneurship

Bornstein and Davis (2010) point to the evolution of social entrepreneurship in the past three decades. We can think of *social entrepreneurship 1.0* as a movement to identify and connect innovative thinkers with social problems, usually as individuals. An illustrative example is the oft-cited Muhammed Yunas, whose creative and successful model of microcredit loans has helped thousands of people on the way to financial self-sufficiency. At its start in the 1980s, his social entrepreneurial work was heavily challenged by skeptics, yet it has been met with positive results and global acknowledgment (he won the Nobel Peace Prize in 2006).

Social entrepreneurship 2.0 was a paradigm focused on organizations and sustainable business practices. This shape of social entrepreneurship is primarily concerned with applying insights from the fields of finance, management, and traditional entrepreneurship to address social problems. Many professionals with expertise in the business sector were drawn to social entrepreneurship at this time as a way to extend their business skills to contribute solutions toward disparities in society. An illustrative example in this mode is that of TOMS Shoes, in which the One-for-One model emerged. Drawing on a traditional commercial retail approach for shoe sales, this company launched as a social entrepreneurial initiative to donate one pair of shoes in high-poverty communities for every one purchased at regular price. Numerous companies have followed suit, spawning a decade of the "socially responsible" buy one/give one model for a variety of products and services. Furthermore, this wave of social entrepreneurship saw traditional nonprofits drawing more than ever before from traditional business approaches. Developing social enterprises—that is, revenue-generating activities with some level of concern for a social issue—reached a new high. In this period of social entrepreneurship, many currently operating social enterprises were born when they "borrowed" traditional business sector designs for their operation of a business, such as identifying revenue sources, a customer base, products, and financing. An illustrative example is Recyclebank, which operates by offering discounts to members for each time that they document earth-friendly disposal behaviors.

The current paradigm, *social entrepreneurship 3.0*, yields a time for the "change-making potential of all people and their interactions" (Bornstein & Davis, 2010, p. xx). This current wave of social entrepreneurship offers a cultural shift in which every individual has the capacity to be a "disrupter" of social conditions by applying entrepreneurial thinking to the problems that surround them. This perspective is well-captured by the Ashoka model of "Everyone a Changemaker," a goal for the world "where each individual has the freedom, confidence and societal support to address any social problem and drive change" (Ashoka, 2016). While action exists to support widespread social entrepreneurial capacity-building, Ashoka's model does still target "Fellows," individuals selected to advance specific social change projects. Many other lesser known organizations also aim to promote the idea that everyone can and should be a changemaker by supporting young people to lead social change in their own communities. This approach has come to be known as "youth social entrepreneurship." In other words, social entrepreneurship 3.0 has readied the environment for any and all youth to become change agents. The coming chapters will contend that this model is mutually beneficial to the actors and communities and thus represents a significant moment in the evolving history of social entrepreneurship.

Social work scholar and author Melvin Delgado portended this movement in his 2004 book, *Social Youth Entrepreneurship*. This publication forecast the growing body of practice that engaged youth and social change as the twenty-first century began. Its prediction that the research needed to support youth-centered social entrepreneurship would grow has not been fulfilled.

Delgado's notable text opened up the ways we conceptualize youth development in relation to social entrepreneurship and has been utilized by many practitioners and researchers of youth-led social entrepreneurship. In his 2004 book, Delgado helped to expand the school-to-career orientation to include community transformation and a multidisciplinary account of youth social entrepreneurship's potential impact, hoping that his volume would do "at least a small part in helping the field of youth development [to] broaden its realm of influence" (p. 14).

Also significant is the focus of Delgado's 2004 book on "undervalued population groups and communities" (p. 16), noting that productive experiences in social enterprises have "added significance when addressing this nation's marginalized groups"(p. 57). In this way, Delgado has helped shape the perspective of youth social entrepreneurship as a matter of equity and disparity, unlike the majority of youth entrepreneurial scholarship. Says Delgado: "Social entrepreneurship as an intervention strategy lends itself to working with marginalized populations" (p. 108). This view sets the stage well for the discussion within this current volume.

Social Enterprises

Youth social entrepreneurship often, but not always, involves a *social enterprise*. Social enterprises tend to be differentiated from *nonprofits* (often referred to globally as nongovernmental organizations or NGOs), but there are relatively minor distinctions. Both constitute "the social sector" and both are essentially focused on "building the social good, the common good. It could be for-profit, it could be non-profit, it could be a cooperative" (Martin & Osberg, 2007, p. 1).

A primary difference between nonprofits and social enterprises is in their tax status (Chhabra, 2015). Nonprofits are regulated under the US tax code as 501(c)(3) organizations. With this status, nonprofits are able to receive charitable donations, and their donors in turn receive tax-deductions. If a social enterprise is for-profit, this tax advantage is not available to them. If they are part of a larger nonprofit or part of a hybrid for-profit/nonprofit, they may access tax exempt status (Pokrasso, 2016). This structuring is legally complicated and best supported by tax law advisors.

Another significant difference tends to be their revenue model. Nonprofits tend to rely heavily on charitable contributions, public funding, and philanthropic foundations to support their programs and operations. A nonprofit that practices social entrepreneurship through a social enterprise, on the other hand, is somewhat less dependent on donor funds because it includes programs that are meant to be self-sustaining. A social enterprise is thus, first and foremost, a business. It has a steady stream of income, and, just like any other company, it takes loans, invites capital investments, and forms partnerships in order to expand its business activities.

The main goal of a nonprofit organization is to create social value without seeking much or any profit, whereas the social enterprise aims for sustainability in the financial, social, and environmental sense while also striving toward social value creation. Yet, unlike for-profit companies, social enterprises serve their mission first, not their shareholders. The products or services they sell are only a means to an end—to achieve their social mission.

Social enterprises often find benefit in partnering across sectors to achieve their goals. In fact, some see social enterprises as the end product of the public, private, and social sectors meshing into each other, making them the new "fourth sector" of the economy (Didienne, 2016). This fourth sector relies on cross-sector convergence, in which the traditional sectors of business, government, and nonprofits overlap to create a newly defined space. These enterprises use various names: benefit corporations, corporate social responsibility, sustainability, cause-oriented marketing and purchasing, venture philanthropy, social investing, micro-finance, and civic and municipal enterprise.

Predicted to grow further into the next generation of social enterprises, this fourth sector is likely to "grow in proportion to the other three [sectors] as a cadre of socially motivated entrepreneurs, supported by appropriate legal and market structures, create enterprises that combine a social mission with a business engine—and refuse to compromise on either front" (Sabeti, 2011, p. 104). To get there requires individuals who are capable of thinking across typical boundaries, people who can maneuver between the "skillsets, language, and inherent trade-offs of the for-profit and the not-for-profit sectors" (Bulloch, 2014, p. 1). This need pertains to two key groups: experienced social entrepreneurs who are particularly open to cross-sector approaches and younger, up-and-coming social entrepreneurs seeking broader, interconnected means to achieve the innovations they imagine. In this way, *young social entrepreneurs* are often deemed the most likely to facilitate social change in communities as well as in industry.

Given the established belief that those within a system are the best equipped and the best motivated to fix it, youth from economically marginalized backgrounds hold significant promise to advance the fourth sector and foster in-novative, sustainable change in society. This potential, though, is hindered by the gap in opportunity to develop the necessary entrepreneurial competencies and the lack of social capital to bring ideas to fruition, as discussed in later chapters within this book.

Social Entrepreneurship and Capitalism

Concerns about the effects of capitalism, while not new, often revolve around the widening chasm between the "haves" and "have-nots" in society. This is no small social problem, especially at a time in American history when the economic disparities between upper and lower classes is particularly stark, and social class mobility is lower than in previous generations (Reeves, 2017). Does involving marginalized young people in capitalist activities via social enterprises alleviate or perpetuate these injustices?

On this concern, some scholars advocate for reducing capitalism's resultant inequalities by equipping individuals to be change agents through competency building while simultaneously improving the systems that unequally prohibit access to opportunity. Youth social entrepreneurship, then, becomes a crack in the wall that separates haves and have-nots, through which individuals can elevate their own economic realities while simultaneously addressing the social conditions of their communities. Parallel attention to the individual (profit) and the common good (social mission) is the bedrock of the emerging fourth sector. In its ideal form, it contributes to improving the system of capitalism at large by way of "reinventing capitalism" (Kayser & Budinich, 2015, p. 196). The view may be criticized as "Pollyanna-ish," but its interconnection of the individual good with benefits for the larger world—community, society, and physical environment—is in line with current popular appetites for change. A new view of capitalism's role takes shape: not simplistically good or evil, but one that flexibly can connect across sectors to raise all boats, as described in this *Harvard Business Review* description of capitalism's potentially more just future:

> Our current model of capitalism has generated prosperity and improved the quality of life, but not without undesirable environmental and social consequences. Calls for its reform are getting louder, and many approaches have been put forth. Whatever their labels—creative capitalism, philanthrocapitalism, new economy, impact investing, blended value, shared value—these approaches are all rooted in the observation that no genuine reform can take place as long as profit-maximizing businesses remain the sole engine of capitalism. Governments and markets must recognize and support for-benefits as an equally legitimate model. As entrepreneurs continue to prove that for-benefit organizations can balance economic, social, and environmental performance, demand for such organizations will grow. For-benefits cannot replace for-profits, governments, or nonprofits; a resilient, competitive 21st-century economy needs all four sectors. But they can fill the gaps created by the failure of the three-sector model. As their DNA takes hold, the entire system will evolve. It will become clear that in organizing their enterprises for benefit, entrepreneurs have been the architects of a new, more sustainable capitalism. (Sabeti, 2011, p. 104)

Critics of involving young people in social entrepreneurship and/or any entrepreneurship fear that they become simply "junior capitalists," perpetuating the very system of inequality from which they are meant to be rising. The counterargument is that by including a critical lens on the systems of power at work in the community, even market-based solutions to social problems will better protect marginalized populations. Better still, adding a social activist mindset to entrepreneurial endeavors may unleash synergies of innovation toward solving intractable social problems. Instead of an "either/or" perspective on the role of capitalism within social entrepreneurship, a more expansive "both/and" holds potential for individuals as well as shifting global economies.

Talking the Talk?

The work of social entrepreneurs is in some ways as old as time: people seeking ways to simultaneously help their communities and themselves. The discourse of this field, though, has exploded in recent decades, and the result is a scattering of terminology, often to define the same phenomena. For example, the terms "social enterprise," "social entrepreneurship," "social impact," "social innovation," "social business," "social-purpose business," and others are used throughout this book and in research and practice. The existence of so many terms for related concepts makes simple definitions difficult and access by the general population even more difficult (i.e., must you study the variations in terms to correctly identify the practices of your organization?).

To further complicate the language around this field, individuals who are unfamiliar with the academic and/or policy approaches to their work often struggle more with understanding the terminology and nuances therein. In one study of mapping missions to support social enterprise ecosystems in the Southern Mediterranean countries, researchers interviewed more than 100 social entrepreneurs, public officials, and leaders in financial institutions in six countries in the Middle East and North Africa (Doumit, 2017). Those interviewed invariably struggled to name "social enterprises" that exist in their countries. When researchers intervened by defining a social enterprise as "an entity that makes a positive social impact and generates revenue to later scale up," the interviewers easily accessed examples to report (p. 1).

In a US example, a student researcher interviewed youth aged 14–18 about their participation in programs identified as youth social entrepreneurship. When asked what they think "social entrepreneurship" means, most struggled to give a full definition, often focusing on "entrepreneurship" as employment within their definitions. Several, in fact, identified the "social" element of the terminology as referring to interacting with other youth or being a friendly, popular person. One youth, for example, replied that a "social entrepreneur is somebody who is willing to interact with multiple people and also be successful and have confidence in themselves about what they're going to be selling" (Shoemaker, personal communication, 2014) apparently differentiating himself from antisocial entrepreneurs!

It is unclear how much of this confusion comes from the terminology, but advocates within the field aim to strengthen the definition and clarify its meaning among diverse stakeholders. One aim of this volume is to help clarify the definitions of social entrepreneurship and especially of youth social entrepreneurship.

2

The Asset-Focus of Youth Social Entrepreneurship

> Problem-free is not fully prepared, and
> fully prepared is not fully engaged.
>
> —KAREN PITTMAN

Introduction

In its essence, this chapter asks: What does it mean to see potential instead of problem? For youth social entrepreneurship, it means centering practices on the identifiable strengths of youth and communities, seeking to build on them and to "unleash" them toward their self-defined goals. The language of the "asset-based" frameworks in both positive youth development and community development helps to shape this approach. Connecting the approach of youth social entrepreneurship to a foundation of the assets-/strength-based paradigm can help mobilize communities for youth development. It fundamentally shifts how adults and institutional leaders think about programming for young people. It also changes the way communities aim to "solve" youth and neighborhood problems, offering assets to build connections—between adults and youth, between programs and individuals, and among programs. This chapter also orients the reader to the link between youth social entrepreneurship's grounding in the central theme of positive psychology: human flourishing. Instead of focusing on the incremental steps toward getting any job at all, the emphasis is on youth capacity for creating a positive career trajectory, supported by exposure to a breadth of opportunity instead of a narrow pipeline. To accomplish meaningful and authentic positivity, the cultural reality of each young person and each community must be included in the experience of development. Therefore, a review of culturally relevant pedagogies and the need for valuing cultural funds of knowledge is included. All together, the asset-focused, culturally relevant practices can foster youth leadership with social entrepreneurship that paves a road toward thriving.

Asset Versus Deficit Focus

A fundamental feature of youth social entrepreneurship is that it builds on the strengths of the youth involved and of their communities. In turn, then, youth social entrepreneurship rejects and actively thwarts a deficit view of both youth and their communities. Deficit perspectives suggest that underachievement and/or pathology are inherent to the individual or system (Valencia, 1997), and cultural deficit models attribute failures to cultural group factors (Silverman, 2011). Since the late twentieth century, a shift in developmental science has pushed the paradigm of deficit views to the fringe. Instead, scholars have rejected deficit perspectives (Volk & Long, 2005) and highlighted a strengths perspective. Also known as an "asset focus"—focusing on what is right instead of what is wrong—this paradigm has infiltrated many fields of the social sector, including community development, health, justice, and urban planning (Lindau et al., 2016). It is also a viewpoint that aligns in powerful ways with the current movement of social entrepreneurship— the "social entrepreneurship 3.0" described in the previous chapter—wherein every individual or group of individuals holds capacity for making positive change. In other words, their strengths hold the power to upend the challenges they or their communities face by leveraging their existing assets.

The field of positive youth development is not only well-aligned with this strength-oriented philosophy, but also has been instrumental in disrupting the deficit mindset in youth work and education broadly defined. Since the 1990s, a strong wave of asset-focused approaches in both youth development practice and research continues to alter the long-standing deficit orientation of previous generations. A deficit view analyzes and addresses all that is faulty or missing from the individual or system being considered. One might think of it as a "glass half-empty" perspective. The focus, then, is not on what contents already exist but on how to fill the glass the rest of the way. This view naturally lends itself to diagnostic questions such as, What caused the glass to be half-empty? What effects does it have on the glass to be half-empty? Who is best suited to fill the rest of the glass? Such a perspective is also known commonly as the "medical model," in which situations of difficulty are always focused on causation and remediation, rather than on prevention or maximization (Mandel & Qazilbash, 2005). Scholars and practitioners in the social sector, such as in social work, have argued against the medical model in their fields, noting that the medical model is "rooted in individual fault and deficiency," which mistakes more effective paths to health and healing and should be overturned in working within social services (Weick, 1995, p. 12).

Continuing the analogy, critics of the medical model suggest a focus on what already exists within the half-full glass. How did it get there? How can it be expanded? Can the glass increase its own contents, given proper supports? This viewpoint, often referred to as "strengths-based," is deeply entrenched in the field of youth development as it currently exists in both research and practice. Like many social workers' core belief that starting with strengths is more successful in both the short- and long-term than focusing on deficits, this perspective rejects the medical model of "curing" the ills of youth and instead orients action toward the thriving of all.

Developmental Assets

A significant force in the emergence of strengths-based youth development was research conducted and disseminated through the Search Institute, particularly at the turn of the twenty-first century. At the leadership helm of Search, Peter Benson first birthed the framework of "Forty Developmental Assets" in 1990, which enabled thinking about adolescents to include both what was missing as well as what was present from a list of 40 assets. The term "developmental assets" was embraced to refer to those features in the youth's life that were identifiable, thus urging youth workers to expand their interactions beyond only addressing the deficits. For example, if a youth identifies having asset no. 3, "Other Adult Relationship: Young person receives support from three or more nonparent adults," but not asset no. 11, "Family Boundaries: Family has clear rules and consequences and monitors the young person's whereabouts," a practitioner has a clear strength—of adults in the youth's life—to consider adding to instead of focusing only on fixing the obstacle of weak family boundaries. Developmental assets are not only used for individual interactions, but also extensively for research and evaluation of communities. Furthermore, this framework is applied widely by curriculum and program designers to centralize a strengths-based approach. While the framework is prominently recognized to address the needs of "all kids" (Benson, 1997), it offers the significant benefit of resilience for youth experiencing higher levels of life stress, such as those who experience housing and/or caregiver instability. Furthermore, Sesma, Mannes, and Scales (2013) point to the consonance of a developmental assets framework with empirically vetted models of resilience. Efforts to target developmental assets as "protective factors" in the resilience paradigm have been documented with positive outcomes in the developmental trajectories of youth (Eccles & Gootman, 2002, in Sesma et al., 2013).

The assets-focused orientation, then, which forms the backbone of the positive youth development paradigm and drives the current work in this field, provides a rich ingredient to the youth social entrepreneurship model. Effective youth social entrepreneurship programs tap the existing developmental assets of the youth involved, aiming to support those toward flourishing simultaneously with bolstering areas of lesser asset.

Furthermore, a focus on developmental assets moves attention from only the single individual youth toward a positive outcome for a broader system within which the youth resides. Another key principle of positive youth development is that youth grow in communities, not programs. Thus, authentic engagement with people in and out of organized youth programs has become a pivotal feature of current practices with youth. In this way, the lived experience and natural contexts of each youth are valued and themselves recognized as assets.

> This work represents a shift away from relying solely on prevention and intervention efforts to the intentional mobilization and engagement of individuals and systems within communities in the service of healthy youth development . . . [and] working toward bringing structure and intentionality to these environments under the banner of positive youth development provides a promising approach to increasing the developmental outcomes for young people. (Sesma et al., 2013, p. 439)

Youth social entrepreneurship as a model for youth development reflects this type of "mobilization" and "intentionality" (as quoted) within larger environments and social systems. Youth who engage in social entrepreneurship become active agents of change in their neighborhoods and broader communities, and, likewise, neighbors and community members are mobilized to support the youth through participation in their enterprising activities.

Positive Psychology

Formidable to the rise of positive youth development has also been the emergence of *positive psychology*. Seligman and Csikszentmihalyi (2000) are among the influential scholars in the field of psychology who put forth a framework for the study of human psychology that centers on strengths and flourishing instead of on correcting deficiencies. Through the early decades of the twenty-first century, positive psychology has multiplied exponentially in its reach and is now included in the preparation of new researchers and clinical practitioners. Larson (2000) helped to make the explicit connection between positive psychology, developmental psychology—which has long resisted the medical model tendencies—and the emerging positive youth development, in highlighting that

> we are often more articulate about how things go wrong than how they go right. We have a burgeoning field of developmental psychopathology but have a more diffuse body of research on the pathways whereby children and adolescents become motivated, directed, socially competent, compassionate, and psychologically vigorous adults. Corresponding to that, we have numerous research-based programs for youth aimed at curbing drug use, violence, suicide, teen pregnancy, and other problem behaviors, but lack a rigorous applied psychology of how to promote positive youth development. (p. 170)

Youth social entrepreneurship leverages the current milieu of positive psychology in its aim to promote thriving in the youth involved. A contrasting view might be seen through employment education, in which a young person from a chronically underemployed community successfully gets a job courtesy of targeted human capital training and social networking. The youth's "first paycheck" experience is potentially a positive one, and one which may usher in a long-standing record of successful employment. Youth social entrepreneurship, on the other hand, aims higher, combining both the first-job experience with a drawing out of the youth's leadership skills and sense of societal agency. In this way, youth social entrepreneurship focuses on thriving over surviving, to use language from the positive psychology field.

For example, Street Bean Coffee Roasters of Seattle, Washington, has engaged street-involved youth in apprenticeships to roast and sell coffee to the local community. Their model is a one-for-one: each purchased bag of coffee funds one hour of training for participant youth. The young people learn all the steps in crafting coffee—choosing beans, roasting, preparing coffee, and serving as baristas. The organization's stated mission is solidly grounded in a positive psychological framework: "to provide an opportunity for street-involved young people to discover and employ their gifts by serving coffee in our community. Our hope is that this experience will serve as a catalyst to move onto successful future employment" (http://streetbeanespresso.org/aboutus/).

Furthermore, Street Bean includes a perspective about their impact on the broader community; they assert that their social enterprise helps to "bridge gaps in our community as a space that fosters conversations that matter over a product that tastes and does good" (http://streetbeanespresso.org/). This recognition of the larger social justice context for their youth apprentices also demonstrates an asset-based approach, investing both in more macro-level change for the future and in the development of a local, community-level asset through their coffee offerings. As framed in their homepage, "your coffee won't just have notes of spice, cocoa, caramel or blackberry—it'll have notes of expertise, impact and community."

Culturally Relevant Approaches

A vital feature of the asset focus in youth social entrepreneurship is its cultural relevance. Though inclusion of value and purpose is beneficial for youth development universally, scholars and practitioners alike see culturally relevant approaches as especially important for historically marginalized youth (Castagno & Brayboy, 2008; Gay, 2010; Ladson-Billings, 1994). Because youth social entrepreneurship is a model of youth development that aims to alleviate the opportunity gap facing American youth of color and low socioeconomic status, if it is to be effective, there must be cultural relevance at its core.

Culturally relevant approaches to youth development are drawn from three decades of research and practice in the field of K–12 education. The work of Gloria Ladson-Billings (1994, 1995) has been instrumental in centralizing culturally relevant pedagogies to today's teacher education and school policy. *Culturally relevant pedagogies* in schools refer to teaching strategies that demonstrate teachers' cultural competence, willingness, and ability to value each student's cultural frames of reference and construct learning that has meaning within that frame. In additional to a teacher's instructional methods, educational researchers and advocates of culturally relevant pedagogies assert that linguistically and culturally diverse students can achieve more academic success when classroom materials directly link their cultural experiences to learning and reflect their culture's values and traditions in the classroom environment. This includes formal curriculum as well as the informal materials of the classroom. Additionally, teacher expectations for student success are high, in part because they are grounded in an asset perspective, and these expectations are communicated to the students through direct and implicit messages. To summarize, culturally relevant pedagogies include any strategy "that empowers students to maintain cultural integrity, while succeeding academically" (Ladson-Billings, 1995, p. 455).

The principles of culturally relevant pedagogy translate well to a broader category of youth work, whether within the traditional school day or in an out-of-school setting. By recognizing and valuing diverse "funds of knowledge," youth development practitioners best engage youth in their own progress, motivating from the center, making the learning process meaningful and lasting (see Chapter 9 for more details on this approach). Youth social entrepreneurship makes use of culturally relevant approaches whenever youth participants connect their real lives with their projects and see their efforts as meaningful and valuable to their community context. For example, Chicago's Good Life Organization (goodlifealliance.org/) includes a youth-led social enterprise in which teens create and sell hip-hop culture–inspired clothing. Their "hip hop(e)" line is grounded in the real cultural context of the youth, and their venture has purpose and meaning in their environment. Roberto Rivera, founder of the organization, ensures that culturally relevant pedagogy is infused in the processes, drawing on a constructed curriculum that was designed for the regional urban environment. In particular, his work with high school–aged males, many on the verge of drop-out or expulsion, engages in culturally meaningful social entrepreneurship that has resulted in improved school attendance and completion (R. Rivera, personal communication, 2016). The cultural relevance of their project acts as both the hook to gain engagement and the line to sustain them through their efforts. As the principles of culturally relevant pedagogy require, both high expectations and supportive relationships are critical to effectiveness. Their initiative embodies this: instead of labeling youth as "at-risk," they have told the students they are being selected for an elite leadership program.

Adult facilitators or program designers of youth social entrepreneurship can exercise culturally relevant practices in many ways. Most importantly, they must cultivate the skill of being responsive to culture, also known as being "sensitive, student-centered, congruent, reflective, mediated, contextualized, synchronized" (Gay, 2010, p. 29). Operationally, this means validating the cultural identities of the youth, combined with a "wider transformative purpose to empower" them (Stairs, Donnell, & Hadley Dunn, 2012, p. 59). Topics of societal power and privilege are explicitly considered, especially among older youth. Program facilitators using culturally relevant pedagogy avoid assimilationist styles of leadership, such as homogenizing youth opinions or aiming to teach youth to "fit in" as society might expect them to (Ladson-Billings, 1995). Such leaders will also seek to infuse the projects and programming with the youth's home cultures and allow youth to engage meaningfully with one another, thus thwarting the "banking model" of education (Freire, 2005) in which the adult and/or teacher is the expert (see Chapter 9).

Culturally relevant approaches to youth practice, such as youth social entrepreneurship, authentically empower youth and put them at center. Simultaneous to affirming the youth's strengths is the furthering of that strength. Karen Pittman famously marked positive youth development with the idea that "problem-free is not fully prepared, and fully prepared is not fully engaged" (Pittman, 1999). Full engagement refers to authentic contribution matched with the development of one's capacities. Thus, youth leadership development has taken center stage in current scholarship within the field of youth development.

Leadership as Part of Youth Development

Youth-focused scholarship related to leadership has increased rapidly in the past 10 years, and more youth practitioners have added leadership expertise to their disciplinary focus or have become professional leadership educators (Komives, et al., 2011). Growth of the youth leadership education field "is evidenced by such developments as new professional associations, dedicated journals, student-centered textbooks and theoretical/conceptual models, substantial research and assessment, and standards of practice" (Komives & Guthrie, 2015, p. 2). An interdisciplinary understanding of youth leadership— that is, consideration of the psychological, developmental, sociological, and economical—can yield holistic approaches to enabling youth leadership skills to flourish in multiple contexts. Youth social entrepreneurship locates youth leadership opportunities in authentic social settings, such as neighborhoods or other targeted communities, promoting "community engagement pedagogy [that] can foster transformative learning on many learning objectives related to leadership" (Wagner & Mathison, 2015, p. 95). Increasingly, scholars on leadership development advocate for "community-centered" leadership in lieu the self- or student-centered models (Hartman, 2016). This is a focus that distinguishes many youth social entrepreneurship programs in which the youth/student and the community are simultaneously considered in leadership objectives. For youth residing in marginalized communities and/or economically depressed neighborhoods, the role of community-centered leadership development becomes a crucial issue, one similar to political organizing as "a place where low-income youth of color build skills and connect to other groups pursuing allied causes" (Ginwright, 2011). To bolster a single young person's sense of self as a leader devoid of the community context is to (a) diminish the lasting impact of culturally relevant pedagogy that aims to validate the youth's identity within that community and/or (b) essentially suggest that the young person apply leadership skills elsewhere. Perhaps this latter outcome points to the oft-cited phenomenon of "accomplished" individuals who disengage and even move away from their marginalized communities (Hardaway & McLoyd, 2009). Youth social entrepreneurship supports young people's contextualized leadership, so that they grow their own sense of their leadership capacity and their ability to impact a community and value that community's strengths within which they are a part. In these ways, it is urgent that the current focus on leadership studies within youth development research and practice prioritize community engagement for all youth, perhaps especially for youth from marginalized neighborhoods or identity groups.

3

The Problem in Youth Social Entrepreneurship

Introduction

After an exploration in the previous chapter of the importance of seeing "potential, not problem," the reader may find it unsettling that the current chapter focuses entirely on problems. Rather, this chapter aims to clarify what is needed to give shape to youth social entrepreneurship as an approach to youth development. It begins with a concern for the lack of prior research specifically on this approach and a potential typology to better frame the work.

Lack of Definition

The youth social entrepreneurship approach lacks a clear definition and a common language to drive its implementation and to support collaboration among stakeholders. Youth practitioners refer to their social entrepreneurship programming as disparate pieces of a puzzle not well formulated, often not even acknowledging the youth development effects of the social entrepreneurship aspects of their program (Kruse et al., 2014). Funders and policymakers interested in supporting youth in social entrepreneurship lack a solid definition on which to base their initiatives. Youth social entrepreneurship has permeable boundaries; for example, "youth entrepreneurship" sometimes includes social justice elements but does not identify them; "community development" efforts often include youth but do not recognize the ways that their work are promoting healthy youth development. This lack of a clear definition is an obstacle for advancing the field.

Fuzzy Boundaries

What constitutes youth social entrepreneurship goes by other names in other forms. Some are relatively new, such as *youth participatory action research* (described later in this volume), and others are quite old, such as "youth volunteerism." Others espouse youth doing social entrepreneurship to improve society but tend to have a high representation of youth from privileged backgrounds. Ashoka's Youth Venture or WE.org appear to fall into this model. In these cases, while "youth social entrepreneurship" is at work, the question must be asked: Is social justice being enacted versus a re-enactment of the social injustice of power and resource already at play?

Still other efforts have social justice at their core but have remained valuable resources only to practitioners and not connected into the academic web of theory and validation. For example, The Freechild Project has offered practical ideas for youth-led social change since 2001. Regionally based intermediary groups, such as Youthprise in Minnesota, help to build local capacity and connect multisector partners for a common purpose: equity-focused youth development. National collectives, such as the Young Women's Initiative, help to create a big umbrella for many similarly minded groups in every state to get under and share support and resources. As potent as each of these—and many others like them—are for driving social change with youth at the center, they do not share common language about their approaches. Many concepts are the same, much of their discourse has a common root, but their terminology is often unique to their purpose.

In its "purest form," I argue that youth social entrepreneurship exists when the three sectors described earlier occur together and in equal measure. Figure I.1's overlapping circles show how these multiple fields meld together. In reality, most programs that may be categorized as youth social entrepreneurship lean more heavily toward one or two of the sectors.

Movement Toward Typology of Youth Social Entrepreneurship

Typologies are useful in providing organized systems both in qualitative and quantitative research (Collier, Laporte, & Seawright, 2008). In an attempt to begin classifying how programs with youth social entrepreneurship-type characteristics might fit together, my colleagues and I systematically reviewed a sample of 30 youth programs in multiple areas of the United States (2014). This study yields insights about the types of youth programs engaging in youth social entrepreneurship. We employed a qualitative analysis of program descriptions, as available publicly on websites and/or annual reports. These were coded and rated to assess the focus of each initiative. Requirements for selection were programs that (1) are established enough to have a presence on the internet, (2) specifically identify as having a youth focus to their programming, and (3) refer to programming that includes at least one of the terms *entrepreneurship, enterprise, business, career skills, employment skills, apprenticeship, job training, management,* or *workforce development.* Programs were sought for this review in the Twin Cities (Minneapolis-St. Paul), Boston, San Francisco, Phoenix, San Antonio, Miami, and Atlanta. Only the Twin Cities, Boston, San Francisco, and Atlanta had example programs that fit the criteria. The relevant description text about each program was extracted and coded by two raters based on a calibrated rubric designed for this project. The rubric categorized the key elements the researchers were studying about youth social entrepreneurship.

1. *Human capital development* (e.g., customer service skills, job-readiness, interpersonal, interview practice, etc.)
2. *Entrepreneurial skills* (e.g., innovation, new products, business development, "running" a business, etc.)
3. *Mentoring/adult-partnerships* (e.g., matched with a community member, meetings with past students, etc.)
4. *Community development* (e.g., connections to community, neighborhood improvement, pride about community membership, etc.)
5. *Level of youth leadership* (i.e., the role youth are given in program)

Ratings were then assessed for interrater reliability, and any divergences were addressed and corrected by the team. Next, rated components were rank-ordered within each program to force the targeted components into a priority order. Demographic data available on program sites were also collected. While limitations to the structure of the study exist, analysis of the ranked data yielded several interesting trends, some of which are useful for this chapter.

Namely, two distinct types of youth social entrepreneurship programs were identified with several variations on each. While many of the 30 programs had a combination of foci, as described in preceding categories, they typically either centralize activities around *economic issues* (employment, job skills, and the like) or centralize around *community issues* (improved conditions for specific neighborhood, opportunities for particular community group, etc.) but rarely were rated high on both. This distinction makes sense when one considers that it is challenging, if not impossible, to prioritize a steady job for youth while also taking risks to make change in a community. The polarization in the ratings for the two categories of employment and for community building mirrored this distinction in practice (Figure 3.1).

The Resulting Typology

First, "economic-transformation youth social entrepreneurship" programs with high ratings in the economic categories exhibit some combination of enterprise activity and employment opportunity. Within this type, there are two subtypes:

1. *Employment-centered*, which predominantly assert their mission as giving transformative economic experience to the youth involved through having a job, a paycheck, learning interview skills, and

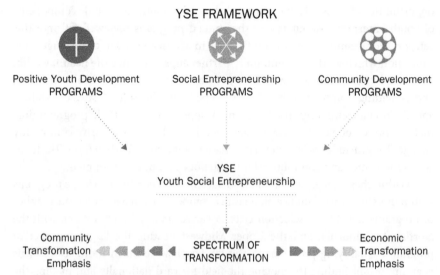

FIGURE 3.1 Youth Social Entrepreneurship (YSE) Framework.
Reproduced with the permission of the Sundance Family Foundation

other employment-related components. About 40% of the programs reviewed for this study prioritized employment and/or human capital development.

2. *Enterprise-centered*, which predominantly talk about affording opportunities for youth to experience leadership, management, and business decision-making. The majority of programs reviewed fall into this category (53%). One example is YE Georgia, in Atlanta, which "teaches students how to become entrepreneurs or to think like one . . . [and] help student[s] learn the value of entrepreneurship and equip them with the skills to add value to their communities and society as a whole" (https://youthentrepreneurs.org/). Their stated goal is to improve communities by enriching an entrepreneurial mindset among youth. A second example is More Than Words, in Boston, which engages youth participants to run the online and retail bookstore and "are integrated into all aspects of the business" (https://www.mtwyouth.org/). Youth facilitate trainings, team meetings, track and forecast financials for the business, and manage all the sales and marketing. They include employment-related training as well, such as customer service and personal bank account management. This program contrasts its model to the "traditional workforce development" by increasing responsibilities, skills, and leadership roles as they earn promotions (https://www. mtwyouth.org/about_us/the_model/).

A second type can be called "community-transformation youth social entrepreneurship." These programs prioritize the betterment of the neighborhood, opportunities of the local area, or a general social mission but include components of youth enterprise. About 15% of the studied programs reviewed fall into this category. For example, Appetite for Change, in Minneapolis is a "change-agent organization which works in community partnerships to change the health, wealth, and social change landscape of [the geographic community], while educating and providing community building leadership to the rest of society" (http://appetiteforchangemn.org/projects/training-opportunities/). Their programming, that is centered on youth, acclaims that "youth are the truth" to drive community change. They include social enterprises like a restaurant and urban farm. The focus is on food justice and community building, not economic development.

Within these categories, or youth social entrepreneurship types, the programs within this study varied quite a bit on other components. In particular, the number of programs that fit the selection criteria varied greatly by US region, with the Northeast, California, and the Upper Midwest hosting the largest number of programs. Qualifying programs in the US South were much more scarce. This is an important finding for moving the field forward nationally and making the unique youth social entrepreneurship experience available more consistently to all youth. Less variation occurred in the demographics: the majority of programs, regardless of focus or location, stated a specific mission to involve youth from low socioeconomic backgrounds. In this way, the program descriptions studied support the idea that youth social entrepreneurship may be a unique approach to reducing the opportunity gap for youth from low-income families and/or marginalized communities.

Lack of Evidence

Without a common framework, no findings can be synthesized to extract larger lessons or reproducible effects. Basic principles of research methodology point to the necessity of identifying common variables before measurement and analysis (Krathwohl, 1993). The programs engaged in youth social entrepreneurship tend to address the variables that are most salient to their concerns—their logic models, their missions, their grant requirements, their stakeholders. Some effort is afoot to connect across a sample of such programs and look for common indicators (Wilder Research, 2016). The aim is to have a first "common evaluation" with which to measure common outcomes of identifiable youth social entrepreneurship programs. Results even of this first endeavor put only a small dent in the lack of knowledge we have about the processes and impacts of youth social entrepreneurship as such. Furthermore, there is a lack of longitudinal studies to investigate the long-term effects of youth social entrepreneurship on the youth participants and/or the communities in which they occur. One has no option but to merely imagine the effects over time of this type of targeted approach.

Learning from studies of similar approaches, or "parts" of the youth social entrepreneurship model, can help inform that imagining. A review of those as potential lessons can be found in the next chapter.

Challenges to Measuring Impact

Even if a clearer framework is established for youth social entrepreneurship, many challenges remain for establishing efficacy as a form of youth development and social justice. The difficulties of quantifying variables at stake are among the top concern, as well as an inability to make conjectures about "best practices" that would pertain to programs in multiple contexts and with diverse youth.

A first challenge exists in any attempt to measure "the complexity of human change processes" (Carnochan, Samples, Myers, & Austin, 2013, p. 1). Outcome measurements rarely can adequately capture the dynamic characteristics of the people involved.

Furthermore, like other approaches in the social sector, the most effective programs are designed for a particular context, with its demographic, historical, economic, and cultural variables in mind. Thus, while there are "evidence-based practices" in youth practice, they cannot be reproduced in identical form to one another. In short, a program that works in Houston cannot be lifted and implemented in Omaha. Social justice work in communities is inherently setting-specific, perhaps especially needing an "ecologically responsive approach to working with black youth" (Ginwright, 2010, p. 147). This reinforces an apples-to-oranges concern about comparing even process measures from one site to another, no less outcome measures.

Last, fidelity to a model will vary from place to place and perhaps relationship to relationship, further complicating attempts to draw conclusions about the effectiveness of a specific model. This variation among individuals further complicates efforts to clearly define outcomes (Carnochan et al., 2013, p. 1).

4

The Potential of Youth Social Entrepreneurship

> Social youth enterprises can effectively help marginalized youth earn
> money in a positive fashion, provide a service to their community, and
> benefit the community in the process.
> —MELVIN DELGADO (2004, P. 56)

Introduction

Despite the established gaps in current knowledge about this model's impact potential, promising results from the field suggest the potential value of
youth social entrepreneurship for its many stakeholders. Currently, recorded
outcomes of youth social entrepreneurship programs are mainly anecdotal, as
has often been the case for complex social sector initiatives. Qualitative data
that have not been documented except for the observations of practitioners
offer a glimpse into the potency of youth and community work. Researchers
and policymakers seek more systematic markers to ensure validity, as is appropriate for their purposes of measuring impact, cultivating theory, and
suggesting best practices. However, it would be folly to overlook the messages
inscribed in the experiences of the youth and community workers as incom-
parable starting points for scholarship and avenues for other practitioners to
traverse. In this way, many small-scale interview data, materials reviews, and
observations give form to what can become a multilayered research agenda.
This chapter summarizes significant examples of such anecdotal yet powerful
findings.

Similarly, the better trodden paths of existing empirical studies in related
areas of study can lead to an initial understanding of youth social entrepreneurship as a model for positive youth development. Like siblings in their similarity,
other models of youth and/or community development offer recognizable
indications to scholars. Examples of this related research are also included in
this chapter.

Promising Results from Related Research

ENTREPRENEURIAL INTENT

The primary extant research on youth entrepreneurship points to the joint role of personal attributes and contextual characteristics. Half a century ago, McClelland (e.g., 1961) highlighted the connection between achievement orientation and entrepreneurial role models, such as parents who are entrepreneurs, in predicting entrepreneurial tendencies in youth. More recently, developmental scientists have focused on individual variables, such as gender, and specific environmental contexts, such as parental involvement and/or role models (see Obschonka, Silbereisen, & Schmitt-Rodermund, 2011).

One large-scale research project that is closely related to youth social entrepreneurship is the Tufts Young Entrepreneurs Study (YES). Begun in 2011, the YES project is a mixed-methods, longitudinal study of the development of entrepreneurial purpose, achievements, and character attributes among 4,000 adolescents and young adults in three regions of United States. The goal of the project is to describe the course of the mutually influential relations between individuals and their contexts as they pertain to entrepreneurship in a sample of late adolescents and young adults. Specifically, this study focuses on identifying the cognitive, motivational, behavioral, and ecological bases of entrepreneurship development. The authors of this work argue that since entrepreneurship is vital for a community or society's well-being via economic growth, entrepreneurial tendencies may be a form of "adaptive developmental regulation" (Geldof, Weiner, Agans, Mueller, & Lerner, 2014, p. 86).

The most salient lessons from this study for youth social entrepreneurship come from the researchers' investigation of young adults' "entrepreneurial intent" (Geldof et al., 2014). Specifically, they examined if personal characteristics (i.e., gender, intentional self-regulation skills, innovation orientation) and contextual factors (i.e., entrepreneurial parents) predicted college students' intentions to pursue an entrepreneurial career. Their findings suggest that several variables have a positive correlation with youth entrepreneurship.

First, this study builds on research that suggests a relationship between self-regulation and entrepreneurial intentions and actions, as asserted by Damon (2008). To do so, the YES participants completed the Entrepreneurial Intentional Self-Regulation (EISR) questionnaire as a way to measure the self-regulation skills relevant to entrepreneurship. This instrument includes items that address how people approach goals, risk, novelty, and challenge, among other subscales. The findings suggest that young people who rate themselves highly on factors of goal selection, optimization, and adaptation—all key elements of self-regulating behavior—are also likely to say that they believe entrepreneurship is important in their lives. For example, youth who considered themselves to be "self-starters" and those who said they "keep an eye out for backup plans" scored higher on entrepreneurial intent than did other participants.

Second, early results of YES identified a correlation with "innovation orientation" and entrepreneurship. Specifically, the researchers measured the degree to which young people rate themselves as generating, implementing, and championing new ideas. Results of this measure were also correlated to entrepreneurial intent, which further supports the long-standing belief that innovative tendencies and entrepreneurship are connected to one another.

Third, Geldof et al. (2014) inquired about the role of having entrepreneurial adult mentors in young people's likelihood to value entrepreneurship. Specifically, through regression analysis they identified that having an entrepreneurial parent positively predicted entrepreneurial intent. Other adult influences were not considered in this study.

The YES study shares many aspects with the youth social entrepreneurship model; namely, recognizing the capacity for innovative and purposeful contributions as dually beneficial to the youth and their contexts. There are key differences in this longitudinal study and the field of youth social entrepreneurship. Primarily, the YES project defines entrepreneurship generally as starting one's own business or organization, while youth social entrepreneurship includes leadership within both startup and established efforts within the social sector. Furthermore, the YES project studies "youth" in late adolescence; that is, late teens and early 20s (e.g., the median age for the 2014 study was 21.1 years; Geldof et al. 2014, p. 84). On the other hand, youth social entrepreneurship activities often include middle-school youth as well as those in late adolescence, following a definition of "youth" closer to the field of youth development as "roughly the second decade of life" (Hamilton, Hamilton, & Pittman, 2004, p. 3).

YOUTH PARTICIPATORY ACTION RESEARCH

Youth participatory action research (YPAR) is a model for engaging young people in collective inquiry and action on community issues. Like youth social entrepreneurship, YPAR endeavors simultaneous community and youth development. In both models, youth and adults collaborate to address issues that affect their daily lives and communities. Like youth social entrepreneurship, YPAR represents an approach to integrating youth leadership into efforts to improve their communities as well as their own personal outcomes. YPAR does this by emphasizing "the improvement of settings that shape adolescent development and health, and can capitalize on developmentally important windows for the development of positive identity, peer social rewards, and exerting an influence" (Ozer, 2017).

Unlike youth social entrepreneurship, YPAR has been well-publicized and studied in recent years in the fields of education and youth development. Numerous studies and publications document the positive impact of YPAR as a tool for promoting positive youth development and carving a path for social justice (Cammarota & Fine, 2008). Furthermore, engaging youth in participatory research helps to "legitimize the perspectives of those who have had little control over scholarly research" (Brown & Rodriguez, 2009, p. 4). YPAR methodology tends to involve qualitative or mixed methods, such as case study, ethnographic, quasi-experimental, phenomenological, and survey (Fox et al., 2010).

YPAR shares a number of key characteristics with youth social entrepreneurship and therefore warrants comparison of possible effects. Namely, three aspects are shared: (1) the centering of youth in the process with authentic youth engagement, (2) the focus on dual youth and community change, and (3) a social justice orientation that seeks to allow historically marginalized youth to hold power. This third element is especially of mutual relevance between YPAR and youth social entrepreneurship in that each model inherently can be implemented with any youth regardless of sociopolitical power, but that is much more impactful when implemented with marginalized youth. In other words, in the United States, white kids from affluent backgrounds can do YPAR or youth social entrepreneurship, but neither model unleashes its full potential until placed in the hands of kids of color and/or from economically depressed backgrounds.

Emerging Research on Youth as Social Entrepreneurs

YOUTH VENTURE

In 1996, Youth Venture grew out of Ashoka, the global association of social entrepreneurs. Since then, thousands of individual social-change initiatives ("ventures") have been launched. Through means such as an international youth council, university partnerships, and a series of workshops hosted by schools and community or religious organizations ("dream it, do it"), young people aged 12–20 engage in identifying a social issue, then developing and implementing their plans to address the problem. Ventures include actions such as AIDS education campaigns, composting in cafeterias, T-shirt companies, skateparks, disaster relief groups, book clubs, tutoring programs, and more (https://www.youthventure.org/). Research on the effects of this programming with youth participants is limited to self-report:

- 92% of Venturers report a high degree of knowledge and capability in the area of leadership, 93% in the area of planning, and 79% in the area of budgeting.
- 77% of Venturers are more involved in leadership roles in their community.
- 70% are more interested in entrepreneurship.
- 94% of Venturers indicated that their participation in Youth Venture increased their confidence in starting and/or leading a project.
- 91% of Venturers report satisfaction with the accomplishments of their projects.

- 72% of youth reported that their Ventures have benefitted more than 100 people in their community, including 27% of youth who reported that their Ventures have helped more than 1,000 people.
- 89% indicate their participation has affected their motivation and preparedness to pursue higher education.
- 81% feel better prepared for their future.

While Youth Venture shares many aspects with the youth social entrepreneurship model described in this volume, a number of significant differences also exist. Most importantly, Youth Venture engages youth from a wide range of backgrounds, including those from high socioeconomic stratifications. A number of the youth "changemakers" in Youth Venture have access to financial and/or political power. Thus, their engagement in social entrepreneurship, while valuable, does not foster unique avenues to opportunity as it does for marginalized youth. In other words, since Ashoka's Youth Venture does not prioritize youth from marginalized backgrounds, youth with existing social and economic mobility tend to fill the role of "changemakers," further adding to the disparity in agency.

REGIONAL YOUTH SOCIAL ENTREPRENEURSHIP

Underway in the Minneapolis/St. Paul area is a foundation-funded research project on local youth social entrepreneurship outcomes. They draw on a sample of 14 qualifying organization whose work with youth conform to youth social entrepreneurship characteristics (http://www.sundancefamilyfoundation.org/). With a goal of establishing common indicators that can help gather and compare measures from the programs in their sample, the evolving tool assesses key variables of work readiness, social-emotional development, and employment outcomes. The sample programs themselves helped to derive a set of common evaluation outcomes. "Work readiness" has been operationalized with staff-report measures of attendance, punctuality, workplace appearance, response to supervisor, quality of work, taking initiative, communication skills, teamwork, problem-solving/critical-thinking, financial literacy, and ability to secure stable employment. "Social-emotional" variables have been measured with self-reporting on personal confidence, stress management, goal orientation, and community engagement. "Employment" data reflect youth completion of high school degree or GED; professional certification while in the program; enrollment in college, military, or postsecondary program; and whether or not the youth has a job after participation in the program. All programs collect demographic and dosage information to contribute to a better understanding of the variables related to the outcomes. Findings from this project will be available in the coming years and will offer a potential approach to a more standardized set of indicators for youth social entrepreneurial endeavors.

STUDIES IN YOUTH LEADERSHIP

Established, empirical research indicates the many positive outcomes of including youth in decision-making and organizational leadership, similar to what is found in models of youth social entrepreneurship. Among the findings are increased youth development and youth commitment to their communities (Zeldin, 2004) and the importance of culturally relevant youth leadership frameworks (Jones, Guthrie, & Osteen, 2016). The scholarship in leadership development supports the positive impact of diverse contexts and diversity among students (Guthrie, Bertrand Jones, Osteen, & Hu, 2013). The field of "youth leadership development" continues to evolve since the 1990s, and a growing professionalization of the field is evidenced by "new professional associations, dedicated journals, student-centered textbooks and theoretical/conceptual models, substantial research and assessment, and standards of practice" (Komives & Guthrie, 2015, p. 1). As leadership skill within their communities, their organizations, and their livelihoods is central to youth social entrepreneurship, interpreting the leadership development research in light of similar practice will be important. Like social entrepreneurship, leadership cannot truly be developed passively by talking about it in the abstract, but only through real-world, concrete experiences connected to making sense of one's environment. Say Wagner and Mathison (2015, p. 85): "Working collaboratively to address real social and environmental issues is a powerful way for students to come to experience the ambiguity and complexity of leadership."

YOUTH ACTIVISM

Young people have a long history of leading social movements in the United States, which offers a precedent to the community change inherent to the youth social entrepreneurship model. From the newsboys' strike of 1899 to the Little Rock Nine of 1957 to the student-led March for Our Lives of 2018, young people have engaged in self-initiated civic activism to make change in society. Sometimes their moments of action have become movements of history, paradigm-shifting waves driven by the energy, optimism, and potential of youth. For this reason, many bodies of research exist on the effects and effectiveness of youth activism that can inform the social change components of youth social entrepreneurship. Within cognitive science, they have given rise to an understanding of collective problem-solving and distributed cognition (Hutchins, 1995). In developmental psychological terms, youth activism "enables participants to forge identities as powerful civic actors. . . . By participating in civic venues, such as school board and city council meetings, youth position themselves—and are positioned by social others—as competent political actors" (Nasir & Kirshner, 2003). Within educational studies, surveys of youth activism described how academic practices were used as tools to accomplish goals that they cared about, rather than viewing school subjects as foreign and alienating concepts. When school subjects are paired with social causes, the youth often demonstrate higher levels of motivation to seek proficiency so that they can advance their activist goals (Tate, 2009). Within political science, youth activism offers political encounters that provide access points for youth to engage the political sphere when their activism addresses civic decision-makers and engages in outreach to community residents and meetings with policymakers. Activism also connects youth to mainstream civic institutions, thus increasing the likelihood of longer term engagement (Kirshner, 2007). For further consideration of youth organizing and activism, see Chapter 13 of this book.

Youth social entrepreneurship programs have the potential to embrace youth activism opportunities that naturally emerge or are intentionally designed through their community change efforts. These efforts are in line with centuries of American youth activists who have gone before them. It is useful to situate the current models into existing lines of research.

Section I

Focal Case Examples

Case 1: SOUL Sisters Leadership Collective

SOUL Sisters' primary purpose is social change in the lives of their targeted community: system-involved girls and young women of color. Their programming reflects a broad array of approaches to accomplish their goals of healing, justice, and empowerment. The inclusion of social entrepreneurship represents one line of programming among many, yet equally committed to the same vision for their youth.

SOUL Sisters Leadership Collective (SSLC) was founded on the philosophy that individual leadership combined with community social justice will result in profound youth growth. The young women who participate in SOUL Sisters have experience in the foster care, juvenile justice, special education, shelter, and mental health systems of New York City or Miami. They are predominantly youth of color and from low-income or extreme poverty backgrounds. With a goal of "young women of color blossoming into leaders with political & self awareness, creative problem-solving skills & strong ethics" (www.soulsistersleadership.org), there are multiple programs within the organization. Participants in the NYC location opted to design a social enterprise as a way to simultaneously grow their skills as leaders, learn a new aspect of the larger world (business planning and marketing), and influence their communities to move toward social change with messages of love and hope (L. Krieble, personal communication, 2016). The approach used by staff to support the young women involved in the youth social entrepreneurship was culturally relevant—drawing on the participants' self-narratives of injustice, they apply a critical lens on the larger system of racism and systemic oppression. In turn, the young women adopted "Spread the Love" as the message they wanted to develop to apply as a healing salve on the realities of the society surrounding them. The culturally relevant pedagogy manifested by staff and peer validation of one another's lived experiences. Furthermore, the staff's intentional plan to allow the girls to "dream big" in their social enterprise and to take on near independence in designing the products communicated to the girls the high expectations recommended by scholars of cultural relevance. Finally, the creation of actual retail products—shirts, handbags, and greeting cards—under the guidance of an actual NYC retail designer made the process fully authentic, grounded in the real world, and meaningful to the youth.

SOUL Sisters demonstrates the positive psychological approach in action. Rather than focusing on "fixing" the participants who have come to the organization through juvenile justice, school intervention, and/or foster care systems, the agency staff orient the nonprofit toward positive action, building "personal and community transformation [using] four pillars: leadership, social justice, healing, and the arts" (www.soulsistersleadership.org). They recognize the strengths of the youth who are with them and seek to draw them out so the youth can more fully "step into their power" (W. Douglas, personal communication, 2017). Because the involved youth have experienced marginalization and often violence in their lives, one of the ways SSLC builds on the assets of the youth is to hold high expectations. "We hold them to high standards, maybe even higher standards than anyone else in their lives ever has" (W. Douglas, personal communication, 2017). This is an act of asset building through challenging the youth to exercise their strengths in the name of progress. The SSLC staff do this in several ways. For example, they help the youth make commitments to complete tasks for their social action projects and then hold them accountable. The fellow cohort members commonly hold one another accountable as well, such that there is youth ownership of the projects.

For a second example of "high expectations," the staff say they that do not water down the concepts they teach regarding social power. Instead, they draw out youth strengths and build on them by assuming the youth will rise to the challenge of learning the "academic language" of social justice. So, they teach about "intersectionality of identity" and "institutionalization of oppression." They believe in these youth as capable, and the youth strive to meet that expectation.

Case 2: Cookie Cart

Cookie Cart itself began as an act of social entrepreneurship by its founder, Sister Jean Therauf. She saw the local problem of neighborhood crime and dangerous activities luring youth, and she sought to disrupt this pattern. Rather than the "traditional approach" of directing these youth to afterschool programs or reprimanding them and sending them home, she opened her house to them and gave them a purpose. By baking cookies together she engaged them in an act of caring, and by guiding them to sell their freshly baked wares, she gave them a path to earnings, albeit modest. Moreover, selling their cookies meant something more: that the youth of this neighborhood had the potential to make something worthwhile and could see themselves as affecting their own futures and making an impact on their community, no matter how small, by sharing their sweet treats where before there were none.

In these ways, Cookie Cart continues to teach youth social entrepreneurship by engaging them in a social enterprise. As an organization, they do not prioritize youth entrepreneurial actions; that is, it is not their focus to help youth develop their own ideas to solve societal problems. Yet their practice of employing and educating the teens, as well as connecting them to new environments while strengthening their local ties, all contribute to an individual young person's capacity to make social change elsewhere. Essentially, they give them the tools to become social entrepreneurs at any point in the youth's life. They assert their model as "one way of doing youth development."

More innovation opportunities do exist for the Cart Captains, those youth who have advanced beyond basic employment. They help manage and lead other youth, troubleshoot organization operations and bakery processes, and contribute new ideas to making and selling. In these moments, they exemplify Drayton's words in Section I's opening. They have not just eaten a fish, nor just learned to fish themselves, but they are learning to change the whole "fishing" industry.

Focal Cases Summary: Key Concepts from Section I

Both SOUL Sisters and Cookie Cart exemplify an asset focus in their youth work by acknowledging and growing the developmental assets of each youth in their respective programs. The positive psychological aspects of thriving are present in both with an intention to help foster youth flourishing—not just problem-free, not even just fully prepared, but also fully engaged (Karen Pittman, 1999). Their approaches to culture differ: SOUL Sisters uses highly specified practice to address their youths' racialized and gendered life experiences, while Cookie Cart applies a more general youth development orientation. Both approaches serve their purposes appropriately.

Regarding the development of "entrepreneurial intent," the programs differ. The youth in SOUL Sisters have opportunities to shape events and enterprises while in the program. Cookie Cart youth learn business skills and approaches that could be replicated after their time in the program. Youth leadership is important within both programs: SOUL Sisters scaffolds leadership opportunities for their participants by age group, while Cookie Cart scaffolds leadership primarily on a young person's length of time in the program.

Last, the development of social-emotional skills is central in both programs. Through using differing approaches, both case examples here show how young people grow their self-awareness, self-regulation, social awareness, relationship development, and responsible decision-making while engaging in their youth social entrepreneurial activities.

Youth Social Entrepreneurship's Potential for All Youth

5

Youth Social Entrepreneurship as Youth Development for All Youth

Introduction

Within the youth development field, there is a distinction between "universal" and "culturally bound" principles and practices. This chapter reviews the universal elements of positive youth development; that is, it explicates the basic foundations of healthy development that are important for all youth, regardless of context or background. Developmental psychology serves as a primary source for the perspectives presented here. Among the key components of this discussion are the principles of the field, a review of relational development theory, and an overview of adolescent brain development. While all of these components are influenced by the broader contexts and environments of the youth, the set of ideas included in this chapter apply to a somewhat decontextualized form of youth development theory as applied to the promise of youth social entrepreneurship. In other words, how is youth social entrepreneurship "good for all kids"? By starting with this frame, we can establish a bedrock of potential for the approach that will then be "tailored" to the contexts of youth who are marginalized in the current US milieu. In other words, after seeing how youth social entrepreneurship can be healthy for all youth, we better see how crucial it might be for youth at the periphery of society, working as an act of social justice to help them reclaim the power that is their right as a part, ultimately, of being "all youth."

Principles and Processes of Positive Youth Development

Over the past two decades, the development and use of positive indicators of child well-being have increased substantially, driven primarily by the positive youth development (PYD) perspective, as explored in Chapter 2 of this book. The challenge to a potentially potent perspective is how to operationalize it—how to make tangible the abstract principles. To that end, PYD has been conceptualized in several ways, and several theoretical frameworks have been suggested (for a review, see Lerner et al., 2011). The most frequently applied framework to operationalize PYD has been through the "Five C's" model: competence, confidence, character, connection, and caring (Table 5.1). A sixth C was added (Lerner, 2007) to mark the importance of "contribution" in adolescent development. Reviews have indicated that the Five C's Model of PYD is the most empirically supported framework to date (Heck & Subramaniam, 2009).

The Five C's were initially created to conceptualize the discrete aspects of PYD as well as to integrate the separate indicators of it, such as academic achievement or self-esteem, based on extensive reviews of the adolescent development literature and input from experienced youth practitioners (Eccles & Gootman, 2002). The Five C's have been linked to the positive outcomes of youth development programs (Roth & Brooks-Gunn, 2003; Lerner, Lerner, Almerigi, Theokas, Phelps, & Gestsdottir, S., 2005). Research also indicates that youth who manifest the 5C's are less likely to be on a trajectory of risk and problem behaviors, such as substance abuse, delinquency, and depression (Benson, Scales, Hamilton, & Sesma, 2007; Irby, Ferber & Pittman, 2001; Pittman, Irby, Tolman, Yohalem, & Ferber, 2003).

The Five C's model provides a common terminology across stakeholders; these "C's" have become prominent terms used by practitioners, adolescents involved in youth development programs, and the parents of these adolescents in describing the characteristics of a "thriving youth" (Roth & Brooks-Gunn, 2003). Although each of the C aspects has some correlation to others within the model,

TABLE 5.1

Definitions of the Five (Six) C's of positive youth development

Competence	Positive view of one's actions in domain-specific areas including social, academic, cognitive, and vocational. Social competence pertains to interpersonal skills (e.g., conflict resolution). Cognitive competence pertains to cognitive abilities (e.g., decision making). School grades, attendance, and test scores are part of academic competence. Vocational competence involves work habits and career choice explorations, including entrepreneurship.
Confidence	An internal sense of overall positive self-worth and self-efficacy; one's global self-regard, as opposed to domain-specific beliefs.
Connection	Positive bonds with people and institutions that are reflected in bidirectional exchanges between the individual and peers, family, school, and community in which both parties contribute to the relationship.
Character	Respect for societal and cultural rules, possession of standards for correct behaviors, a sense of right and wrong (morality), and integrity.
Caring	A sense of sympathy and empathy for others.
Contribution (resulting in this 6th C)	Active participation and leadership in a variety of settings; making a difference.

From Lerner et al. (2005) and Lerner (2007).

such as increased "competence" affecting increased "confidence," recognizing each as distinct makes them manageable for practitioners and researchers. In this way, the C domains are interactive with one another, and youth require healthy development in all of them. The 5(6) C's emphasize a strength-based orientation toward youth development, aiming to leverage youth experiences toward each of the C's to manifest a young person's potential.

Youth social entrepreneurship as an approach to youth development aligns nicely with the 5C's framework. Both models share the goal of engaging youth in activities that positively influence their strengths and allow them to grow. Though empirical research to support the direct link between youth social entrepreneurship and the 5C's is needed in the scholarship, examples from practice that appear to connect the models abound, as described here.

First, "competence" in the 5C's is the ability "to act effectively in school, social situations and at work" (Lerner et al., 2005). In youth social entrepreneurship programs, youth competence is paramount. Each program varies on what aspects of youth lives are targeted. For competence "in school," some youth social entrepreneurship initiatives include school achievement, but many others do not. One example application of this target is increased school competence via grades, attendance, or college acceptance.

Many include "financial literacy" as a competence goal. In this case, the youth develop skill in first-hand management of finances, both of their enterprise and of their "first paycheck." In youth social entrepreneurship, the youth learn skills relevant to the enterprise specifically, be that coffee brewing, t-shirt making, bike repair, urban gardening, or other.

Second, the 5C's model purports "confidence" as "a sense of self-worth and mastery; having a belief in one's capacity to succeed" (Lerner et al., 2005). Youth social entrepreneurship initiatives lend themselves to fostering this outcome. Developmental research about confidence highlights the importance of authentic achievement to create confidence; that is, "artificial bolstering" of a youth's ability to succeed is not effective (Erik Erikson in Coles, 2001, p. 124), but rather only real accomplishments of value in one's own context are meaningful: "meaning in their culture." In other words, the so-called self-esteem movement of the 1990s, meant to increased student confidence as a means to increase accomplishment, failed primarily in the absence of authentic and meaningful actions. A person's confidence is impacted by experiences of success, not by lip service to skills or undocumented mastery. Research on self-efficacy underscores this critical variable to the development of confidence. When youth have opportunities to exercise authentic leadership within social entrepreneurial settings, they experience the "authentic and meaningful" accomplishment of which Erikson and others have spoken.

Third, the 5C's model includes the development of "character," defined as "taking responsibility, a sense of independence and individuality; connection to principles and values" (Lerner et al., 2005). While the concept of "character" can take on slightly different meanings in different disciplines—for example, philosophy of ethics versus psychology of morality—it always relies on the centrality of an individual's responsibility toward a set of values. In youth social entrepreneurship, which character traits or principles are a focus might vary from place to place. However, when positive youth development is present in the setting, the character variable of resilience is likely to be paramount.

Next, "connection" is a key aspect of the 5C's of PYD, defined as "a feeling of safety, structure, and belonging; positive bonds with people and social institutions" (Lerner et al., 2005). Youth social entrepreneurship, as a PYD approach, emphasizes connective bonds for youth within their contexts. Maslow's theory of motivation suggests that fulfilling the human need for belonging is imperative before a young person can engage in challenge or growth opportunities. Effective youth social entrepreneurship initiatives include active attention to the creation and maintenance of bonds among the youth.

Furthermore, "contribution" is a vital element of PYD, defined as "active participation and leadership in a variety of settings; making a difference" (Lerner et al, 2005). As described earlier, as a characteristic of "confidence," an individual's experience of agency relies on making a meaningful impact. Youth social entrepreneurship offers a unique opportunity for youth to experience making real contributions, both to the enterprise itself (growing a business) and to the communities in which they are based. Said one youth named Davion "I work hard and lately I've been helping a lot of the new hires. I show them what to do in the bakery and how to act and just talk to them. It helped me when I first started that the older employees made me smile and showed me basic stuff, so now I'm doing that" (Cookie Cart, 2016).

Last, the development of "caring" is an aspect of the 5C's framework, defined as "sympathy and empathy for others; commitment to social justice" (Lerner et al., 2005). Some youth social entrepreneurship programs emphasize the social justice aspect more than others. In these cases, the aspect of "caring" could be seen as being held in higher importance than the others. Nonetheless, fostering a sense of caring comes part and parcel with teamwork, which is present in nearly all youth social entrepreneurship initiatives. In a youth social entrepreneurship, it is critical for youth to have empathy for peers while on their learning trajectory. Leaders can support this by bolstering perspective-taking among the youth and by the youth with their stakeholders—customers, community members, and others. Recent studies in learning underscore the long-term effects of empathy ("caring"). Individuals who report a higher sense of this construct may be considered as embodying *emotional intelligence* (EI). EI, defined by Salovey and Mayer (1990), connects thinking and emotion so that "caring" might be seen as both a cognitive and affective action.

> Emotional Intelligence includes the ability to engage in sophisticated information processing about one's own and others' emotions and the ability to use this information as a guide to thinking and behavior. That is, individuals

high in emotional intelligence pay attention to, use, understand, and manage emotions, and these skills serve adaptive functions that potentially benefit themselves and others. (Salovey, Mayer, & Caruso, 2008, p. 516)

In this way, the "caring" C may be operationalized by youth experience of attending to the emotional state of others and acting accordingly. This EI aspect pervades the youth social entrepreneurship world among the youth, between youth and adult partners, and perhaps especially in youth–customer interactions.

Youth Interests ("Sparks")

Late in his career, Benson pointed to the importance of what he called youth "sparks" in each young person's development (2008). He defines "sparks" as the passions, interests, and strengths that are discoverable in every person, with special concern for adolescents. Among the sparks noted by youth, the arts (visual, performing, and music) are most commonly identified, as well as athletics, service, and leadership. Business is also named as a spark. Youth social entrepreneurship activities can be seen as drawing on many of these sparks, allowing youth to ignite their individual interest area through hands-on, meaningful tasks toward a communal goal.

Using a national sample of more than 1,800 racially and ethnically diverse youth (mean age, 15 years), developmental researchers investigated the adolescents' deep passions or interests (their "sparks"), the opportunities and relationships they have to support their development of those sparks, and how much personal agency they feel they have to make civic contributions (Scales, Benson, & Roehlkepartain, 2011). Their findings point to several notable lessons: first, 100% of the youth studied claim that they understand the concept of "spark" and want to have a spark, and 62% of them say they can name their spark. This suggests that the concept is understandable and relevant within adolescents' conceptions of themselves and that identifying sparks is an accessible task, though one that may require facilitation for some youth.

Second, fewer than half of the youth were able to identify an adult who supports their spark. This supports the need for more connecting of youth to guides, role models, mentors, and the like who can take personalized attention to cultivating a teen's interest toward potential. Such an adult–youth interaction has been called a "developmental relationship," defined as "close connections through which young people discover who they are, cultivate abilities to shape their own lives, and learn how to engage with and contribute to the world around them" (Search Institute, 2017).The adult half of the relationship helps the youth half to set and achieve goals for growing their sparks and applying their interest to a greater good, such as community development. Five categories of behaviors are suggested for the adult to best foster a developmental relationship: (1) express care, (2) challenge growth,

(3) provide support, (4) share power, and (5) expand possibilities (http://www.search-institute.org/research/developmental-relationships).

Third, the Scales, Benson, and Roehlkepartain (2011) results supported the alignment of an adolescent's spark with opportunities to effect change in his or her environment, such that having "a sense of voice and supportive opportunities and relationships" has positive effects on other outcomes. In particular, "prosociality," or care and concern for others, includes community engagement activities. Other studies of sparks offer converging evidence that relates to positive developmental outcomes (Ben-Eliyahu, Rhodes, & Scales, 2014). Specifically, this growing body of research demonstrates that adolescents who can identify a spark or passionate interest and who have people in their lives who help them nurture that spark are more likely to express commitment to social contributions that benefit their broader communities.

Youth social entrepreneurship offers an ecosystem wherein young people can take their natural "sparks" and create a meaningful experience for themselves while making a positive impact on communities. This is an issue of social justice in that it may give those in underrepresented groups access to power that has not been possible in the past (Bornstein & Davis, 2010). In the United States, there is unequal access to enrichment opportunities for developing individual interests/sparks. Youth social entrepreneurship can bridge this access gap by helping youth to grow their own sparks, thus aiming to bolster positive developmental outcomes.

Relational Developmental Systems

The model of the PYD process constructed by Lerner, Lerner, and their colleagues explicitly has drawn on the individual ↔ context relational developmental systems conception as its foundation. This model has been elaborated in the context of the longitudinal study of PYD conducted by Lerner, Lerner, and colleagues: the 4-H Study of positive youth development. This research seeks to identify the individual and ecological relations that may promote thriving as well as have a preventive effect in regard to risk/problem behaviors.

The relational developmental system acknowledges how contextualized each individual's growth is in contrast to a one-sided cause–effect framework, which is often a false dichotomy of "nature" versus "nurture." Instead of this traditional understanding of development as "additive," the relational system offers a holistic view of the individual with fully interdependent parts that cannot be extracted for isolated development or examination (Overton, 2015). This meta-theory offers the youth practitioner a more robust understanding of how all aspect of each youth's development, including individual, social relationship, community, institutional, cultural, physical, ecological, and historical factors, are involved in his or her growth. Using concepts from

Bronfenbrenner's classic ecological theory of human development (1979), each level of organization within the ecology of the youth "is fused with variables from all other levels; the structure and function of one variable is thus governed, or regulated, by the structure and function of other variables" (Lerner, Johnson, & Buckingham, 2015).

The implications for research are significant. To accept the interdependence of variables in youth development requires a willingness to grapple with heightened levels of complexity. Potentially, though, it also means an opportunity to better draw dynamic representation into theories of human development that reflect reality and "may be argued to be the 'really big' question for science and society." What actions, of what duration, with what youth, in what communities, at what points in ontogenetic and historical time, will result in what features of PYD and contributions to self, family, community, and civil society? Or, more simply, we may ask the question, "How do we foster mutually beneficial relations between healthy youth and a nation marked by social justice, democracy, and liberty?" (Lerner & Overton, 2008, p. 252). These are questions that youth practitioners aim to address in every interaction, every day, everywhere.

Embracing a relational developmental systems theory holds promise for the progress of a strength-based focus, both in research and in practice. Due to the dynamism of the theoretical system, opportunities exist to enhance multiple variables at once by essentially matching youth with targeted environments and fostering targeted relationships to elicit "maximum" (or something approximating maximum) growth.

> Capitalizing on the strength inherent in all individuals because of the potential plasticity of their structural and functional attributes, the developmental scientist, in the service of increasing the probability of positive development, is interested in identifying how best to align the strengths of people with the resources for positive development present in their contexts—as both individual and context change. Understanding such alignment between individuals and the actual contexts of their lives, and specifying and studying ways to enhance these alignments across time, embeds the work of developmental science in the actual, key settings of human development, such as the family, school, and community. (Lerner & Overton, 2008, p. 247)

Specific implications for youth social entrepreneurship can be construed as the need for opportunity-rich settings to foster the "alignment" of each youth's strengths. Environments and activities that elicit authentic youth engagement and allow youth leadership to impact larger settings in meaningful ways result in the positive transactional individual ↔ context model of relational developmental systems theory.

Adolescent Brain and Youth Social Entrepreneurship

The rise of neuroscientific findings over the past three decades offers many insights for the field of youth development. Namely, the field has gained "new" understanding of the biological bases for adolescent perspectives, attitudes, needs, and opportunities during the teen years. Educators in middle and high schools and youth workers in out-of-school settings have scientifically derived approaches to their work with youth, often lending physiological credence to practices they have long employed anyway. Yet perhaps one of the most important outcomes of neuroscience findings about adolescence is the further dismantling of a deficit focus in the field. Advocates for PYD have developmental neuroscientists to thank for revealing the ways in which the adolescent brain is uniquely suited for productive and healthy activities versus being protected from the negative, sequestered to avoidance of risk behaviors without positive alternatives. Neuroscience obliterates the myth that youth in their teen years are simply immature and need to "just grow up." Instead of this being a time period to simply survive, many developmentalists see it as an opportunity to thrive and to progress through the biological changes in healthy ways that lead to successful adulthood.

In his book, *Brainstorm: The Power and Purpose of the Teenage Brain*, Dan Siegel (2013) advances the idea that adolescent brain change carries with it both potential and challenge. He structures these changes as having four key characteristics: novelty seeking, social engagement, increased emotional intensity, and creative exploration. Each of these marks the transition of the human nervous system on the way to adulthood, regardless of one's context, yet impacted by the surroundings and experiences encountered. Youth social entrepreneurship as an approach during the teen years fits in well to maximize much of the age-specific potential identified by interpersonal neurobiologists such as Siegel. What follows here is an exploration of each of these adolescent period characteristics in relation to the specific aspects of the youth social entrepreneurship model.

First, the adolescent brain experiences heightened "novelty seeking." This results from an increased drive for rewards in the brain's circuits. During the teen years, as the brain grows and restructures, there is an increase in activity of those neural circuits that use dopamine, the neurotransmitter that is key to seeking reward. Starting in early adolescence, this heightened dopamine release causes youth to gravitate toward "thrill" and to more frequently feel "bored" without novel stimulation. The increase continues until a peak in mid-adolescence, and then tapers to a more moderate level. Research suggests that, at this time, the baseline level of dopamine is lower than in adults but that its release in response to experience is much higher. This brain chemistry dynamic can elicit impulsive behaviors, with the adolescent taking risks to achieve dopamine release without consideration for broader consequences. Similarly, it increases susceptibility to addiction: the dopamine release fueled by drugs, alcohol, and high-glycemic foods is part of the addictive cycle. Additionally, studies show that in the adolescent brain, increased reward drive can result in "hyperrationality" (Siegel, 2013, p. 69). When youth place more weight on the exciting potential benefit of their actions, they often disregard the negative consequences, even though they are aware that they exist. In other words, the brain is biased in favor of a positive outcome to a behavior because of the dopamine desire.

Together, these phenomena contribute to the adolescent's inclination to make risky choices and "take chances." This diminished inhibition results in teens having disproportionately high levels of automobile accidents, overdoses, and other "preventable" deaths. Yet such tragic outcomes comprise only one side of this dopamine story. The other side is an openness and enthusiasm for novel situations. Many youth programs seek to satisfy this in healthy yet thrill-seeking ways, such as Outward Bound hikes, mountain climbing, or zip lining. Youth social entrepreneurship leverages the adolescent drive for reward by granting teens a chance to achieve a dopamine release via pushing out of their comfort zones. Whether pitching an enterprise idea to a community investor or selling a product to a new customer, many participants in youth social entrepreneurship programs cite these new experiences as having a thrill factor. In short, by its very nature of doing something different from what youth typically do—or have been given the chance to do—youth social entrepreneurship engages their extra-sensitive reward system and, in many cases, gives them an exciting surge of dopamine to keep them coming back. Youth social entrepreneurship is usually the opposite of "boring"; hence, this approach suits the youth age group particularly well.

Second, Siegel (2013) references "social engagement" as uniquely significant during the adolescent period of brain growth. During the years of adolescence, the role of connection with others changes as youth seek a larger sphere of friendships and interactions and push away from family and smaller scale environments. From an evolutionary standpoint, this action is the necessary work of youth on the way to an independent adulthood. As social mammals, if older adolescents did not commonly move into connection with the larger world, the species would risk inbreeding and unhealthy genetic patterns (Siegel, 2013, p. 75). In this way, the act of "leaving the nest" is adaptive not only to the individual but to the collective human family. During this time period, adolescents turn more toward their peers for interdependence.

Youth social entrepreneurship offers a well-timed opportunity precisely for this adolescent branching out behavior. Most youth social entrepreneurship initiatives involve interactions with a broader set of relationships both within the program as well as with vendors, stakeholders, and customers. The skill set to enact social engagement is fostered in youth social entrepreneurship because program planners tend to include explicit instruction and support for interacting with unfamiliar others. This setting satisfies the "social engagement" aspect of brain development for the adolescent age group in ways that traditional school or after-school environments do not. For example, former youth participant of Juma, Jannylee, explains of her vending work at Seattle sports venues:

my customer service skills greatly improved. I grew accustomed to having face-to-face interactions with customers in a high intensity environment. I learned to be approachable, professional, and I always kept a smile on my face even if my feet were cramping, or legs were giving out from walking so many stairs. Through the physical struggles, I gained mental strength that would help me later in life. Whether it was keeping cool and calm under pressure, or maintaining professionalism while a rude fan was unpleasant to me, vending prepared me for what was to come later in my career. (http://www. juma.org/youth-stories/)

Similarly, Tuyen says of her work with Juma:

I have grown so much working with Juma. At first, I wanted to give up because I thought I wasn't ready for all these new things. Meeting over a thousand people during every shift, talking and using customer service skills, was all overwhelming. I didn't have the confidence to do it but Juma has taught me confidence and customer service skills. Before I didn't know I could talk and interact with so many people in one day. Using this skill, I became a person who is more outgoing and not scared of talking in front of a large group of people. (http://www.juma.org/youth-stories/)

Furthermore, in youth social entrepreneurship programs that intentionally bring a community change perspective to their program, the involved youth gain opportunities to exercise their growing capacity for social cognition. The so-called social brain changes rapidly. Cognitive neuroscientists point to altered activity during the performance of social cognitive tasks, such as face recognition and mental state attribution in the medial prefrontal cortex and the superior temporal sulcus, as suggesting an impact on adolescent brain development. Research also indicates that, in humans, these parts of the social brain undergo structural development, including synaptic reorganization, during adolescence (Adolphs, 2009; Blakemore, 2008). Recent research by Rosen, Sheridan, and Sambrook (2017) suggests that the adolescents' greater sensitivity to shifts in the emotions of others is likely to promote flexible and adaptive social behavior. Meeting new people—"thousands" says Tuyen—but also thinking about the "mental state" and/or needs of others exist at a new level for youth in their teen years. Youth social entrepreneurship that facilitates youth actions on the larger community directly tap into this significant time of neural change.

Third, the neurobiology of the adolescent is characterized by intense emotionality (Siegel, 2013). Understanding the root cause of this intensity can help adults engaging with youth better grasp the meaning of their emotions. Furthermore, given the established importance of emotional regulation skill as protective against unhealthy behaviors (e.g., aggression and substance abuse), youth practitioners can better promote skill acquisition to align with the key developmental tasks of adolescence (Modecki, Zimmer-Gembeck, & Guerra, 2017). Viewed through a positive lens, the intense emotionality of the teen years is a source of passion, a driver of the "sparks" described previously. If cultivated carefully by committed adult partners within developmental relationships, this intense emotionality becomes fuel for passionate growth toward potential.

Adults, including parents and youth practitioners, can help to facilitate healthy emotional regulation of the intense emotionality in moving toward positive outcomes. Specifically, research indicates that the emotional support of adults, such as the use of "emotion coaching," is associated with more effective emotion regulation in adolescents (Morris, Criss, Silk, & Houltberg, 2017).

To conclude, adolescence involves significant and often rapid brain changes that are observable as high-risk, high-social, and high-emotion youth. These heights can be startling and concerning to nearby adults, peers, and community members, and they have led to G. Stanley Hall's famous "storm and stress" identifier of the age group more than a century ago. Today, we have the technology to peek directly into the changing brain structure to see the storm and to better navigate it, in part by reducing the stress and focusing on the strengths brought by the unique characteristics of youth. By tapping into these energetic changes, rather than stubbornly resisting them or attempting to rein them in, youth have healthier developmental outcomes and are able to provide better contributions to their communities, present and future. Many examples of youth social entrepreneurship directly embrace and leverage the specific characteristics of adolescent brain development described here to the benefit of both the young people and those in relation with them.

SOCIAL-EMOTIONAL LEARNING

Attention to and support for social-emotional learning in schools and in out-of-school settings grew rapidly in the past decade. New research, publications, and funding opportunities abound that point to both the positive outcomes of explicit social emotional instruction and to the best practices for teachers and youth workers in this field (Durlak, Domitrovich, Weissburg, & Gullotta, 2015). "Social-emotional learning" is generally defined as the "cognitive, affective, and behavioral competencies necessary for a young person to be successful in school, work, and life" (Beyond the Bell, 2015, p. 1). The Collaborative for Academic, Social, and Emotional Learning (CASEL) has developed a framework that identifies five competencies that comprise social-emotional learning:

1. *Self-awareness*: The ability to understand one's emotions and how they influence behavior
2. *Self-management*: The ability to regulate emotions, such as calming one's self down when upset, setting goals, and working toward them
3. *Social awareness*: The ability to recognize what is appropriate in certain settings and to empathize with others

4. *Relationship skills*: The ability to communicate well, to listen and respond appropriately, and to negotiate conflict
5. *Responsible decision-making*: The ability to make decisions that take into account social standards, consequences, and context

Youth social entrepreneurship holds the potential to address all five of these competencies. For example, many such programs include running an enterprise, which requires the ability to set goals and regulate behavior toward those goals (competency 2), relationships with teammates (competency 4), and well-informed, responsible decision-making (competency 5). Many programs also include customer service skills and practice interacting with adults in professional settings, which requires the growth of astute social awareness (competency 4). In some cases, youth social entrepreneurship endeavors include attention to self-awareness as they seek to build a critical consciousness of oneself as part of a larger system to make social change. This practice hinges on the ability to identify one's emotions and manage them for one's purposes (competency 1). In these ways, youth social entrepreneurship seems to hold promise as a structure into which the development of social-emotional competencies can most naturally flow.

Social-emotional learning advocates sometimes talk about these competencies as being either "caught" or "taught," which is to say either explicitly directed or implicitly included in the environment and relationships of a program, such as through observing role models. While afterschool programs and community-based youth development have long embraced and succeeded in their role as significant sources for social-emotional learning (Durlak, Weissburg & Pachan, 2010), they can benefit from increasing the intentional value of this area of outcome. Two ways this increase is happening is through well-planned assessment and targeted funding. Youth social entrepreneurship programs offer a strategic advantage to occupy this space, grow their programs, and enhance the social-emotional learning of their involved youth.

6

Youth Cultures and Contexts

Introduction

Knowing that a decontextualized understanding of youth development cannot be adequate, an examination is needed of the most relevant youth contexts in the United States at this socio-historical point in time. To do so with any accuracy requires drawing on multiple fields of inquiry—youth contexts are not solely the study of developmental scientists. Thus, this chapter reviews prominent theories of cultural theorists, sociologists, educational researchers, and political scientists to establish a depiction of the contemporary American youth context. The aim is a macro-level view of the policies and practices influencing the individual youth micro-level, including in the reader's frame of reference. Such a frame will inform perspectives in later chapters that concern narrower groups of youth (such as youth with few or no developmental relationships, those known as "disconnected youth"). Section II continues, then, with a more "universal" portrayal of youth culture in the United States before turning to Section III, which situates youth social entrepreneurship as a tool for social justice against the backdrop presented here.

A central point of concern here is that youth who lead social change are often portrayed as either "cute" or "dangerous," with both views disparaging their efforts and undermining their credible power. A brief examination of current cultural narratives about young people can inform analysis about these limiting parameters of cute or dangerous, when a more accurate and beneficial reaction would be gratitude, admiration, and even inspiration.

CONTEXT 1: YOUTH CULTURE

The concept of *youth culture* has vexed research sociologists for nearly a century in their attempts to measure and define how adolescents share group norms, values, and practices unique to their development. Early sociological research on youth subcultures in the United States predominantly concentrated primarily on the deviant aspects of youth (Williams, 2007). In popular discourse, "youth culture" often refers to the phenomena of the late 1950s into the 1960s of "hippie, punk, heavy, and techno cultures" (Salasuo & Hoikkala, 2012, p. 76). Scholarly discourse has tended to focus on the inner-city cultures in which young people dwell, influenced by the 1920s sociological focus on urban gangs and studies of delinquent behavior. More recent scholarship focuses on the subcultural aspects of youth style, such as music and dress; youth interaction with broader society, such as resistance to power; and youth social spaces, such as social media. Despite change over time within the field and dissent among scholars on the most productive approach to understanding the culture or subculture of youth, a practical lens suggests that there is value in acknowledging the shifting cultural norms of youth and the ways that they influence youth development. As it has been said, youth culture used to change "every Tuesday" when new music videos would come out depicting latest trends or styles. Current social media now means that youth culture changes daily, perhaps hourly. In short, an understanding of youth culture is a moving target that can be helpful to practitioners seeking attentiveness and acceptance of change.

The field of youth studies draws conceptualizations from a wide array of disciplines, including anthropology, criminology, education, psychology, sociology, social work, critical theory, and gender studies (Lesko & Talburt, 2012). In youth studies, the category of "youth" itself is produced to cater to social institutions such as schools, labor market, correctional facilities, families, and scientific study, rather than a biological reality based on chronological age (Wyn & White, 1997). This is in contrast with most developmental psychological as well as medical viewpoints, which are more apt to embrace the physiological aspects of "youth" in relation to the constructed social contexts. Pulling from these two separate, if not opposing, epistemologies can offer interdisciplinary researchers, youth workers, funders, and advocates a way to develop a well-rounded and well-grounded handle on the aspect of youth studies upon which they agree: that social constructions of youth, contexts, or both are never static. The ever-changing nature of both context and scholarship may result in "a shot in the dark" when attempts are made to secure a measurable reality. Observing the approaches to study and work with youth, in fact, may tell us more about academic research and social conditions that anything about actual young people (Valentine, Skelton & Chambers, 1998, p. 21).

Scholars across disciplines related to youth studies seem to agree on one more thing: that, across history, youth have never been enfranchised by the research conducted on their lives (Talburt & Lesko, 2012). Furthermore, a body of scholarship exists to document the harmful consequences of the many problematic representations of youth in academic research (Fine, 2012). As a structural inequality itself, troubling categories of youth advanced by decades of academic research play out in youth work and policy matters. In particular, young people have been studied through ideological lenses that either demonize or diminish them, and, in turn, they experience those effects in the institutions of schooling, justice, and health systems. Seen then as inferior, subservient, or delinquent, youth have been forced to participate in a youth culture that limits them by its very definition. In these ways, the pressure for youth-focused organizations to embrace "research-based practices" demands consideration of those unintentional consequences that defeat the organization's very purposes.

An illustrative example is youth interaction with television and film. Scholarly research and subsequent practices focus on the impact of young people's usage of media as consumers. Decades of research in psychological science has focused on the negative outcomes of media depictions of violence and aggressive behavior. Having established that viewing media violence in experimental laboratory conditions elicits negative effects (e.g., Bandura, 1973), resulting practices include advocacy for elimination or reduction of violent images from media. This perspective, though, neglects to acknowledge the active role of young people involved in the viewing. Far from passive recipients, their interaction with media images is much more complex and multifaceted than the simple 'cause-and-effect' models suggest (Osgerby, 2004). Rather, more recent research fills in a more full-bodied representation of the young media viewer as capable of critical consumption. Work on "critical media literacy," for example, demonstrates the alternate angle taken by scholars to document how viewers actively make meaning of the televised images they witness. In turn, practices aim to help build capacity for youth to be critically media literate as well as to reduce/eliminate the violent images available.

Similarly, academic research on youth development that has been disconnected from a youth perspective has resulted in assumptions of youth passivity and subsequent practices that aim to disrupt passivity. By contrast, youth social entrepreneurship and related models aim to harness engagement and activity, building on an assumption of young people's inherent desire to make progress and create livelihoods and community improvement. Tuck (2009) refers to this "desire-based research" in contrast to "damage-centered" analyses. No matter how well-intentioned the damage-centered frameworks of understanding are—and often they are—they are steeped in an underlying belief of inferiority and/or deficit. Desire-based frameworks, on the other hand, assume that "youth make the best choices they can, based on the information available to them" (p. 21). A close cousin to the asset-based perspectives described in Chapter 2 of this book, desire-based research frameworks reject the aim to document problems ("deficits"), including pain, loss, and even devastation of communities. Instead, they seek to understand the "complexity, contradiction, and self-determination of lived lives . . . dismiss[ing] one-dimensional analyouth social entrepreneurships of people, communities, and tribes as flattened, derelict, ruined" (p. 20). In this way, one may see that desire-based researchers safeguard their subjects' agency, which in turn connects it well to the movement of positive developmental psychology. Here, agency is defined by "the interplay between a person and the action space surrounding him or her" (Little, Walls, & Malmberg, 2009). Assuming personal agency within a research framework means assuming that youth have the ability to actively shape their environments, even within constrained systems of action (like a typical school day!). In other words, environments counterexert in ways that either help or hinder the actor's intended outcomes. For proponents of youth social entrepreneurship, this is a key assumption.

Desire-based research on youth social entrepreneurship, then, seeks to represent how the young people involved have multifaceted lives, with complex identities and perspectives, set against a "moving target" of youth culture, yet oriented always to positive aspirations.

CONTEXT 2: ECONOMY AND POLITICS

Economic and political milieus influence the contexts of youth development in significant ways. The foundational formulation of Bronfenbrenner's ecological theory of development includes, among its five nested systems, a macrosystem that reflects a society's cultural values and related public policies (1979). The macrosystem offers a backdrop for the developing microsystem (the immediate environment) that includes an individual's socioeconomic status, societal power, and privilege. The macrosystem is constructed through cultural patterns and values, specifically the individual's dominant beliefs and ideas, as well as political and economic systems. Research and practices in youth development are also influenced by the larger macrosystem, such that the pressing concerns and dominant beliefs of a society push viewpoints of young people in directions aligned to the particular macrosystem existing within the socio-historic setting.

While developmental psychologist like Bronfenbrenner strive to acknowledge the powerful influence of the macrosystems—within the nested group of other direct and indirect environments—on the individual, cultural theorists offer a vantage point that sees the specific "color" of the macrosystem. A key example relevant to youth development is Giroux's cultural critique of modern capitalism.

Giroux's analysis of the "disposability of youth" (2013) suggests an American macrosystem that devalues its young and practices those values via public policy. Through virulent sources of current Western society's economic and political values, Giroux and theorists like him depict a modern "war against youth" (p. 16) via neoliberalism and authoritarianism. The result is systemic disinvestment in the contexts where society's younger generations can grow healthfully and access necessary conditions for social justice and equity.

Concretely, realities such as a "bloated defense budget, prison-industrial complex, and environmental degradation" (p. 11) point to a disregard for the upcoming adult members of a society. Economically, this disregard plays out through the high value of individualism, privatizations, and deregulations that elevate the market above the individual. Politically, it plays out through a political elite bent on totalitarianism, religionization of politics, and an intense attachment to partisanship over the collective good. Against this backdrop, American youth live and grow, but the resulting microsystem limits their development. They are hindered by an "ongoing militarization of public schools" (p. 73), a dehumanizing curriculum and instruction, and a lack of critical thinking exercises that result in "America's education deficit" (Giroux, 2013).

Furthermore, the systemic racism embedded in America's history and present continue to shape its macrosystem, such that youth of color are further terrorized by the political and economic values of the day:

> Poor minority youth . . . are not just excluded from the American Dream but have become utterly redundant and disposable, waste products of a society that no longer considers them of any value. Such youth, already facing forms of racial- and class-based exclusion, now experience a kind of social death as they are pushed out of schools, denied job training opportunities, subjected to rigorous modes of surveillance and criminal sanctions, and viewed less as chronically disadvantaged than as flawed consumers and civic felons. (p. 111)

It is against this backdrop that youth social entrepreneurship as a model aims to intervene. By shifting power to youth, by participating in capitalist practices but with the critical perspective of acknowledging its effects, and by centralizing collective good and community development, youth social entrepreneurship can step into the social responsibility emphasized as necessary by Giroux, Freire, and other critical theorists of modern oppression. While youth culture in contemporary America is characterized by limited empowerment and limited access to independence, youth social entrepreneurship aims to disrupt these patterns by arming youth with authentic leadership and agency.

CONTEXT 3: SCHOOLS

The current era of American public education has been marked by concerns of *accountability*, most notably driven by the 2001 federal policy of No Child Left Behind and continued in general style by the 2009 Race to the Top. In both approaches, schools and districts are in competition with one another for funding based on demonstrated success. Here, "success" refers to the measured achievement of students primarily through test scores. The advent of state standardized tests and the growth of high-stakes graduation exams only cemented the sense of competition for resources in the world of K–12 education at the start of the twenty-first century. The focus on school accountability and measurable achievement became grossly distorted during this period, with its full reliance on standardized multiple-choice testing. Says educational historian Diane Ravitch (2010): "The problem was the misuse of testing for high-stakes purposes, the belief that tests could identify with certainty which students should be held back, which teachers and principals should be fired or rewarded, and which schools should be closed" (p. 150).

Many notable negative outcomes resulted within the testing culture of the 2000s. Nichols and Berliner (2007) traced 10 identifiable consequences to education's growing reliance on standardized test scores through a systematic scouring of news outlets and scholarly journals for accounts of the impact of high-stakes testing, amassing a "significant collection of evidence highlighting the distortion, corruption, and collateral damage that occur when high-stakes tests become commonplace in our public schools" (p. 10). The higher the importance of the testing (the "stakes"), the more the negative consequences seem to be present.

In addition to the inadequacy of a single score to accurately reflect student learning (thus marking it as a low-validity measure), the standardized testing movement brought collateral damage including a narrowed curriculum, lower teaching morale, and an in-class pedagogy that disproportionately favors multiple-choice thinking over creative, open-ended learning. Supplemental and "enrichment" opportunities for learning flourished to make up for this gap, including summer programs and for-profit educational centers like Kumon. Many of these options are well beyond the financial reach of low-income and even middle-income families. Other out-of-school-time (OST) programs sought to fill the space left by standardized teaching-to-the-test via free or affordable after-school programs in arts, sports, and service. While after-school program funders continued (and, to some extent, still continue) to target an "academic achievement" impact with their grant-making, this score-based obsession waned in the second decade of the 2000s, giving way to a more holistic learning focus on social-emotional student growth.

Youth social entrepreneurship is among one of the OST movements that has filled in learning opportunities where standardized testing has left off. In youth social entrepreneurship initiatives, adolescents experience the kind of hands-on learning that is directly opposite of what the standardized-testing culture offers. *Authentic tasks*—actions that fit into real-life, everyday settings—have been long demonstrated to be effective for lasting learning. Foundational principles of educational psychology indicate that students are more highly motivated by authentic activities. In turn, when they find tasks more meaningful and interesting, their engagement is higher and their long-term retention is improved (Pugh & Phillips, 2011). Examples of authentic learning tasks in youth social entrepreneurship programs abound. They include planning how to address the identified community need, researching approaches, forming groups to implement plans, speaking with community members, creating products for an enterprise, and more.

Another well-researched approach to learning that counters the standardized-testing culture is *problem-based learning*. In this method, students are given real-world problems that do not necessarily have a single right answer. Instead, they must use high-order thinking to synthesize what they know and apply solutions, often working in groups to do so. As a type of authentic task itself, problem-based learning has been found to positively impact student interest, engagement, and long-term memory (Anderman & Anderman, 2010). Examples of problem-based learning in youth social entrepreneurship programs abound. They include seeking solutions to ill-defined problems in a neighborhood, navigating group dynamics among community stakeholders, managing peer behavior within a social enterprise, applying limited resources to manage product creation, and more.

Since the period of No Child Left Behind educational policy (2001–2015), the continued effects of the high-stakes testing movement linger in the culture of education. A narrowed curriculum leads to both limited opportunities for students to explore topics of interest beyond what will be tested and limited chances to engage in authentic tasks and problem-based learning. OST programs like youth social entrepreneurship are vital for the well-rounded and engaged development of adolescent students.

As noted earlier, *school pushout* is another deleterious effect of the testing movement of the 2000s. Students of color and/or from working and impoverished social strata have disproportionately been affected by "school pushout" experiences, defined as the conditions in which school administrators and their policies compel adolescent students to permanently leave school due to factors such as "disrespectful treatment by teachers and other school personnel, violence among students, and the insurmountable presence of high-stakes testing" (Tuck, 2012, p. 1). As a term, "school pushout" directs attention to the environmental context that results in students not completing high school versus "dropout," which suggests they have full autonomy to withdraw, thus suggesting they have made a choice not to complete.

Even in the earliest years of the No Child Left Behind legislation, the concerning trend of student dropout/pushout patterns was well-noted. A 2001 report by the New York City Board of Education warned that increasing high-stake standards has an evidenced negative impact on "the most at-risk students" and that interventions must be applied consistently to reduce the related high risk of dropping out (Tuck, 2012, p. 79).

Extensive educational research has explored the impact of after-school, OST, and/or extracurricular activities to reduce school dropout/pushout. While results suggest that additional activities alone do not act as a "magic bullet" for youth leaving high school before completion, many findings support the positive influence these programs tend to have. Perhaps the most notable is the Eccles, Barber, Stone, and Hunt (1999) longitudinal study, which reported a positive association between after-school/extracurricular participation and education completion. They found that generally all types of activities, ranging from church groups to student government and cheerleading, were associated with a higher likelihood of full-time college enrollment at 21 years of age. Upon further investigation, they identified peers as the mediating variable that associates activity participation with positive academic outcomes; simply put, the youth participating in afterschool activities tend to have peer groups who plan to complete high school and attend college and were also doing well in school. Multiple additional studies have demonstrated this finding as well: a positive relation between extracurricular activity and staying in school, especially among "at-risk adolescents" (see Feldman & Matjasko, 2005 for a review).

Mahoney and Cairns (1997) reported that school dropout rates among students with identified dropout risk factors were significantly lower for those in extracurricular activities than for those who did not participate. Among at-risk but academically and socially "competent" students, higher dropout rates were found only in cases in which students did not participate in any extracurricular activities. Mahoney and Cairns determined that linear increases in activity participation were accompanied by large reductions in dropout rates. In addition, Mahoney (2000) reported that participation in at least one extracurricular activity was associated with reduced rates of early dropout among high-risk boys and girls. On the basis of previous work, Mahoney (2000) asserted that it was not the activity that led to lower dropout rates. Rather, it was the social networks that adolescents acquired through participation that kept them engaged with their schools and prevented them from dropping out (Feldman & Matjasko, 2005).

The power dynamics of the testing movement has also contributed to school pushout. Many researchers point to the cultural bias often present in the forms and values of standardized tests. In literacy measurement, for example, high-stakes standardized testing seem "to build upon the legacy of dominant power relations in the state in its ability to sort, select and rank students and ultimately produce and name some youth as illiterate in contrast to an ideal white, male, literate citizen" (Kearns, 2013). Thus, school becomes another space where a youth of color and/or without educated parents is considered inferior and where he or she feels left out and ultimately pushed out. Effective OST, which youth social entrepreneurship programs can and should be, may become havens for thwarting the social power dynamics that deeply damage so many adolescents' future pathways. Instead, they can offer the healthy space for exercising personal power and "literacy," as defined by the authentic settings of their social enterprise and community. These spaces can become a balm to begin the healing of the "structural trauma" induced by the high-stakes, high-pushout contexts created and perpetuated within standardized testing schools (Ginwright, 2016).

Section II

Focal Case Examples

The young, free to act on their initiative, can lead their elders in the direction of the unknown . . . The children, the young, must ask the questions that we would never think to ask, but enough trust must be re-established so that the elders will be permitted to work with them on the answers.

—MARGARET MEAD

Case 1: SOUL Sisters Leadership Collective

At SOUL Sisters Leadership Collective (SSLC), many intentional practices are engaged to promote the positive youth development of their participating youth members. SSLC programming involves young women and girls of a broad age range: an average of ages 11–18, but with some programming that begins at age 8 years. Hence, their staff design curriculum to be age-appropriate and adjust practices to fit the age level of each specific cohort. In this way, they apply an awareness of the relevant neurobiology of their youth, recognizing the need to alter plans to meet these young people at their point of development.

Furthermore, they explicitly engage youth in learning about brain development, including mindfulness about emotional reactivity and impulses. In this way, they are promoting emotional regulation, as described in Chapter 5. A focus for them is on recognizing one's "individual triggers" (W. Douglas, personal communication, 2017). Because many of the SSLC youth have experienced trauma in a number of forms over their lifetimes, a careful attention to trauma-informed practices is well-warranted. Basic characteristics of trauma-informed practices include realizing the widespread impact of trauma and understanding potential paths for recovery; recognizing the signs and symptoms of trauma in clients, families, staff, and others involved with the system; responding by fully integrating knowledge about trauma into policies, procedures, and practices; and seeking to actively resist retraumatization (SAHMSA, 2018). To this end, SSLC staff say they are explicit in their use of trauma-informed practices, thus empowering their youth to better understand themselves and identify their needed pathway to health. This is what Siegel (2014) has referred to as "name it to tame it." Siegel's well-known "handy model of the brain" is an often-used part of the SSLC prac-tice. Teaching the youth an applicable way to think about the neural processes involved in their experiences of emotional dysregulation, such as anger, fear, and stress, helps them to intervene in it, thus increasing prevention and improving re-covery. Learning when emotional dysregulation causes you to "flip your lid" helps youth—and adults!—better regulate their emotional state and retain neural inte-gration (Siegel, 2013).

Furthermore, Soul Sisters' use of this approach demonstrates attentiveness to their youth's changing neurobiology in relation to their contexts of trauma. Sensitivity to their development in this way is in line with the relational devel-opmental systems theory, acknowledging the dynamic and complex interplay of the young women's developing selves. Yet the asset-focused approaches of this program empower the youth to retain emotional regulation, thwarting the deficit view that they are "broken" and need to be fixed.

The SOUL Sisters program encourages their youth to become involved in a self-designed social entrepreneurship work, known as their "Social Action Project." Each cohort collaborates to plan, research, and implement this project based on the needs of their community and on the identified strengths of the young women in the cohort. In this way, SSLC embodies the igniting of youth "sparks," as described in Chapter 5. The staff partner with the youth to consider their interests and investigate the contexts in which they will act. They then create a "desire-based" project, the implementation of their group's aspirations for the community. Examples include hosting a community healing circle for 200 people in Miami to address police shootings (July 9, 2016) and projects of "theater, spoken word, film, and photography, among other art forms, to explore issues impacting young women of color" (https://www.soulsistersleadership.org).

The consistently asset-based approaches of SSLC toward the healing and lead-ership of their youth also embody an antithesis to the culture of "youth dispos-ability" fermenting in US society (Giroux, 2010). SOUL Sisters helps youth and their communities by creating the spaces and opportunities for the young women to essentially prove that they are not disposable but instead are purposeful, mean-ingful, and productive people who deserve and demand the creation of a society that values them.

Case 2: Cookie Cart

Cookie Cart also incorporates numerous elements of the concepts raised in Section II of this book. Their program design takes youth development into ac-count first by considering age. Director of Development Marit Michels says, "15–17 is our sweet spot"; the young people are old enough to work in the bakery and learn the program curriculum, but are still within an age that they have not been significantly disconnected (simultaneously out-of-school and out-of-work).

Keeping the principles of youth development central to their work, the walls of the bakery display the organization's long-term impact goals for their youth, painted on separate walls as a visual commitment: Connectedness to new communities, Strengthened future goal orientation, Improved interpersonal skills, Enhanced critical thinking skills, Increased employment readiness skills.

The youth program at Cookie Cart demonstrates each of the 5(6)C's of PYD:

1. *Competency*: Cookie Cart bakers complete a Safe Food Certification process that teaches them restaurant industry standard skills in the areas of personal hygiene, allergens, time and temperature control in food preparation, cross-contamination, cleaning, and sanitation (Cookie Cart, 2016, p. 11). This is a real-world competence that can bolster a young person's sense of purpose and ability to have applicable skills. Furthermore, they build competence in managing the financial responsibility of having a paying job. This "hands-on curriculum" covers the "building blocks of personal finance: budgeting and saving, checking accounts, and personal credit" (Cookie Cart, 2016). Their process is considered effective, with 165 teens in an average program year completing this training and 89% reporting that they see themselves at more competent to "use a bank, budget, and save money" (p. 7).

   Competency goals of youth social entrepreneurship frequently include business skills such as customer service. Program participants who also complete customer service training apply these skills at the shop's front counter and/or at the "pop-up" sales locations around the city, including at Major League baseball games. Youth often report the ability to talk to potential customers to sell the Cookie Cart product and represent the program as a new competence area. In 2016, 69% of the involved youth said that they learned interpersonal communication skills. Says one youth named Jada, "Cookie Cart is helping me build my communication skills because before I started working here I couldn't look you in the eye, but I got used to doing it here and to greeting everyone when I see them." (Note: all youth quotes in this section are publicly available at http://cookiecart.org/about/blog, 2017.)

2. *Character*: At Cookie Cart, youth are expected to learn from mistakes and embody a growth mindset (Dweck, 2006) that sees failures as a necessary part of learning. Said Jada at Cookie Cart: "When I made four 20 dozen boxes and I tried to put them on the top of the shelf and they all fell down on me and I had to throw them away, but I didn't know I had to throw them away. So I was just was going to put them back up, but then everybody in the bakery was like 'you can't do that', I was embarrassed, but I didn't let it get to me though. I learned something."

3. *Confidence*: Cookie Cart's program builds confidence by supporting youth to move out of what is comfortable to them. The experience of

mastering new tasks yields increased confidence. Said one youth named Antiquita: "when we sold out at the Twins Home Opener, I stepped out of my comfort zone twice—once through talking to everyone passing, making sure they noticed us, and second by going further out from the cart into the crowd."

4. *Caring*: At Cookie Cart, training on customer service is a fundamental element of their preparation, not only scaffolding the young bakers to be professional in their customer interactions, but also caring of the perspectives of their cookie buyers. Furthermore, Cookie Cart programming is designed to engage the youth with one another in a collaborative culture of the kitchen. Said one Cookie Cart youth named Elijah: "I used to not like talking to people I didn't know, but now I like learning everyone's story and sharing my own and finding things we have in common."

5. *Connection*: One of Cookie Cart's key missions is supporting the young bakers in retaining connections to their communities and creating new connections outside of their communities as well. The latter happens during cookie sales in public venues, as well as through strategic partnerships with corporate volunteers who make cookies with the youth and practice job readiness activities. Connections are also reflected in the connectedness among the youth, many of whom attend different schools and are meeting for the first time. Said one youth named Pheng: "It's been fun working here from the start because everyone is welcoming and made me feel part of the team. I thought it would be challenging to work in the bakery, but it's not because we're a team."

6. *Contribution*: Realizing that you are capable of making meaningful contributions to others and even to your larger community is an important part of this "C." Cookie Cart fosters a sense of meaningful contribution for a group of youth by providing a plethora of opportunities to share cookies—their very own handiwork—with communities nearby, the local neighborhood, and even the downtown corporate community, among others. Through their handmade and edible contribution, the youth's cookies provide tangible evidence to themselves and their world that they can make a contribution—and are not thereby "disposable" (Giroux, 2010). Their contributions as individuals are also vital because of the interdependence of the bakery operations, as noted by Cookie Cart youth Jada's delight in contributing to the team: "In the bakery, I show a lot of leadership, like if anybody doesn't know what to do, or looks confused, I'll just go over there myself and ask them if they need help. Even if I don't know how to help, I'll still refer them to Ashley. I also try to be friends with everyone—talk to the new hires and all the volunteers, even when I'm not on the clock I still try to talk to them. And I'm just always so happy."

Last, as an antidote to the school disengagement described in Chapter 6, baking cookies may be the "ultimate" authentic learning task! The youth bakers are entirely hands-on in their learning, experimenting with the process of cookie making: mixing, prepping, and handling the ingredients. The project-based learning happens in many ways—many of which are called Chocolate Chip, M&M, Chocolate Chocolate Chip, Snickerdoodle, Peanut Butter, Gingersnap, Oatmeal Raisin, and Coconut Toffee. Like all truly authentic, project-based learning experiences, mistakes are not only expected but welcomed, as is collaborative problem-solving. As described by a Cookie Cart youth named Cirea: "You get to learn from your mistakes. When I first started, I dropped a cookie on the ground and I thought you could pick it up, but everyone was nice and helped me learn that you can't do that. Everyone helps you if you have questions and helps you figure out another way to do things."

This is an unusual experience for many youth in the high-stakes testing era of recent decades, especially those in high-poverty schools where testing and accountability pressures are the most severe. "We're the world's most inefficient bakery," jokes Michels, referring to their high value for the authentic learning process and of mistakes as part of youth experience.

Focal Cases Summary: Key Concepts from Section II

Both SOUL Sisters and Cookie Cart operate within the broader macrosystem of youth culture, American education policy, and volatile economic and political climates. They aim to counter the numerous disempowering pressures affecting their involved youth by providing concrete opportunities to hold power, both within their programs and taken out into public spheres (e.g., cookie sales for Cookie Cart and public events for SOUL Sisters).

Both programs apply PYD principles of igniting youth sparks—interests that capture their motivation and energy—and of building healthy developmental relationships within their programs through intentional design. SOUL Sisters takes this healthy holistic development a step further with embedded curriculum for neuroscience-based stress management strategies and trauma-informed practices (see Chapter 9 for more on this).

Youth Social Entrepreneurship's Role in Social Justice

7

The Economic Opportunity Gap

What if young people were activated, not to just to solve problems
on a test, but to solve problems in their lives and in society as well?

—ROBERTO RIVERA, *FOUNDER OF THE GOOD LIFE ORGANIZATION*

Introduction

For as much potential toward positive youth development (PYD) that youth social entrepreneurship programs offer, their potency for impact may be even more
notable within a specific population of youth; that is, those for whom similar
opportunities are not accessible. For this population of young people, youth social
entrepreneurship holds a twofold benefit: reducing the equity gap in enriching
experiences that affect one's future, as well as empowering a young person to confront the system's underlying disparity in the first place. In simpler terms, youth
social entrepreneurship has the potential to lessen the opportunity gap and, in so
doing, enable youth to improve their local communities and the broader societal
context because they have the resources to do so. This is the crux, then, of youth
social entrepreneurship as an issue of social justice.

This chapter explores the demographic trends in the United States of youth
for whom youth social entrepreneurship may have these effects, framed by the *opportunity gap*. This gap has been conceptualized by the field of education to better
explain outcome disparities for youth of color and/or from low-income families.
Academic disciplines and the nonprofit sector have embraced this framework
and furthered it by identifying the youth "haves" and "have-nots" depending on
their access to opportunities of many kinds: educational and economic among
them. Youth without, or with fewer, opportunities tend to also lack connections of
many kinds that can inhibit their educational, employment, housing, and health
outcomes. This, then, is the central concern of this chapter: What is lost when a
young person does not have equal or ample opportunities and becomes *disconnected*? What are the means for ameliorating the disconnection, and how can
youth social entrepreneurship be a part of that solution?

Opportunity Youth, Disconnected Youth

Since 2010, discourse around disparities in education has shifted to account for critical input factors instead of focusing only on the outcome of "educational achievement." Prior to that, much attention—research and policy—centered on the established "achievement gap," which had been illuminated by the growing big data from standardized tests across the United States. This disaggregated data evidenced the stark disparities in educational variables by social group, race, and socioeconomic class.

The language of the "achievement gap" helped move national attention to the inequity that hounds traditionally marginalized groups in the United States. News coverage, politicians, and average citizens became better versed in the quantified reality of persistent disparities. This gap is operationalized by statistically significant lower grades, standardized test scores, course selection, dropout rates, and college completion rates for students of color and/or of low-income backgrounds.

Finding a proper way to frame a problem gives us not only a better understanding of it but also impacts the ways in which we address the problem and work so solve it. Shifting the frame from looking at measures of educational outcomes to examining what students actually experience in schools results in a very different way of describing disparities among students in schools. This new frame calls attention to the fact that African American and Latino students are less likely than white students to have teachers who emphasize high-quality mathematics instruction and appropriate use of resources.

For example, by the eighth grade, 91% of African American and 87% of Latino students are not proficient in mathematics, as measured by the National Assessment of Educational Progress (NAEP, 2007). This stands in stark contrast to the lower proportions of Asian American (53%) and white (63%) students who are not proficient. In fact, twelfth-grade Latino and African American students perform as well as eighth-grade white students on NAEP's mathematics assessment (Flores, 2007).There is also a considerable gap in mathematics test performance between students from poor families and those from non-poor families. Only 13% of students from poor families are at the proficient or advanced levels, compared to 38% of students from non-poor families (Wiener, 2006, in Flores, 2007).

Simultaneous to the shift to "opportunity gap," economic development entities launched an initiative to understand unemployed and undereducated young people as "opportunity youth." Defined as youth aged 16–24 who have been disconnected from school or work for at least 6 months, opportunity youth comprise a segment of the population in need of targeted intervention to improve experiences and prospects. There are an estimated 6.7 million young people in this category (Warland, Applegate, Schnur, & Jones, 2015). These youth are disproportionately male and from minority groups, though substantial rates are found for all youth groups. Common causes for young people to become part of this category are:

- dropping out of high school or college and been unable to find work;
- being involved in the criminal justice system;
- having mental or health conditions that have inhibited their activities; or
- having caregiving responsibilities in their families that prevent them from engaging in wage-producing labor and/or schooling.

"Opportunity youth" refers to older adolescence intentionally because young people in this age group experience distinct developmental milestones on their way to becoming healthy, connected, and productive adults. While this developmental phase is rich with possibility and the promise to make more independent decisions, create career goals, and engage in meaningful relationships, it is also during this time that young people transitioning to adulthood experience increased vulnerability and risk (see Chapter 5 for details). This is a significant time period for youth to become disconnected from family, school, or work. They are more likely than younger youth to lack access to physical and mental health care and may engage in risky or unsafe behaviors. This "disconnection" to adult supports makes the time period for opportunity youth unique from the admittedly intense needs of early or middle childhood.

In the United States, approximately 3.4 million young people are "chronic" opportunity youth, meaning that they have never been in school or work after the age of 16. Another 3.3 million are "underattached" opportunity youth; despite some schooling and some work experience beyond 16, these youth have not progressed through college or secured stable employment. Both categories share the challenge of failing to build their own "economic foundation for adult independence" and of being a costly burden on society through reliance on government supports, increased criminal activity, and worse health outcomes (Belfield, Levin, & Rosen, 2012, p. 1). The economic impact is significant: researchers estimate that each opportunity youth imposes an immediate taxpayer burden of $13,900 per year and an immediate social burden of $37,450 per year (2011 dollars) for each year that a youth is identified as having opportunity youth status. Aggregate taxpayer burden amounts have been projected to $1.56 trillion in present value terms, with an aggregate social burden of $4.75 trillion. Opportunity youth are disproportionately from racial minorities in the United States; while the overall 2011 unemployment rate for 16- to 24-year-olds was 18%, for young African Americans and Hispanics it was 30% and 20%, respectively (Statistics Portal, July 2017).

Youth social entrepreneurship programming often aims to engage youth who would be categorized in this way. A potential benefit to the field of practice is to situate the youth social entrepreneurship model within the nation's economic need for opportunity youth to find meaningful connection and employment.

Unemployment

According to the Bureau of Labor Statistics (2017), in 2016 11.5% of all American young people 16–24 years old were counted as "unemployed": defined as not employed, yet available for work, and had actively looked for a job sometime during the prior 4 weeks. Disaggregated by racial group, the following trends in unemployment are detected, suggesting disproportionate unemployment for African American youth (Summer Youth Labor Force News Release, 2017):

- White youth: 9.9%
- Black or African American youth: 20.6%
- Asian youth: 10.0%
- Hispanic youth: 11.3%

Notably, the Workforce Innovation and Opportunity Act (WIOA) was signed into law in 2014 (Pub. L. 113-128), designed to help job seekers access employment, education, training, and support services to succeed in the labor market and to support employers with the skilled workers they need to compete in the global economy (Department of Labor, WIOA Overview, 2016). WIOA was the first legislative reform of the public workforce system in 15 years and was passed by Congress with an unusually wide bipartisan majority. The US Departments of Labor and Education undertook the process of implementing WIOA to revamp the nation's workforce training programs, involving $20 billion in funding. The WIOA offers many things: strategic alignment of workforce development training programs, increased accountability and transparency, and support for regional collaboration that coordinates job development within states. Most significant to the field of youth development, though, this policy change included a revitalized focus on young people who have been detached from school or employment. WIOA is notable in its goal of making "key investments in serving disconnected youth and other vulnerable populations" (Department of Labor, WIOA Overview, 2016). For example, organizations that receive WIOA funds are required to spend 75% of funding on out-of-school youth versus 30% under a previous law (Families & Youth Services Bureau, March 2016). Furthermore, local areas must spend at least 20% of youth funds on work experience activities such as summer jobs, pre-apprenticeship, on-the-job training, and internships so that youth are prepared for employment. While the long-term effects of the WIOA are yet to be identified, in the short-term, dozens of partner programs have been bolstered by this policy approach.

Youth social entrepreneurship offers a unique space for opportunity youth. A number of programs have aimed to fill the employment void and increase educational outcomes. For example, YouthBuild is a long-standing agency with locations worldwide that engages opportunity youth in meaningful job experiences to disrupt patterns of underemployment while simultaneously boosting the infrastructure of their communities. The youth involved tend to have previous incarceration and/or school dropout experiences in their background.

The YouthBuild program has five components: construction, education, counseling, leadership, and graduate opportunity. Community development is simultaneous to individual youth development: the young people who participate in YouthBuild "pursue a dual mission: to create a meaningful and productive life for themselves and their families while giving their best energies to improve the world around them" (www.youthbuild.org/what-we-do/we-serve).

Students spend every other week on a job site, learning the construction trade by building homes for their own communities, thereby creating housing opportunities for low-income people while simultaneously giving the youth new and marketable job skills. On the alternating weeks, the youth attend a YouthBuild classroom with the goal of attaining their high school diploma, often via a GED. YouthBuild programs provides new pathways to livelihoods and productive future "by unleashing the positive energy of low-income young people to rebuild their communities and their lives, breaking the cycle of poverty with a commitment to work, education, community, and family" (www.youthbuild.org/what-we-do).

There are 260 urban and rural YouthBuild programs in 46 of the 50 United States, with a total capacity of about 16,000 students yearly, and there are similar programs under way in more than 15 countries. In 2014, 2,000 units of affordable housing were constructed, and 8,000 YouthBuild graduates were placed into jobs or continuing education.

YouthBuild is a type of youth social entrepreneurship because, in addition to traditional school completion and trade skill development, it fosters youth empowerment so that young people can become leaders in their communities and work for social change: "YouthBuild USA promotes the voice of youth at every level. We sponsor an annual Conference of Young Leaders and an annual Hill Day in which students speak with elected officials about their realities, and organize the 1000 Leaders Network to become involved in public affairs" (www.youthbuild.org/lifting-youth-voice). A core value of the organization is that "young people are capable of playing a leadership role and if encouraged to do so will bring enormous energy, creativity, and imagination to the work, as well as ideas that are well informed by the reality they face."

Commonly, opportunity youth need help overcoming barriers to employment and accessing the labor market because they face significant challenges such as extreme poverty, homelessness, and justice system involvement. Hence, programs for opportunity youth offer more intensive assistance in entering and keeping employment. In YouthBuild, for example, counseling is provided to address underlying stressors or health concerns that can limit a young person's ability to progress in his or her plans.

The foundation-convening body known as "Youth Transition Funders Group," aims "to guide investments and support improved well-being outcomes for vulnerable young people" (Langford & Badeau, 2015, p. 4). To this end, they highlight the means by which the multiple systems in the life of opportunity youth can best promote healthy outcomes. These systems include formal education, child welfare, youth employment, and youth justice. Furthermore, they have produced a "Well-Being Framework for Vulnerable Youth and Young Adults" to addresses the holistic development of all youth, but especially disconnected youth (whom they call "vulnerable"). The six domains of well-being are cognitive, social-emotional, mental health, physical, and economic. While youth social entrepreneurship touches on many of these domains, it may hold *unique value* for disconnected youth in the area of "economic well-being."

This framework acknowledges that while all young people should have the opportunity, education, and supports to obtain and retain steady employment that provides a living wage and a career path, youth who are disconnected need targeted support to gain work experience as well as exposure to a range of career options. To this end, they benefit most by having "a range of work and career options, soft-skills training, educational requirements, and financial aid resources available to help them achieve career goals," which can be intentionally supplied by the personal or public contacts in their lives (Langford & Badeau, 2015, p. 24). Additionally, they need opportunities to achieve a high school diploma and to gain work experience that matches their interests and abilities through part-time, after-school, and summer employment, including volunteer service, internships, work-study programs, and career exploration activities, many of which are available through out-of-school programs. Youth social entrepreneurship programs, in particular, lend themselves naturally to developing this economically related learning. The "Well-Being Framework for Vulnerable Youth and Young Adults" also points out that youth need to obtain all necessary documents required for entry and success in the workforce and to obtain financial management skills, including skillsets and mindsets that help them save and accumulate assets. The report advocates for collaboration to implement such opportunities:

> Public and private leaders should work together to ensure that young people have access to a broad range of post-secondary options, including two- and four-year colleges, apprenticeships, certificate programs, and other vocational, service, or interest-oriented post-secondary opportunities, as well as the financial and other supports needed to successfully complete such programs. Community leaders must always work to grow the employment base and the local economy, while exposing youth to entrepreneurship and self-employment options. (Langford & Badeau, 2015, p. 24)

Economic Asset-Building

In his seminal volume *Assets and the Poor: A New American Welfare Policy* (1991), Michael Sherraden proposed what was at the time a radical social policy concept: the importance of individual asset accumulation as a way out of poverty for both individuals and their communities.

Sherraden introduced Individual Development Accounts (IDA) in which "the main idea is to offer a development account to everyone that begins at birth. Money could accumulate in these accounts and matching would be progressive, with lower-income families receiving a higher contribution." In the 25 years since then, IDAs have been adopted in federal legislation and in more than 40 states (Martin, 2011). Social economic research suggests that incentivized savings help low-income families "get a toehold in the financial world and increase financial literacy" (McKernan & Ratcliffe, 2009, p. 5). In this way, asset-building is an important movement in anti-poverty policy and community development, which is "not only about fairness, but about enabling all Americans to become stronger and more productive citizens" (Sherraden, 2001, p. 4).

Disruption of Financial Patterns

Some research has indicated that parental savings, particularly for college, is predictive of teen savings behavior (Pritchard, Myers, & Cassidy, 1989). In a related finding, Beverley and her colleagues (2003) report that 60% of participants in IDA programs say that they are more likely to make educational plans for their children because they are saving. A number of studies suggest that assets are also related to relationship and familial stability. For example, Bracher, Santow, Morgan, and Trussell (1993) have demonstrated that, while controlling for a number of other social and economic factors, asset accumulation via homeownership reduces the risk of marital dissolution.

Asset development seems to also have positive effects on physical health. In one example study (Stronks, van de Mheen, van den Bos, & Mackenbach, 1997), asset accumulation via a socioeconomic measure that includes homeownership is positively related to health (fewer chronic conditions and better perceived health), even when controlling for the effects of occupation, education, and employment status. Graduation rates are positively correlated to homeownership, and research finds that a substantial proportion of the effects of homeownership on child graduation rates are due to increased residential stability, especially for low-income children (Green & White, 1997; Aaronson, 2000).

Acknowledging the established importance of financial asset-building in the life of individuals, their households, and their larger communities—via health and behavioral outcomes—the impetus exists to situate development of asset-building habits and capacity earlier in life. Adolescents capable of earning income are prime candidates for targeted support toward the asset-building goal. Two assumptions shape this perspective (Beverly, 2013): the first is that young adults need assets because they help fund postsecondary education and training and finance independent living (housing, transportation, basic needs). The second assumption is that the current distribution of assets—which is dramatically skewed by income, education, race, and other indicators of socioeconomic status—is problematic within the larger society and for the youth themselves. Therefore, addressing the asset-building aspect of youth development is critical at both the individual and societal levels. Since psychological and sociological research suggests a notable influence of parents on youth asset-building attitudes and behaviors (Otto, 2013; Webley & Nyhus, 2013), proponents argue that programs and policies are needed to provide intentional and consistent support for youth, especially those who are disconnected from adults with healthy financial habits. It's no surprise, then, that many youth social entrepreneurship initiatives include financial-asset-building as part of their programming.

An illustrative example is provided by the expansive youth social entrepreneurship organization known as Juma. Juma is "one of the country's largest youth-run social enterprise operations—and the first to provide financial capability and matched savings accounts to teens" (www.juma.org/our-mission-history/). As a basic part of their "Youth Connect" programming, Juma "opens a savings account for each youth in our program and provides youth with financial capability training to ensure they use those accounts wisely" (www.juma.org/our-mission-history/). They emphasize that financial asset-building must be one of the legs of a three-legged stool for disrupting the cycle of poverty for their opportunity youth. This goal of "Save" is balanced alongside the other two legs—"Earn," which is being placed in a job, and "Learn," which is support through career and academic skill-building. Their program mission names Financial Exclusion as one of the key problems facing opportunity youth.

Based in San Francisco, Juma operates in nine US cities with more than 20 social enterprises. "Juma," which means "work" or "gathering together as a group of people" in several African languages, began at a single-location youth center by connecting youth in need of employment with a local ice cream shop (Ben & Jerry's) in the early 1990s (Maran, 2003). In the more than 20 years of its existence, Juma has employed more than 6,000 low-income students who have generated $29.4 million in enterprise revenue, earned $8.1 million in wages, and saved $5.8 million for higher education. Each year, another 1,100 young people engage in the employment, learning, and savings program offered by Juma. The primary locations for Juma's youth employment are sports and entertainment venues, such as NFL stadiums, MLB ballparks, NBA arenas, MLS stadiums, convention centers, concert amphitheaters, and music festivals. After job training, the youth participants work within concessions at the sites. In addition to the significant enterprise revenue generated by the youth (approximately $3.3 million each year), Juma attracts massive corporate and philanthropic funding partners to help with operations and matched-savings program.

Says Lorenzo, a second-generation Nicaraguan-American and a former participant of Juma:

As a Juma youth, I worked as a vendor at AT&T Park but also received academic support and financial literacy training. Juma helped build my confidence and work ethic while learning responsibility and time management skills. For students like me who had to work through school, we learned how to manage extra responsibilities. Juma taught me a newfound work ethic. Instead of hanging out with friends on the weekends, I worked vending at football games. Having a savings account and learning financial capability also taught me better spending habits. Juma was my first experience going to school and working at the same time. Juma prepared me for college. . . . Like many of my Juma peers, I defied the statistics, proved my elementary school teacher wrong, and broke the cycle of poverty. I pushed beyond the limited perceptions that others had of me, built a successful career as a privacy and public policy lawyer in Silicon Valley and I credit much of what I have today to my beginnings with Juma. (https://www.juma.org/student-stories/lorenzo-2)

Embedding a program focus toward financial asset-building can be an important first step for existing or newly created youth social entrepreneurship initiatives. Key economic well-being–related questions for policymakers and programmers are offered by Langford & Badeau (2015):

- What opportunities and resources are available in our community to provide youth and young adults with access to work opportunities and safe, affordable housing?
- Do young people in our community have access to mentors and financial aid to support their success in postsecondary education, vocational training, employment readiness, and employment? Are there gaps or barriers that need to be addressed?
- In what ways do laws, policies, and opportunities support the economic well-being of all young people, or do we need to make changes to mitigate the impact of implicit and explicit racial, linguistic, ethnic, or gender-based bias in our educational, employment, and/or housing systems?

In addition, the authors offer the following tips:

- Provide young people with a variety of employment training options, including self-paced, competency-based, flexible schedule, and work-based programs that match young people's interests and abilities and offer early work experiences (e.g., job shadows, internships, paid employment) to ensure connection to the world of work.
- Provide youth with opportunities to build their skillsets, demonstrate mastery, and earn industry-recognized credentials through formal and informal systems.
- Create centers or programs focused on re-engagement of young people who have fallen off track.

- Provide policy incentives for employers to create and support employment pathways and ladders to careers for youth and young adults.

Preparing Practitioners for Youth Financial Asset-Building

Given the established importance of individual asset development versus an orientation simply to income generation, the resulting focus on *financial capability and asset-building* (FCAB) in youth and social work policy and practice is not surprising. Multiple studies reveal the concern that social workers and other helping professionals often lack preparation, knowledge, and skills to tackle increasingly complex financial problems facing their clients (Birkenmaier, Curley, & Sherraden, 2013). Financial "literacy" has long been a focus for programs working with low-income individuals, including and perhaps especially youth. *Financial literacy*, which generally refers to the skills and knowledge to make informed and effective decisions with financial resources, is indeed an important part of economic well-being. The competency areas tend to include understanding of personal spending, borrowing and debt, and banking (www.hsfpp.org/about-the-program/modules. aspx). The National Standards in K–12 Personal Finance Education (Jump$tart Coalition, 2015) include "investment strategy" as a key component of personal finance knowledge and ability. Yet many teachers, youth workers, social workers, and other so-called front-line youth staff lack the capability to provide adequate financial guidance (Loke, Watts, & Kakoti, 2013). Most notably, there is evidence that service providers often lack knowledge of public benefits and investments. To wit, one study found that social service providers "tend to be less knowledgeable than the general population" when it comes to the asset-building field (Loke et al., 2013, p. 265). Speculated reasons for this fact range from practitioners having a shared demographic with their program participants, which means a limited experience with wealth creation, and the lack of a common curriculum for financial asset-building within the field of social work. In either case, bolstering the professional development of youth practitioners to support their clients toward both financial literacy and asset-building is needed. While many youth social entrepreneurship programs include the support of their staff toward these economic goals, not all have or are able to do so.

Lastly, youth social entrepreneurship impacts youth asset development because, as a model, it aims to bring together scholars, policymakers, and practitioners to implement action that produces opportunities for financial asset-building for low-income, disconnected youth. Beverly (2013) encourages this symbiotic movement: "imagine the creative ideas that might be providers of financial education, and others generated when developmental psychologists, scholars thinking about institutional theory, come together to think about asset-building initiatives" (p. 55). The result could be meaningful and effective policy and programs to improve the immediate outcomes of youth and their communities and to instigate a longer term disruption to cycles of poverty.

Education Gap

The correlation between level of schooling and economic well-being has been well noted across the literature in multiple fields of inquiry (Card, 1998). A lack of educational attainment predicts lifelong depressed economic opportunity. In this way, the economic opportunity gap begins with disengaged students even in the early years of schooling.

Most opportunity youth commonly experience low levels of school engagement, operationalized as regular school attendance, school work completion, and high school graduation. Opportunity youth in the United States show a high school graduation rate that averages 18 percentage points below the overall rate, even at the age of 28. The college gap is even larger: at age 28, only about 1% of opportunity youth have achieved as much as an associate's degree or bachelor's degree, relative to 36% in the general population (Belfield et al., 2012). Given what is known about the established opportunity gap in the United States, these lower levels of education may actually be an underestimate since they do not account for the lower quality of preparation in schools with poorer resources. Furthermore, with current rates of postsecondary completion, the nation will likely fall short by 5 million skilled workers needed for 55 million job openings by 2020 according to a report by the Georgetown Center for Education and the Workforce (Carnevale, Smith, & Strohl, 2013).

Youth social entrepreneurship programs can aim to fill this void by providing meaningful and productive experiences for youth to learn employable skills within a context that values academic achievement. For example, while a typical entry-level food service position provides a paycheck and work skills, it often does nothing to foster achievement motivation that will encourage the young employees to stay in school. Furthermore, fast-food positions can actually deter school completion by denying young workers time to pay attention to their school work within the demands of the employment schedule (Allegretto et al., 2013).

The consequences of school disengagement can be significant, most notably in young people not achieving a high school diploma or equivalency. School dropouts are defined as individuals, aged 16–24, who are not currently enrolled in school and have not completed high school or obtained a GED. Overall, this rate has greatly declined, from 17% of American students in 1967 to 7% in 2014 (Child Trends, 2015). While rates have since declined substantially for each group, disproportionality exists for youth of color in the United States. This long-term decline is at least in part related to increased incarceration rates among young black and Hispanic males, a group that disproportionately affects dropout rates. Because the incarceration rate for this group more than doubled between 1980 and 1999, it removed them from the population base (noninstitutionalized civilians) used to calculate these estimates. The effect is not only on individuals, but also on the larger society and economy. Dropouts never catch up with high school graduates on any measure. They are less likely to find work at all and more likely to live in poverty, commit crimes, and suffer health problems. Life expectancy for dropouts is shorter by 7 years than for those who earn a diploma (Rumberger, 2011).

Students start disengaging long before they drop out of high school. Schools and communities pursue a number of approaches to intervene in school disengagement, a framework within which youth social entrepreneurship also resides. Out-of-school-time programs have long toiled to counteract the negative effects of school disengagement, offering an antithesis to the standardized curriculum often offered in traditional K–12 schools as well as aiming to "rebuild self-efficacy" toward learning success (Harpine, 2013). Developmental theorists suggest that after-school programs in which youth experience leadership and "mattering" can thwart some effects of school disengagement. Eccles and Templeton (2002) found that adolescents directly involved in community service through their after-school program were at a lower risk for school failure than their peers (p. 60).

Youth social entrepreneurship programs offer similar efforts to renew self-efficacy, leadership, and mattering for youth who have become disengaged in traditional schooling. One illustrative example is available in the Chicago-based Good Life Organization. Their national project, known as "Fulfill the Dream," offers educational curricula that centers on hip-hop culture and social change, including a youth social entrepreneurship component. They aim to increase youth engagement in school, recognizing the extensive research that "engagement is associated with positive academic outcomes, including achievement and persistence in school; and it is higher in classrooms with supportive teachers and peers, challenging and authentic tasks, opportunities for choice, and sufficient structure" (Fredricks, Blumenfeld, & Paris, 2004, p. 5).

To further engage the often disconnected youth of their community, "Fulfill the Dream" offers a culturally relevant program. They focus on "activating communities to challenge the negative trends facing youth and encouraging them to create change." Their movement of "hip-hop(e)" seeks to reduce "the youth violence rate, high school dropout rate, murder rate, and incarceration rate focusing on youth between 8 and 18 years old" (http://goodlifealliance.org/about/). At present, Fulfill the Dream is available in seven urban locations in the United States: Los Angeles, Chicago, Providence (Rhode Island), Cincinnati, Milwaukee, and in Madison and Beloit, Wisconsin.

The results of this program are promising. A pilot program of Fulfill the Dream of four middle-school classrooms demonstrated significant youth academic and social outcomes. The involved students improved in their grade point average (GPA), attendance, and behavior. In fact, the group's average GPA overall increased half a point in just 10 weeks. Follow-up interviews with youth, administrators, and parents provided qualitative evidence pointing to Fulfill the Dream programming as a major factor in the improvement. Furthermore, at an alternative high school, Fulfill the Dream was implemented with seniors. After completing the program, the school reported its first ever 100% graduation rate. A study of the program's effectiveness on youth social-emotional learning found that the youth identified the importance of establishing authentic relationships with the facilitators, developing critical consciousness, and engaging with issues and concepts that are relevant to their culture (Slaten, Rivera, Shemwell, & Elison, 2016, p. 139).

Fulfill the Dream's founder Roberto Rivera points to the crucial value of social entrepreneurship activities with youth to help them reach their academic outcome goals:

> The urgent need is that many urban cities in the US and around the world, have a dropout epidemic. Schools have become places that leave many youth feeling de-genius-ized, full of deficiencies, and feeling disempowered. Many of these youth who drop out, end up in one of three places: 1. Dead; 2. In Jail; 3. In a dead-end job. The system of education is crashing, and we have the system upgrade. . . . We have come up with a pedagogical approach, and practical tools that allow youth workers, educators, and parents to engage youth in strength-based, holistic, and relevant ways that empower them to reach their potential. We help to bring districts and organizations into the 21st century by training and equipping them with tools to engage the next generation of leaders, innovators, and change agents. We support educators in creating an educational foundation that teaches 21st century skills like thinking critically, working creatively, and acting collaboratively that meet the current needs of academic systems academically while also preparing youth with the transferable skills necessary to thrive in the new knowledge economy. (Unreasonable Institute, 2013)

Rivera, who founded Fulfill the Dream and was named one of the "Top Young Change Agents in America" by the Search for Common Ground Coalition, describes his work as "connecting positive youth development to community development using culturally relevant methods" (http://goodlifealliance. org/the-team/). He emphasizes that effective social entrepreneurship is about building youth's capacity and is "reciprocally transformative for communities" (personal communication, 2016). Rivera recognizes this impact from leading youth for more than a decade and from his own experience as a disconnected young person himself. As a self-proclaimed "hope-dealer," Rivera's work is as a capacity-builder for positive development of youth, which explicitly identifies the connection between democratic participation, academic achievement, and developmental outcomes. Says Rivera: "If we dig into it and do it right, deep within here is the real purpose of education: to disrupt systems" (personal communication, 2016).

8

The Social Opportunity Gap

It is hardly possible to overrate the value . . . of placing human beings in contact with persons dissimilar to themselves, and with modes of thought and action unlike those with which they are familiar. . . . Such communication has always been, and is peculiarly in the present age, one of the primary sources of progress.

—JOHN STUART MILL

Introduction

One step toward addressing the established opportunity gaps facing American youth is to recognize the unequal distribution of social capital. Like other forms of capital, this inequality is associated with other gaps and with reduced chances for change in the future. In fact, social capital is tied closely to social mobility, that centrally American belief that one's birth status is not a predetermination of wealth. Not only is there a yawning gap in the social capital of youth from high-income versus low-income households in America, but low-income youth of color also are disproportionately less likely to be able to participate in upward social mobility (Reeves, 2017). Youth social entrepreneurship offers practices to help raise the social capital of individual youth as well as cultivate increasing community capital via social change efforts. This chapter reviews the principles of social capital and provides examples of the study of social capital, as well as linking its theories into the model of youth social entrepreneurship.

Furthermore, individual empowerment and agency are accompanying components of many youth social entrepreneurship programs, as well as the establishment of a hopeful future. Key questions about practices around these topics are explored here, advancing the consideration of youth social entrepreneurship's role as a tool for social justice.

Social Capital and Networks

The basic idea of social capital is that a person's family, friends, and acquaintances are themselves important assets, ones that can be called on in a crisis and leveraged for material gain (Woolcock & Narayan, 2000). These *social networks* (who you know) have collective value, in part because of the inclination of the members to do things for each other. The helpfulness among members of a social network is known as *norms of reciprocity*. In short, the concept of social capital operationalizes the long-standing maxim that it's "who you know, not what you know" that matters for life success.

In the 1990s, the concept of "social capital" rose to considerable prominence across all the social science disciplines (Castiglione, Van Deth, & Wolleb, 2008). It has been referred to as "one of the most successful 'exports' from sociology to other social sciences and to public discourse during the last two decades" (Portes, 2000, p. 1). Situated within the discipline of sociology, the first systematic contemporary analysis of social capital was produced by Pierre Bourdieu, who defined the concept as "the aggregate of the actual or potential resources which are linked to possession of a durable network of more or less institutionalized relationships of mutual acquaintance or recognition" (Bourdieu 1985, p. 248). Social capital can be understood as part of the "family" of capitals wielded by individuals or communities, which also includes human capital and financial capital (Lin, 2002).

Halpern (2005) refers to social capital as "the social networks, informal structures, and norms that facilitate individual and collective action" (p. 5). The central idea of social capital, according to Robert Putnam, whose seminal work on social capital is captured in *Bowling Alone: The Collapse and Revival of American Communities* (2000), is that networks and the associated norms of reciprocity have value. They have value for the people who are in them, and they "enable participants to act together more effectively to pursue shared objectives" (Putnam, 1995, 4).

Two forms of social capital form an individual's social network. First, *bonding social capital* results from reciprocity of close-knit groups and reflects the degree of social connectedness that individuals have with others in their immediate lives, such as friends, families, neighbors, and co-workers. In this way, bonding social capital occurs within a community of individuals, such as a neighborhood. Second, *bridging social capital* is a property of individuals' and networks' connections to other individuals and networks not immediately in one's circle, and located perhaps very far from it. Bonding social capital is a necessary antecedent for the development of the more powerful form of bridging social capital. Bridging social capital occurs when members of one group connect with members of other groups to seek access or support or to gain information. Examples of bridging social capital include calling a city department to voice a complaint about public services or forming a neighborhood group to conduct a protest. In our work, bridging social

TABLE 8.1
Channels of social capital

Channel	Examples
Information flows	Learning about jobs, learning about candidates running for office, exchanging ideas at college
Norms of reciprocity (mutual aid)	"Bonding networks" that connect folks who are similar sustain particularized (in-group) reciprocity. "Bridging networks" that connect individuals who are diverse sustain generalized reciprocity.
Collective action	The role that the black church played in the Civil Rights movement; the PTA within a school
Broader identities and solidarity	Translating an "I" mentality into a "we" mentality

Adapted from Putnam (2000).

capital is defined as residents' efforts to extend contact beyond the members of the neighborhood; collective action is the product of bridging social capital.

In the past 20 years, an extensive body of evidence has documented social capital's value on economic growth, health, education, and crime. These effects are noted not just for individuals, but also in many cases for social groups, including neighborhoods. For example, communities with an abundant and diverse set of social networks are in a stronger position to confront the vulnerabilities that come with crises, including those of poverty. For a description of the multiple channels through which benefits from social capital flow, see Table 8.1.

Criticisms of the social capital theory point out that it lacks clearly agreed-upon definitions and empirically measurable values. Despite compelling theoretical arguments that support the role social capital plays across a variety of settings, there remains little empirical evidence regarding the effect of social capital in neighborhoods (Fulbright-Anderson & Auspos, 2006). Further in question may be social capital's role within economic development for individuals in poverty. This example depicts the conflict (Woolcock & Narayan, 2000): new entrepreneurs initially depend on their immediate neighbors and friends (bonding social capital) for credit, insurance, and many similar supports. but then "outgrow" their community space as their businesses expand and they require access to more extensive markets. In other words, economic development for low-income individuals has them drawing initially on their social capital but then requires them to acquire a broader networks that transcend their community as they progressively join the economic mainstream.

Unequal Distribution of Social Capital

Research has also shown that the *absence* of social ties has an equally important impact. Individuals in poverty are most commonly *not* members of—and may even be actively excluded from—certain social networks and institutions that could be used to secure employment and housing (Woolcock, 1998). Furthermore, research suggests that while bonding social capital may be more uniform across neighborhoods of varying socioeconomic status, bridging social capital tends to be found in greater amounts in neighborhoods of higher socioeconomic status, which allows them greater success when mobilizing to improve their neighborhoods (Altschuler, Somkin, & Adler, 2004).

Research suggests that although social capital is not contingent upon socioeconomic status, bonding social capital and bridging social capital exist in unequal measure based on socioeconomic status. Therefore, encouraging the development of bridging social capital for poor and moderate-income individuals "may require revealing the operating procedures of the municipal 'system' in an understandable manner" (Larsen et al., 2004, p. 75).

Examples of youth social entrepreneurship square well with the concept of building individual-level social capital. Because parental social capital has been shown to be an important predictor of adolescent social capital (Weiss, 2012), it follows that youth whose families are marginalized may experience lower levels of social capital. To this end, youth social entrepreneurship can enrich youths' social networks by supporting interactions with a broader set of individuals. Facilitated development of relationships could thereby grow an individual young person's social networks, eventually affecting their future opportunities.

Connections and Protections

In addition to growing social and financial capital, engaging disconnected youth in meaningful employment, such as in a youth social entrepreneurship program, can result in the development of protective factors. *Protective factors* are seen by developmental scientists as characteristics "at the biological, psychological, family, or community (including peers and culture) level that are associated with a lower likelihood of problem outcomes or that reduces the negative impact of a risk factor on problem outcomes" (O'Connell. Boat, & Warner, 2009, p. 18). Protective factors are related to the developmental assets described in Chapter 2, with some differences in their constitution and metrics. Examples of protective factors include positive physical development, high self-esteem, emotional self-regulation, good coping and problem-solving skills, and engagement and connections in two or more healthy contexts (e.g., school, with peers, in athletics, employment, religion, culture). In short, connections help to develop protections against unhealthy outcomes.

A common feature of youth social entrepreneurship programs is that they connect youth into protective contexts, whether through a job or a social action team. In most instances described in this book, that engagement is formal; that is, an organized effort or program is designed with the intent to provide youth with targeted positive experiences. However, youth social entrepreneurship as a concept does not have to operate that way. In other words, youth social entrepreneurship occurs any time youth are in empowered roles within their communities, roles that foster mutually beneficial protective assets. For example, a recent news story described four young men who got summer jobs working for their community housing after months of persistence (Wanshel, 2016). At the LaGrange Housing Authority in Georgia, the African American teens, aged 13 and 14, had asked the head of the Housing Authority for employment but were turned down due to their age. She says, "I thought they just wanted to work for money." However, as the school break for summer began, she found that the four of them had been approached to join gangs and were asking for jobs as a way "to stay out of trouble." They told her they had each been approached by gang members to join them but came to her to say, "We just don't want to be in gangs." The Housing Manager "hired them on the spot," and they spent the summer tending to a community garden, passing out flyers, and performing other odd jobs around LaGrange Housing Authority for $7.25 per hour. They built new picnic benches for the community and helped with the newly acquired community chickens. Only time will tell how future summer breaks will go for these boys, but for that summer, at least, they experienced gang protection alongside developing protective factors, all because the management of the housing organization decided to give them the chance and allow them to become empowered actors within their physical community and within their own lives.

Agency and Empowerment

The opportunity gap may very well cause exponentially deleterious effects, the amount of which neither scholars nor society can truly measure. When an individual is deprived of opportunities that others are given, the gap grows not only between their potential and the others', but between how they see their potential— the lost sense of hope described in Chapter 7.

Youth social entrepreneurship aims to rectify this loss by introducing new pathways of personal agency for youth. By engaging them in an active role within the program and the community, youth may construct an increasingly empowered social identity. The social psychology of participation points to the importance of social identity. Actions are ultimately structured by social identity. Social representations, including social identity, strive to explain "the production of knowledge in everyday life and the manner in which groups come to form a shared view of the world" (Anand & Lea, 2011, p. 285). Taking social identities and social representations into account may be especially necessary for resolving the opportunity gap experienced by disconnected youth. An important piece of that goal is the development of *critical consciousness*—awareness of the larger contexts that influence youth's outer experiences and contribute to the internal sense of self (see Chapter 9 for further discussion). Awareness of such systems' effects on personal identity opens the door to new paths of individual agency. Empowerment, then, comes from both knowledge and the opportunities to act. The need is most critical for youth who are marginalized, as explained by Ozer (2017, p. 173): "While promoting a sense of agency and empowerment is developmentally salient for adolescents generally, it is crucial for youth who must negotiate structural barriers such as poverty, racism, and heterosexism in their journey toward positive development and identity."

Collective Hope to Counter Disconnection

One way that youth social entrepreneurship can disrupt the cycles of disconnection for opportunity youth is through collective hope and informed action. *Collective hope* has at least three features (Ginwright, 2016). First, young people have "shared experiences" related to the condition of their lives. These shared experiences reflect neighborhood conditions, power dynamics in interactions, and familiarity with crime and violence, among many other aspects. Shared experiences elicit shared perspectives about fairness of conditions, such as perceived injustice and negative attitudes about law enforcement.

Youth involved in youth social entrepreneurship programs typically have some shared experiences. Grassroots initiatives typically bring together youth who know each other through shared living spaces (such as neighborhoods or housing projects and/or going to the same schools), which result in some degree of shared conditions and common perspectives. Top-down youth social entrepreneurship initiatives typically recruit youth from similar backgrounds by ethnicity, immigration status, gender identity group, or other organizing factors. In this case, the involved youth also have a shared experience through their common identifying factor.

Second, collective hope requires "radical imagination" (Ginwright, 2016, p. 23). *Radical imagination* hinges on informed awareness of the injustice experienced by the group that results in a desire for change. It is a collective agreement that the status quo is unwanted and must be overturned. Radical imagination relies on a creative vision for what might be possible beyond the current condition.

The creation of any youth social entrepreneurship involves extensive radical imagination because it creates something where there was nothing. Part of youth social entrepreneurship's radical imagination is the empowering of youth who previously lacked power in their environments. It is radical in its vision that change is possible for communities and for youth regardless of their immediate past, including incarceration, or broader obstacles such as generational poverty.

Third, collective hope requires "critical action." This happens when members of a group commit to act toward a central goal, a mutual intention based on their shared experiences and their radical imagination. In turn, critical action fosters a sense of control that can subvert the powerlessness they might have felt via their shared perceptions of injustice. This sense of control engenders a future orientation, which focuses the group on their capacity to address future events. In this way, a perception of future control fuels collective hope in the drive for change.

Youth in youth social entrepreneurship programs drive the critical action. They are the actors who embody a collective hope about control over future events in a vision for the future that exists beyond the injustices of the status quo. They are the dreamers of new ways to address community needs and the doers of the actions that help create new enterprises or new organizations that reflect their radical imaginations for a more just society.

In the context of poverty, writes Ginwright, collective hope is part of healing from the harm caused by psychological, cultural, spiritual, and/or physical injury related to membership in a societally marginalized group. Healing comes from justice strategies rooted in love and civic vision. It empowers from deep within each individual and community. Thus, Ginwright and other activist/scholars point to the role of schools and community organizations to help "move young people's individual experiences to a collective awareness, to collective action" (2016, p. 54). Working together for social change is therefore an act of healing and an act of hope. Youth-led social entrepreneurship embodies collective effort toward a hopeful vision for the future.

In these ways, youth social entrepreneurship aims to dismantle the boundaries of social class by fostering low-income youth's access to economic opportunity in their own geographic communities; by developing the strengths of youth as they are, not as adults think they should be; and by harnessing the social change power of neighborhoods and grassroots enterprise. Understanding this multidisciplinary youth practice as a form of multicultural education promises to enrich efforts toward equity of social mobility and access to opportunity.

9

Addressing Systems of Power and Oppression

> Because love is an act of courage, not of fear, love is a commitment
> to others. No matter where the oppressed are found, the act of love is
> commitment to their cause—the cause of liberation.
>
> —PAULO FREIRE

Introduction

An imperative for social justice organizations and activists is to grapple with
entrenched structures of power and injustice. Empowering all young people to
identify the uneven social order and to recognize power hierarchies as social construction is to engender change that lasts beyond this generation. Taken further,
empowering all young people, with special consideration for those who are or
could be marginalized, to confront societal disparities is to cloak them in their own
power, striving to heal what has been harmed and aiming to reduce the yawning
gaps in access to education, to employment, to opportunity. This chapter traces the
practices of critical pedagogy; the processes of critical consciousness toward social
change; and the healing potential of collectivism, hope, and caring. Youth social
entrepreneurship examples embody such practices in varying degrees. Insofar as
any program or youth social entrepreneurship activity aims to disrupt the pre-
vailing disparities in contemporary American society, an understanding of critical
perspectives and pedagogies is essential. That is to say, aiming for social change
requires a clear awareness of current social order. This chapter offers a primer of
key concepts and applications toward the goals of social justice.

Critical Consciousness

Structural inequality refers to a system of power imbalances maintained by social
norms, organizations, policies, and individual behaviors informed by a society's
dominant ideologies. Groups of people are marginalized within this system of
power and do not then experience the same rights and opportunities as the dominant population. Structural inequality is often considered in two domains: privilege

and oppression. Whereas structural inequality is the presence of privilege and/or oppression, structural equality is the absence of privilege and oppression. Privilege and oppression both have internal and external forms. For instance, believing that one is genetically superior or inferior when compared to others is a form of internal privilege or oppression. An example of external oppression includes a store clerk suspiciously watching customers due to the color of their skin.

Incarceration practices in the United States offer an example of structural inequality and, specifically, of external oppression: a disproportionate number of African Americans are incarcerated due to racial profiling, increased police presence in low-income neighborhoods, and harsh mandatory sentences for drug possession. After incarceration, their ability to resume productive lives in the community is sharply limited by privileged legislators, employers, and community residents who deny them access to welfare support and limit their ability to compete for certain types of jobs, apply for financial aid to attend school, and enjoy basic human rights.

Critical consciousness focuses on the role of oppression and privilege in creating and sustaining social inequalities and dysfunctions, including disproportionate unemployment, crime, homelessness, and/or lack of access to education. From a critical consciousness perspective, such dysfunctions are a direct consequence of structural and internalized inequality.

Paulo Freire introduced critical consciousness ("*conscientizacao*") as a way to address the oppression of impoverished people in Brazil. He pointed to their lack of knowledge as a key tool of their oppression. Freirian theory holds that, in addition to the acquisition of knowledge, critical thinking skills are necessary to actively resist oppression. Freire's work has influenced people working in education, community development, community health, and many other fields. Freire developed an approach to education that links the identification of issues to positive action for change and development.

> The pedagogy of the oppressed [is] a pedagogy which must be forged with, not for, the oppressed (whether individuals or peoples) in the incessant struggle to regain their humanity. This pedagogy makes oppression and its causes objects of reflection by the oppressed, and from that reflection will come their necessary engagement in the struggle for their liberation. And in the struggle this pedagogy will be made and remade. (Freire, 1970)

More recently, social justice scholars such as Julio Cammarota have helped advocate for critical consciousness-raising among youth of color as a way to transform their perspective. These scholars argue that critical consciousness helps young people to "see the real purpose of an uneven social order and encourages them to see how the dominant group arranges social structures to make certain the subordinated continue to experience exploitation" (Ginwright, 2016). In line with the original Freirian philosophy, both reflection and dialogue become essential processes to meaningful work with youth and/or their communities. Reflecting on experience and communicating about its impacts leads to true "praxis," or action toward both internal and external forms of transformation (Freire, 1973). Says Cammarota on this role of critical consciousness in social change:

> The internal form involves the Self reflecting on a particular situation and then transforming the perception of the reality driving the situation, leading to knowledge of how to implement change. Internal transformation requires a movement of thought, a Self-action so to speak. (Cammarota & Romero, 2009, p. 32)

Youth social entrepreneurship holds many opportunities for developing critical consciousness. Namely, intentional reflection and dialogue can be part of the developmental aspects of a program's design. The aim should be to disrupt the "culture of silence" regarding oppression (Freire, 1970). Youth involved in the initiative take pause to reflect on their life experiences in the communal setting of a shared enterprise. Older youth and/or youth workers facilitate dialogue about the power structures experiences, offering opportunities to acknowledge the inequalities witnessed and the oppression experienced in the youth's school, home, and community life. Inclusion of the language of "systemic oppression" can help make meaning of young people's experience, as in "the bias that teacher showed me might not be specifically about me but about people like me who don't look or speak like her and that bias is couched in a deep history of oppression that is much bigger than just her life or mine."

Educators and youth workers aim to advance the critical consciousness of youth in a variety of ways from which youth social entrepreneurs can learn. Given the goal of supporting young people to critically analyze and change the socioeconomic and physical conditions in their communities, they may practice analytic methods on case examples before engaging in the social problems of their lived experience. Simulated exercises are designed to enhance youth understanding of societal conditions, while action-oriented ones are designed to bring about real change. In all instances, the goal is to "increase critical consciousness by deepening understanding of the root causes of [social problems] and by showing students how to bring about desirable . . . change" (Luter, Mitchell, Taylor, 2017, p. 4).

Reflection and dialogue lend themselves then to praxis, which is the action that could be at the heart of social entrepreneurship—the informed and passionate commitment to making change for the better. Ginwright and Cammarota (2007) call this "critical civic praxis," providing access to the networks, ideas, and experiences that build both individual and collective capacity to pursue social justice for their communities. Critical civic praxis is an empowering approach to youth work because it acknowledges the structural constraints in youths' communities but also views the young people as active, capable participants in creating social change, such as in their own neighborhood conditions.

Popular Education

Freire's work has had an enormous influence on the educational and social work practitioners who work with people who are poor, oppressed, and
exploited. His approach to *popular education* as a means of social change is
documented in an extensive body of literature devoted to related applications.
In popular education, Freire argues that the content of education should draw
on the lived experiences of the learners. For youth and community workers,
this means avoiding standardized curricula and instead pursuing local knowledge and issues as the basis of educational initiatives. Popular education is in
contrast to what Freire calls *banking education*, the traditional relationship of
teacher and student, which is a dysfunctional, oppressive system (Freire, 2005).
In banking education, the teacher retains control and takes on the role of an
oppressor, while the student is expected to be a passive, unthinking follower.
The teacher deposits information into the student, who is assumed to be a pow-
erless, empty receptacle for these deposits. Popular education includes an analysis of the nature of inequality, exploitation, and oppression and is informed
by a clear political purpose. Rather than a focus on alleviating or managing
poverty, popular education strives for a more just and egalitarian social order
altogether. The model of youth social entrepreneurship is inherently oriented
toward Freirian popular education in that the lived experiences of youth within
the context of their culture and communities is central. This programming
value contrasts the banking education that many youth experience in their
formal schooling settings, in which a top-down, hierarchical structure is more
common. Program designers of youth social entrepreneurship would do well to
keep this framework in mind as they structure their activities, moving toward
more authentic youth engagement and leadership to allow a more fully popular
education model to flourish in their sites.

Problem-posing education is also part of the Freire's alternative to the banking
model of education. Problem-posing education is structured to encourage critical thinking in students. In this form of education, the teacher and the student
become partners and dialogue to mutually reach conclusions about problems.
The solutions must not be predetermined by the teacher, but instead be co-
created during the process of dialogue. In a dialectical relationship, the teacher
and students learn from each other. Youth social entrepreneurship can provide
opportunities for problem-posing education when adults and youth partner in
mutually respectful and reciprocally beneficial ways. This nonhierarchical interaction takes cultivating and is only achieved with care and intention. (An exploration on this partnership is provided in Chapter 13.) Furthermore, there is an
inherent problem-posing nature of addressing community change through social
entrepreneurship. Recognizing this characteristic and framing it within Freirian
theory may help bolster the work of youth social entrepreneurship practitioners
and advocates.

Funds of Knowledge and Cultural Capital

Funds of knowledge, as defined by researchers Moll, Amanti, Neff, and Gonzalez (1992), are "the historically accumulated and culturally developed bodies of knowledge and skills essential for household or individual functioning and well-being" (p. 133). While this concept has been pivotal within the field of education, and especially in language and literacy instruction, it has great relevance within youth development work as well. Funds of knowledge counter the cultural deficit model, a long-prevailing belief among educators that underachievement is attributable to students' socioeconomic status and familial origin. That is to say, the deficit theory holds that "racial/ethnic minority groups do not achieve as well as their White majority peers in school and life because their family culture is dysfunctional and lacking important characteristics compared to the White American culture" (Salkind, 2008, p. 216). This belief has been held in both explicit and implicit ways. An explicit example occurs when children with limited English-speaking skills are asked to sit in the back of the classroom because it is assumed they cannot participate and benefit from the classroom instruction until they gain English language fluency. A more implicit manifestation occurs through lowered expectations, such as a teacher or youth worker assuming the young person with limited English proficiency will not be able to learn as much and, in turn, asking less of that youth.

Instead, with a viewpoint that values diverse funds of knowledge, the educator can investigate the cultural and cognitive resources brought by this youth. These resources can then inform culturally responsive and meaningful lessons that tap the student's prior knowledge. Youths' funds of knowledge are useful in that they emphasize "strategic knowledge and related activities essential in . . . functioning, development, and well-being . . . pertaining to social, economic, and productive activities" (Moll, Amanti, Neff, & Gonzalez, 1992, p. 139). This perspective demonstrates deep concern, respect, and appreciation for youth and reflects a belief that young people's insights and well-being are central to community change processes to foster healthy environments.

Furthermore, acknowledging diverse funds of knowledge shows appreciation for cultural capital that may not be valued within the larger systems in which the youth live. This moves away from a deficit view of marginalized youth as having "cultural poverty disadvantages . . . instead focuses on and learns from the array of cultural knowledge, skills, abilities and contacts possessed by socially marginalized groups that often go unrecognized and unacknowledged" (Yosso, 2006, p. 89). Culturally responsive teaching (Gay, 2010) in educational research and practice offers a well-established set of approaches to interactions between teacher–student or youth worker–youth participant that both values multiple of cultural frames of references and adapts to the individual as needed. Culturally responsive teaching is most significant for application with learners/

youth whose identities are marginalized in the setting. The effectiveness comes from leveraging the students' unique cultural strengths and nurturing them to promote student achievement and a sense of well-being about the student's cultural place in the world. Culturally responsive teaching affirms a young person's cultural identity, legitimizes the youth's own funds of knowledge, and connects new learning to their social experiences and prior knowledge, rendering the learning much more meaningful than the one-size-fits-all curricula of traditional schooling and some after-school programs.

Anti-oppressive Practices

Grounded in the field of social work, an interdisciplinary model of anti-oppressive practices states that, "Within this definition, there is a clear understanding of the use and abuse of power within relationships on personal, family, community, organisational and structural levels. These levels are not mutually exclusive—they are interconnected, shaping and determining social reality" (Burke & Harrison, 2002, p. 132).

Like the praxis-oriented approaches previously described, the driving force of anti-oppressive practice is the act of challenging inequalities. The process of the challenge produces opportunities for change. This is most impactful in the concurrent addressing of micro- and macro-level strengths and challenges. The framing of vacillating attention to micro and macro can be understood in that the personal is political: "the everyday life experiences of individuals need to be located within social, cultural, political and economic structures which are historically and geographically specific" (Burke & Harrison, 2002, p. 132). In youth social entrepreneurship, this means a recognition of the power structures at work that both limit and exploit youth agency in their community, yet seeking to partner with youth opportunities to disrupt this status quo.

Preparing youth and community practitioners to engage in anti-oppressive approaches while enacting cultural responsivity is a need and challenge explored by scholars like Sakamoto (2007):

> Instead of adhering to the Eurocentric social work models that automatically assume the Whiteness of the social worker, I assert that we must shift our focus from trying to understand the cultural other towards interrogating the power-laden contexts in which the process of othering occurs; towards naming and subverting the dynamics of power that allow for the culturally different to be deemed as "other" in the first place. In short, I advocate a re-visioning of cultural competence that is simultaneously framed by anti-oppressive principles while also being open to different ways of knowing. (p. 110)

Trauma and Healing

Some developmental theorists, educators, and activists emphasize the need for *healing* in communities facing oppression before engaging in social justice action. In particular, education scholar and activist Shawn Ginwright connects youth critical consciousness to healing as a developmental process among many marginalized youth. Youth who have been disconnected from healthy adults, who have experienced oppression first-hand, who have lived in the conditions of poverty with its related stressors, violence, and disease have much trauma to be healed. In *Hope and Healing in Urban Education* (2016) Ginwright explores the necessary elements for trauma-informed youth to re-engage in their own healthy development. The key for him is "understanding how to move young people's individual experiences, to a collective awareness, to collective action" (p. 54).

An example method used is through "healing circles," based on indigenous people's practice of circle. In circles, all participants take turns speaking with the use of a "talking piece" and the aid of facilitators (often called "circle keepers"). Howard Zehr, widely considered the grandfather of restorative justice, refers to the circle process as "the closest thing to a 'universal' model of addressing harm and conflict" (2014, p. 21). Circles are considered a primary process in *restorative justice*, an approach that emphasizes correcting and healing the harm of caused by other individuals or by broader societal systems. It is best accomplished through cooperative processes that include all stakeholders and can lead to transformation of people, relationships and communities:

> Rather than asking traditional questions like "What law or rule was broken?;" Who broke it?;" and "What consequences or punishment do they deserve?;" restorative justice asks "Who has been affected?;" "What are their needs?;" "Who has the obligation to address the needs, right the wrongs and restore the relationships?" It's an effective approach that seeks to engage, heal and transform both the victims and the perpetrators of a crime simultaneously. (Surowidjojo, 2015)

TRAUMA

Restorative justice fits well with the principles of trauma-informed practices because both aim to heal sources of struggle and "use inclusive practices to repair harm" (Swaringen, 2017, p. 1). The concept of trauma has garnered increasing attention in the past decade, in part due to the growing recognition of the neurological responses to experiences that previously may not have been considered traumatic. That is to say, the psychological effects of an event may result in trauma for an individual even if it is not objectively understood by outsiders to be classified as trauma. Therefore, the standing statistics about trauma are in question: that "25% of children and adolescents will experience at least one traumatic event during their lifetime, including life-threatening accidents, disasters, maltreatment, assault, family and community violence" (Ko et al., 2008, p. 397). Rather, the number of youth affected by trauma is potentially much higher. Copeland et al. (2007) suggest that more than two-thirds of youth reported at least one traumatic event by age 16 years. Sources of trauma commonly include psychological, physical, or verbal abuse; home or school violence; natural disasters; terrorism; sudden or violent loss of a loved one; sexual assault; refugee and war experiences; and military-family stressors. As a response, the use of *trauma-informed practices* and *trauma-informed systems* of care delivery (Ko et al., 2008) have expanded in recent years to accommodate the increased awareness and increased incidence of childhood trauma. Similarly, *toxic stress* is defined in neuroscientific theory as the central biological mechanism representing the social conditions, experiences, and personal interactions that "shape and reshape brain and body development, especially in early childhood, with resultant effects on later educational and occupational attainment as well as on health" (McEwen & McEwen, 2017, p. 450). This involves "frequent or sustained activation of the biological stress system" and is triggered by chronic negative social conditions. The result can be impaired development of neural circuits involved in the self-regulation of emotions and behavior.

Youth work that incorporates trauma-informed practices and/or focuses on broader healing can help promote healing of identity, agency, and personal purpose in the lives of youth and their communities. The result can be transformative as it cultivates critical hope and allows students to imagine ways they can thrive despite socially toxic stress (Camangian, 2017).

TRAUMA-INFORMED YOUTH PRACTICE

Emerging empirical work suggests that best practices in trauma-informed youth work may help address underlying barriers to opportunity that disconnected youth are prone to through traumatic experiences. Trauma-informed practices can help youth who have experienced trauma to feel safer and more in control of their environments. In short, these practices include assessment of youths' direct experience or exposure to violence, especially family violence in the home, as appropriate, which can help identify stressors for the young person. Next, youth workers can help youth feel more comfortable in addressing their trauma by not forcing conversations, by being consistent in their relationship with and commitment to the youth, and by not downplaying emotional responses, such as saying "don't worry." Furthermore, youth workers should help connect to professional help if youth are acting on a trauma experience in ways that pose a danger to themselves or others. Last, youth workers must develop their own plans for resolving personal issues and addressing the job stress connected to supporting youth trauma (Whitman, 2007).

Trauma must be addressed at both the individual and community levels. Examples of individual trauma are physical and/or sexual abuse, emotional and/

or psychological maltreatment, neglect, witnessing violence, and serious accident or injury. Examples of community/collective trauma include natural disasters and events or circumstances inflicted by one group on another, such as usurped homelands, forced relocation, servitude, or mass incarceration, or any other ongoing exposure to violence in the community. The trauma that results from such situations is often "transmitted from one generation to the next in a pattern often referred to as historical, community, or intergenerational trauma" (SAMHSA, 2014, p. 17).

INDIVIDUAL TRAUMA

Trauma has become recognized as a "predominantly sensory process for many children and adolescents that cannot be altered by cognitive interventions alone" (Steele & Malchiodi, 2015, p. xix). The Substance Abuse and Mental Health Services Administration (SAMHSA) defines trauma in this way (2014, p. 7):

> Individual trauma results from an event, series of events, or set of circumstances that is experienced by an individual as physically or emotionally harmful or threatening and that has lasting adverse effects on the individual's functioning and physical, social, emotional, or spiritual well-being.

To engage in the best practices of trauma-informed approaches, youth workers must address "4R's" (SAMSHA, 2014):

1. *Realization*: Program staff should realize that trauma is widespread among their populations and that there are many paths to healing. For those working in youth social entrepreneurship, this means awareness that many or possibly most of the young people have experienced traumatic events and may be continuing to experience the adverse effects in their day-to-day lives.
2. *Recognition*: Program staff must be prepared to recognize the symptoms of trauma in their youth participants. Such symptoms may be "gender, age, or setting-specific" and can be best recognized via trained "trauma screening and assessment" (p. 9). Professional development and supervision practices are recommended to reach this goal, in all youth work, including youth social entrepreneurship sites.
3. *Response*: Youth workers need to respond to evidence of trauma by integrating their knowledge of trauma into program practices, policies, and procedures. For example, program leadership should "promote a culture based on beliefs about resilience, recovery, and healing from trauma" by stating their organizational commitment to trauma reduction. This might include visual signage claiming the space to be a physically and psychologically safe zone, inclusion of trauma statements into their staff handbooks, and the organizational design practices of including

program participants on their advisory boards and planning. For youth social entrepreneurship, these responses may include attention to youth trauma before encouraging youth to engage outside of their comfort zones, such as with customers or within leadership roles. Certainly, ensuring a trauma-free environment is a minimum expectation for effective youth social entrepreneurship programs, as it must be for all program development agencies.

4. *Resist retraumatization*: Youth program staff should intentionally work to prevent any possible instance of triggering painful memories of traumatic experiences for youth who have trauma histories. Intention is necessary here to mitigate even unintended retraumatization. For example, trauma-informed youth workers would resist "using restraints on a person who has been sexually abused or placing a child who has been neglected and abandoned in a seclusion room [which] may be re-traumatizing and interfere with healing and recovery" (p. 10).

Thus, the program goals must be broader than PYD and the social entrepreneurship goals of a venture. Instead, trauma-informed practices must become a natural part of the environment, especially in settings where high numbers of youth have trauma histories. Given the disproportionately high levels of trauma experienced by youth from marginalized backgrounds—by income, race, language, and sexual and gender orientation, among other identities—youth social entrepreneurship program staff in these settings require extra support for and attention to trauma-informed practices to help support youth participants to reach their potential.

Trauma-informed practices within youth social entrepreneurship programs aim to engage youth with "sensory, neurosequential experiences to help restore a sense of safety and bring about a renewed sense of empowerment" (Steele & Malchiodi, 2015, p. xx). Youth should be guided into practices that help soothe the "survivor brain," such as somatic, body-oriented activities including but not limited to mindfulness, meditation, deep breathing, and visualization exercises. These practices offer coping mechanisms for individuals who have experienced trauma. Equally important, trauma-informed practices help youth to develop healthy relationships with others, thus improving attachments and safety. They are also scaffolded to more healthfully communicate their trauma experiences to themselves. In so doing, they enhance self-regulation and trauma integration, moving from "victim thinking" to "survivor thinking" and eventually to "thriver" status (Steele & Malchiodi, 2015).

In some cases, trauma-specific interventions may be needed for a young person to be able to comfortably engage in the activities of a youth program, even if it offers a trauma-informed environment. Youth workers must be prepared to provide referrals to appropriate trauma treatment, defined as "based on the best available empirical evidence and science, are culturally appropriate, and reflect principles of a trauma-informed approach" (SAMHSA, 2014, p. 13).

COMMUNITY, OR COLLECTIVE, TRAUMA

The fields of youth and community development are shifting from understanding trauma solely at the individual level to also including a clearer view of collective trauma. Despite the increasing recognition of the widespread nature of trauma as an epidemic at a community level, the predominant focus for addressing trauma remains at the individual level (Pinderhues et al., 2016). Collective trauma occurs when a community is subjected to a "community-threatening event, have a shared experience of the event, and have an adverse, prolonged effect" (SAMSHA, 2014, p. 17). Youth social entrepreneurship programs with a mission to involve specific populations who have, or likely have, experienced collective trauma are particularly responsible for providing community-level trauma-informed practices because they aim to address a community need or social problem in their work. In this way, experiences of collective trauma must be recognized and addressed (Frantz, 2014).

Research suggests that "the most effective strategies [for community trauma] build on indigenous knowledge, expertise and leadership to produce strategies that are culturally relevant and appropriate" (Pinderhues, Davis, & Williams, 2016, p. 5). Three areas of strategy address improvements to (1) the socio-cultural environment, such as promoting community assets and connections among community members; (2) the physical environment to enhance health, safety, and general well-being; and (3) the economic opportunities of the community, including job readiness, education access, and livable wages.

The model of youth social entrepreneurship is inherently well poised to engage such improvements. Examples of active programs are described in this book and include practices that result in improvements in each of these three strategic areas.

Addressing historical, transgenerational trauma likely requires direct attention to the source of the identity that carries the trauma. To this end, the cultural identity of the community must be at the center of healing practices.

> Cultural interventions work by infusing cultural awareness and teaching as the primary goal of interventions. Cultural activities are the keystone of these interventions. . . . These interventions are meant to mold and reinforce identity, so as to facilitate the healing process. (University of Calgary report, 2012, p. 10)

For example, the youth social entrepreneurship program First Person Productions focuses on media training for American Indian youth in order to produce public service announcements (PSAs), short films, and documentaries on issues of importance to the community and to assist community nonprofits and businesses with promotional videos. Youth complete 200 hours of media training through a local university partnership before engaging in the creation and distribution of American Indian content (migizi.org/our_program/first-person-productions/) as their social enterprise. This program operates under a larger organizational umbrella known as MIGIZI, which was "founded with a goal of countering the misrepresentations, inaccuracies, and falsehoods promulgated about Native Peoples in the major media." For decades, they have trained American Indian journalists who created the first nationally distributed American Indian radio news magazine in the country to provide "a venue for Indian people to tell their own stories and a primary source of accurate information about Native Peoples for thousands of non-Native listeners" (migizi.org/about/). In these ways, their organizational practices facilitate movement toward the healing progress of historical, collective trauma inflicted on the indigenous peoples.

CARING

In *Black Youth Rising: Activism and Radical Healing in Urban America* (2010), Ginwright asserts that caring—in the face of oppressive systems and trauma—is a political act in and of itself. Caring reflects "trust, dependence, and mutual expectations," but, in the context of oppressed communities, caring is political because it "builds hope, political consciousness, and the willingness to act on behalf of the common good" (2010, p. 56). The role of fostering caring relationships toward social justice is suggested as part of a healing process at the individual, community, and broader societal levels. Ginwright argues that adults provide a form of care when they offer opportunities for young people to engage in activism as legitimate political actors. The care these opportunities show is reciprocated by the youth, who begin to see political engagement as their responsibility and within their capability.

At the level of one-on-one relationships and at the organizational level of defining a program, youth social entrepreneurship should embody caring. With the aim of advancing youth and community development, expressions of authentic caring within youth social entrepreneurship take several forms: reciprocal, meaningful adult–youth partnerships in the work; intentional spaces for collective and individual healing while engaging with one another; and the inclusion of critical consciousness that results in praxis in designing a social enterprise. Caring, then, is a vital ingredient to impacting social change: "Community organizations are responding to this crisis by creating opportunities for healing through caring relationships, strong social networks, and action taken to improve social conditions. These organizations are weaving together threads of hope that, ultimately, form the fabric of civic life" (Ginwright, 2011, p. 39). At its core, caring involves love, perhaps the radical love described by Freire, which holds potential for dismantling oppression and opening pathways for all to a more equitable future.

Section III

Focal Case Examples

Case 1: SOUL Sisters Leadership Collective

SOUL Sisters Leadership Collaborative (SSLC) places culturally relevant practices with a social justice orientation at the heart of their programming. While they do not include a focus on disconnected youth, the young women who participate are systems-involved, often on their way to "disconnection" through school disengagement and pushout, given their trajectories. SSLC addresses the trauma resulting from their youths' experiences within the systems of juvenile incarceration, foster care, homeless shelters, and underresourced schools. To this end, the programming designed by SOUL Sisters founders Caitlin Gibb and Wakumi Douglas reflects numerous restorative practices drawn from established restorative justice. They explain that they do not implement formally structured restorative justice, but that their activities, customized specifically for their young women, are highly informed by the restorative justice paradigm. For example, SSLC includes the circle process in all of their meetings as an act of healing and a sign of mutual respect and caring among their community members. They include a Talking Stick, a signature feature of the circle process, which cultivates equity among the participants.

The circle process as part of restorative justice reflects cultural relevance, because it stems from a ritual of indigenous people. By making it a focal part of their practice, SSLC shows honor for the traditions of native people and for cultural acts that are outside of the dominant culture. SSLC applies this culturally relevant healing circle process to all aspects of their program, including the Social Action Project, which is their social entrepreneurship component. In this way, they support young people's empowerment to think critically about their communities and plan innovative solutions to problems with a culturally relevant structure. Says Wakumi Douglas of the use of routine and ritual, such as Circle, "[it] allows us to go deeper faster" (personal communication, 2017). Another important ritual for the SOUL Sisters is the use of communal recitation. At each meeting's closing, the youth recite the "Assata Chant":

> It is our duty to fight for our freedom
> It is our duty to win
> We must love and respect each other
> We have nothing to lose but our chains.

The words are attributed to Assata Shakur, the noted activist in the Black Liberation Army and a member of the Blank Panthers. Their routine follows the same pattern each time: they repeat the verses three times, at three different volumes. First, they whisper it together. Next, they speak it at a conversational volume. Last, they yell it as loudly as they can—"they love this," says Douglas, "it's so different from what they are usually allowed to do, especially in a site like a school. It feels defiant and very powerful" (personal communication, 2017).

These practices emphasize one main goal: to help the youth "step into their power." Given the socially toxic stressors and potentially trauma-inducing experiences associated with the systems of which the young women at SSLC have been part, having this space of empowerment may be the healthiest environment available to them. Staff apply trauma-informed practices as appropriate, expressing care for youth affective state and vigilance about the stressors affecting the participants. This awareness alone fosters new approaches: SSLC facilitates the youths' learning about their own triggers and how to manage the resulting reactions, as described in Section II.

Recognizing the sources of their oppression is a necessary step in the dismantling of it. To this end, the SSLC program is designed on a Freirian-inspired model of "popular education." Staff model a co-construction of learning that frames their shared power. In their practices with the youth, the staff commonly "go back and forth between the macro and micro," linking the youth personal, first-hand experiences with the broader societal realities and systems at work (Gibbs & Douglas, personal communication, 2017). This intentional drawing out of the participants' personal experiences as sources of information (funds of knowledge) shows value for the cultural capital of their communities and squarely places them at the center of their learning, as Freirian models advise.

Leading the youth toward critical consciousness, SSLC staff use engaging and intricate instruction about oppression. For a specific example, they use a "tic-tac-toe game" to teach about the "-isms" (Douglas, personal communication, 2017). Explicating the forms of oppression that are internalized versus institutionalized, the participants identify how homophobia, racism, xenophobia, and sexism play out in real-life examples. When they identify them correctly and get "tic-tac-toe," there are fun rewards. As described in Section II, the terminology used to describe these realities is academic language, expressing the staff's belief and expectation that the youth can handle high-level concepts. Furthermore, it is a matter of equitable access to information; that is, they have the right to be told truthfully about the oppressive systems underlying their experiences. It is a matter, after all, of sharing power.

Case 2: Cookie Cart

Cookie Cart prioritizes employing young people who are on their way to becoming "opportunity youth"; because they focus on aged 15–17, their young bakers have not accrued years of disconnection. Most are anxious to become employed—in fact, Cookie Cart continues to have a waiting list as more youth apply for each cohort than they can accommodate despite their recent expansions (see Section IV). Cookie Cart is located in neighborhoods of high unemployment, intentionally aiming to intervene in patterns of unemployment and underemployment for the local teens. By targeting young people in high-need communities, Cookie Cart aims to create opportunities for employment where it does not exist.

Cookie Cart's program model aims to build social capital with the participating youth. As young people growing up in economically depressed communities, their access to social capital is commonly limited. That is to say, their "who you know" tends to be comprised of social networks within the community, not beyond it. Such opportunities to connect outside of the immediate low-income neighborhood can offer bridging ties. Examples of this practice within Cookie Cart are plentiful. Part of the mission of the organization is supporting youth interaction with new communities, usually professional and academic settings. Knowing that the youth who seek employment at Cookie Cart come from low-income homes, generally with little bridging social capital—opportunities for connections and enrichment beyond their immediate context—the program recognizes their role in helping to fill in this gap. "We're compensating," Marit Michels says of their intentional programming to arm youth with diverse new experiences that can connect them to future opportunities as well (personal communication, 2017). To this end, every cohort of young bakers experiences college campus visits, field trips to corporate sites, and one-on-one connections with professionals from outside of their community through mock job interviewing or informal interactions with volunteers. The college campus visits are intended to help the youth "see" the possibility of entering college after high school. Most of the youth at Cookie Cart do not come from college-educated households, so the process and environment of higher education may require more support, as has been documented by those who work with first-generation college students (Shelton, 2011). Field trips aimed at "career exploration" take youth to corporate work sites and broaden bridging capital because they bring the youth physically into novel environments to help them imagine future options. A notable example is Cookie Cart's group trip to Dairy Queen's international headquarters, located in the same city as their program. In addition to exposure to the business side, they young bakers visited the "ice cream lab," where food scientists experimented with novel flavor creations, demonstrating the applications of science within the food industry.

Another example from a few years ago brought Cookie Cart youth to an area amusement park. Before enjoying the rides, the youth learned about the field of hydraulic engineering with a behind-the-scenes tour. The career field trip was grounded in information about engineering career opportunities via a volunteer from a nearby mechanical engineering firm. Cookie Cart youth were also able to learn about degree and certificate options that could make that career path a reality (http://cookiecart.org/hydraulics-are-fun/).

While the bridging ties created in the previously described activities may possibly be fleeting, an argument can be made that exposure to diverse social settings increases comfort and familiarity, thereby increasing the likelihood that a young person will transfer that day's learning into another situation in the future. They may, for example, apply for a job one day at that same venue and reference their visit, revealing a deeper knowledge about the site than they would have had otherwise. Furthermore, there is the potential to create new *weak ties*, acquaintances who, research shows, are more likely that even one's close family and friends to make connections to employment and opportunities.

Of equal importance, Cookie Cart fosters deepened bonding social capital as well. These ties represent the families, friends, and neighbors of the youths' local community. As an organization, Cookie Cart participates in neighborhood events and encourages community use of their spaces, creating and affirming the connections that exist among the youth and their geographical community. The young bakers serve cookies at community gatherings and represent Cookie Cart at events all around the town. The participating youth are encouraged to be committed to their families and communities of origin, as demonstrated in their Employment Tips: "Applicants will provide examples of being responsible in their home, school and or community" (http://cookiecart.org/media/R-E-A-D-Y.pdf). Care for their bonding ties, then, is put on a level playing field with other factors, such as academic achievement (maintaining a grade of C or higher) and a "can do" attitude in the bakery.

Though Cookie Cart does not deploy a culturally specific model of youth development, the cultural backgrounds of their youth are relevant within the programming. Staff maintain an awareness of the changing demographics of the neighborhood over Cookie Cart's decades of operation, changes that reflect the mobility and immigration patterns of the city. While African American youth make up a significant number of the young bakers, the number of recently immigrated East African youth has risen sharply. As a tight-knit ethnic group, youth from this population tend to apply for Cookie Cart en masse; that is, in a groups of siblings and cousins. As familial word-of-mouth becomes a recruiting norm, the program has adapted by considering these values within their "hiring" or acceptance process and honoring the extended family applications (Michels, personal communication, 2017).

Focal Cases Summary: Key Concepts of Section III

Cookie Cart is especially focused on building individual financial assets, as described in Chapter 7, heavily influenced, it seems, by the Sherradenian concept of individual asset accumulation as a way out of poverty for both individuals and their communities. Their program design also attends to the families of the youth bakers in a way that aligns with Sherraden's view of the next stage of economic improvement: "twenty-first century social policy is very likely to move beyond the simplistic idea of consumption support, aiming for greater development of households, communities, and societies as a whole" (Sherraden, 2001, p. 9). By contrast, SOUL Sisters is less oriented toward economic capital opportunities, but focuses instead on social and cultural capital development.

Critical consciousness is a central feature for SOUL Sisters, comprising its primary approach for the youth to interrogate and disrupt the systems of oppression around them. SOUL Sisters' programming also includes restorative justice and trauma-informed practices, while these are not as formally present at Cookie Cart. Principles of trauma-informed practice appear to shape Cookie Cart's work, though, given the centrality of a safe environment for these youths' "first jobs."

Both programs embody problem-posing education because they are structured through hands-on, active partnerships aimed to solve a defined need in a mutually beneficial way. The result is critical thinking, empowerment, and the careful cultivation of Ginwright's collective hope.

Entrepreneurship, Employment, and Youth Social Entrepreneurship

10

Entrepreneurship Education

> Entrepreneurship holds a secret weapon against apathy and anger.
> It presents an ace in the hole for anyone who wants to build a
> community. Entrepreneurs are inveterate optimists! They usually don't
> know what they can't do. This optimism, this belief in the possible, is a
> remarkably potent resource for building community.
>
> —SMILOR, *1997, P. 8*

Introduction

The social innovations that undergird the programs and processes in youth social entrepreneurship draw heavily on entrepreneurship as its root source. With a long history (perhaps as old as humans themselves), entrepreneurship is about people thinking creatively to add value to their environments. This chapter explores how entrepreneurship has been structured and taught with the purpose of adding clarity to this dimension of youth social entrepreneurship. Whether or not a youth social entrepreneurship initiative includes a revenue-generating enterprise, this brief study of the principles of entrepreneurship can inform practice and help frame research and evaluation. The definition of entrepreneurship shaping the ideas of this chapter is a broad one (Moberg, Stenberg, & Vestergaard, 2012):

> Entrepreneurship is when you act upon opportunities and ideas and trans-
> form them into value for others. The value that is created can be financial,
> cultural, or social. (p.14)

This breadth sets up an examination of *design thinking* and *human-centered design* as the newest, cross-sector movement related to entrepreneurship. This chapter asks the reader to explore the concepts, apply them to the model with youth thus far described, and imagine how diverse practices of innovation can advance the causes of social justice and where they may impede progress.

Entrepreneurship and Education

Education and entrepreneurship are not inherently odd bedfellows: as societal values have existed and continue to grow for both self-created economic resources and/or for "entrepreneurial thinking," so, too, has instruction for being an entrepreneur been welcome in youth education. Entrepreneurship education is the "creation of knowledge, competencies and experiences that make it possible for students to initiate and participate in entrepreneurial value creating processes" (Moberg et al., 2012, p. 14). Advocates say that entrepreneurship is an independent discipline and thus can be taught, as is being done in increasing quantity and quality globally (Vanevenhoven & Liguori, 2013). Our current era brings entrepreneurship into education and youth work to "an unprecedented degree" (Hess, 2006, p. 1), including models of schools spawned by private-sector entrepreneurs. Perceived opportunities for new economic growth in the areas of knowledge and service have contributed to the surge of interest and programs in entrepreneurship education (Boyle, 2012). To wit, entrepreneurship education programs have grown extensively in higher education—from 400 universities in 1995 to more than 2,000 in 2012 (Tompkins-Bergh & Miller, 2015), rising from an initial group of 16 or so offering courses in 1970 (Kauffman Center, 2001). This trend has been well-documented in the United States as well as throughout Europe (Johansen & Schanke, 2013). Youth social entrepreneurship can learn much from the wealth of established work in entrepreneurship education.

Approaches to and Effects of Entrepreneurship Education

Research findings suggest that entrepreneurship education has an impact on student propensity and intentionality. The extent to which such education impacts on later entrepreneurship or whether it enables students to become more effective entrepreneurs is not yet established (Pittaway & Cope, 2007). Junior Achievement (JA) is the most prominent, long-standing example of youth entrepreneurship education, and the program is often a subject of such research. Founded in 1919 as an after-school program for high school students interested in business, JA now offers both in-school and out-of-school-time programming in all 50 American states and in about 100 countries through JA Worldwide. In the United States, JA involves 4.8 million youth per year. Thus, its history and reach is extensive.

The JA mission is for youth to access the "knowledge and skills they need to own economic success, plan for their futures, and make smart academic and economic choices" (www.juniorachievement.org/web/ja-usa/about). Their programming includes work readiness, financial literacy, and entrepreneurship. They offer a curriculum whose scope and sequence spans from elementary (grade 5) through high school (grade 12). While some JA programs focus more on basic economics, "JA Be Entrepreneurial" is available to grades 9–12 and highlights the "essential components of a practical business plan and challenges them to start an entrepreneurial venture while still in highschool" (www.juniorachievement.org/documents/20009/63782/JA+Scope+and+Sequence+Elementary.pdf).

An empirical inquiry of JA offers many findings, some studying the long-term impact of JA on entrepreneurial entry, performance, and survival. In one longitudinal study (Elert, Andersson, & Wennberg, 2015), JA alumni of Sweden were followed for 16 years after high school graduation. They found that JA participation increased the long-term probability of starting a firm as well as entrepreneurial incomes and increased the expected entrepreneurial income. However, participation did not affect survival of the created businesses. Youth social entrepreneurship programs may benefit by considering the curricular opportunities of the far-reaching JA organization, as well as attend to the limits on the long-term effects on business-related outcomes.

The field of entrepreneurship education for youth today tends to focus on understanding the determinants of entrepreneurial intent, the link between intent and action, and the pedagogical recommendations. Across the multitude of institutions offering entrepreneurship education, there exists a wide variety of programs and pedagogies with little uniformity in content and approach (Vanevenhoven & Liguori, 2013), so a movement toward best practices is challenging. Though there are many theories and approaches for preparing youth to become entrepreneurs, there is a great lack of knowledge on which interventions and approaches work best for their given context and aims. The field of "entrepreneurship programmatic research," which creates information that can help programs, remains at a relatively early stage despite the vast amount of resources spent on entrepreneurship education by numerous institutions (Chambers, 2015). Reasons for this include (1) programs have loose definitions of context and goals, (2) no direct opponents to entrepreneurship education programs exist, and (3) there is a lack of research using methodologies that truly identify the effect of an intervention. Efforts are afoot to advance the knowledge and practice in this area though. For example, the Entrepreneurship Education Project is a global, longitudinal research initiative of entrepreneurship researchers and education administrators seeking to determine the impact of entrepreneurial education. Based on traditionally aged college students, the study focuses on both the motivational processes underlying a student's entrepreneurship through the entrepreneurial process and the process of personal growth from student to entrepreneur (http://www.trepeducation.com).

Furthermore, the connection between concept and application for entrepreneurship education is often lacking. Vanevenhoven (2013) points out that "many of the linkages between entrepreneurship education and entrepreneurship in the 'real world' remain largely underspecified" (p. 466). True experiential education seems to be of utmost importance in entrepreneurial education: that is, first-hand experience with the activities and environments of an entrepreneur, which adds value to student learning (Plumly et al., 2008).

Advocates who want to see entrepreneurship education expanded point to the multiple benefits that would positively affect individual youth as well as communities and broader society. Based on their original research, Kourilsky and Walsted (2007) encourage the addition of entrepreneurship into academic curriculum as a way to prepare all young people to "control their means of production and future livelihood, no matter what their background, history, or aspirations" (p. 152). Drawing from each young person's own fund of knowledge, entrepreneurship education, they argue, can help youth "recognize their own strengths and expertise as grounded in community and family experiences" when they see opportunities of their own creation (p. 153). Researcher suggests that there is an elevated benefit for "students from low-income communities for whom entrepreneurship is the optimal strategy for economic and social mobility" (p. 154).

Youth Entrepreneurship and Youth Social Entrepreneurship: Distinctions and Connections

Since experiential pedagogies are paramount within entrepreneurship education, youth social entrepreneurship offers a potentially effective way to deliver entrepreneurship education by engaging students in the real-world, hands-on experiences that are arguably necessary for effective learning. "Entrepreneurship education development will be better informed on teachable elements based on this exploration of the complex interaction between the entrepreneur and the opportunity" (Vanevenhoven, 2013, p. 467). In this way, the similarity between the field of entrepreneurship education and youth social entrepreneurship lies in the shared pedagogical values. Just as youth social entrepreneurship as a model for youth development is inherently experiential and project-based, so, too, is entrepreneurship education, which stands in contrast to current, traditional forms of schooling: "Standardized, content focused, passive and single-subject based curriculum in traditional education is contrasted with an individualized, active, process-based, project centric, collaborative, experiential and multidisciplinary approach in entrepreneurial education" (Lackéus, 2015).

Furthermore, there appear to be central elements of entrepreneurship education that are also needed for any youth social entrepreneurial venture. These can be seen as the key "entrepreneurial competencies" (Lackéus & Williams-Middleton, 2014) that an individual might need to begin a start-up, whether seasoned or new to the area, whether focused on a social problem or working strictly for-profit. Entrepreneurial competencies are defined here as knowledge, skills, and attitudes that influence the willingness and ability to act as an entrepreneur. In all, there is *explorative value creation,* which refers to innovative, novel responses to existing stimuli. These offer "new ways of doing things," in contrast to "how things have always been done." Entrepreneurial competencies fall into three categories, each of which has been well-studied in the field of entrepreneurship education. Some applications for youth social entrepreneurship follow.

Entrepreneurial Competency: Cognitive Category

Teaching students how to *understand* entrepreneurship includes specific content such as risk and probability models, accounting, finance, technology, marketing, and the like. In general, entrepreneurs need to have knowledge about "how to get things done without resources" (Lackéus, 2015). In traditional entrepreneurship education programs, this content might be taught in textbook format or as a teacher-led lecture. In youth social entrepreneurship, this content might be taught through the application of the business model or explorative value creation.

Entrepreneurial Competency: Skills Category

Teaching students how to *apply* entrepreneurship knowledge includes assessing the marketplace, conducting market research, creating financial plans, dealing with customers, and communicating a vision (Fisher, Graham, & Compeau, 2008). New entrepreneurs need competence to also recognize and act on business opportunities, develop product or service ideas, and lead and motivate others. Furthermore, skills must be cultivated to cope with uncertainty and to set goals and strategies. In traditional entrepreneurship education programs, this content might be taught through practical case examples or by having students try the skills out on imagined scenarios. In youth social entrepreneurship, this content tends to be facilitated by watching peers exercise the skills in action if it is within an existing youth social entrepreneurship or by applying the skills toward a new value creation enterprise.

Entrepreneurial Competency: Attitudes Category

Teaching students the emotional and attitudinal states needed for successful entrepreneurship includes encouraging them to develop self-efficacy, innovativeness, perseverance, passion, proactivity, and tolerance for ambiguity (Krueger, 2003). As risk and failure are counterparts to all experimental endeavors, personal "resilience" is another important attitude for entrepreneurs. In both traditional entrepreneurship education programs and in youth social entrepreneurship, these attitudes are notably difficult to "teach"; instead, effective instruction involves role-modeling and individualized facilitation of positive attitudes, or individualized interventions if needed. As many of the entrepreneurial competencies in the category of "attitudes" tend to resemble "noncognitive factors" (Lackéus, 2015, p. 12), it may be wise to borrow from the vibrant body of teaching practices for social-emotional competence to develop these entrepreneurial attitudes.

In another configuration, the entrepreneurial characteristics that are mirrored in social entrepreneurship—and that can therefore be facilitated through education—are fivefold. Martin and Osberg (2007) describe the five characteristics as foundational to any innovation. First, entrepreneurship involves *inspiration* to make change in an existing situation. Entrepreneurs see an opportunity to disrupt an "unpleasant equilibrium" (p. 33) and experience a strong desire to pursue it, often because they are recipients of the unpleasantness. Similarly, youth social entrepreneurship often includes inspired ideas to improve the circumstances of an existing situation. For example, the founder of Old Skool Cafe in San Francisco, a youth-run supper club, was inspired to engage recently incarcerated youth in productive employment and leadership. As a corrections officer, she witnessed the unpleasantness of youth incarceration, crime, and recidivism and became passionate about disrupting it (www.oldskoolcafe.org/our-story).

Second, entrepreneurship involves *creativity* to innovate through original solutions, not "to optimize the current system with minor adjustments, but instead find a wholly new way of approaching the problem" (p. 33). Similarly, youth social entrepreneurship exercises creativity to engage youth, allow youth leadership, and address community needs. To continue the same example, Old Skool Cafe expanded on the employment and training pathways in hospitality and culinary arts by connecting history (jazz-era design), music, food, and culture. The youth plan, prep, and serve a menu referred to as "Comfort food from around the world," claiming:

> For centuries, families and communities have gathered around the dinner table to "break bread," and recipes are passed down from generation to generation. Our youth come from many different cultures and traditions of food. We take the home recipes that our youth have grown up with and help transform them into dishes that are inspiring, as well as delicious. We believe that food nourishes the body and the soul. (www.oldskoolcafe.org)

Third, entrepreneurship involves *direct action*. After being inspired and securing a creative approach to solving the identified problem, entrepreneurship does not wait "for someone else to intervene or try to convince somebody else to solve the problem," (Martin & Osberg, 2007, p. 34). In this way, entrepreneurship and social entrepreneurship differ from advocacy, organizing, or activism. Though these efforts may involve action, the direct nature of the entrepreneurial endeavor distinguishes it. In the Old Skool Cafe example, the founder started small but directly: she created a supper club in her apartment to be run by youth in need. This direct action led to larger scale attention and support to get their own building a couple of years later. Ten years since then, they are expanding to an even larger facility and include off-site catering among their services.

A fourth characteristic of entrepreneurship is the need for *courage* to take the action step. This element draws heavily on the knowledge (risk modeling) and attitudes (resilience) competencies described earlier as being part of entrepreneurship education. Preparation for social entrepreneurship is no different: courage is necessary to take any direct action in the face of significant risk of failure. The Old Skool Cafe example reflects notable courage: the restaurant industry itself is a high-risk venture with approximately 60% of traditionally run restaurants failing in their first year of operation (Parsa, Self, Njite, & King, 2005). To add the dimension of a restaurant run by youth who have been incarcerated, homeless, and/or in foster care requires an undeniable courage.

Fifth, entrepreneurship involves *fortitude* to persist despite the inevitable "setbacks or unexpected turns, and . . . to be able to find creative ways around the barriers and challenges that arise" (Martin & Osberg, 2007, p. 33). This characteristic is akin to the resilience factor noted as a competency in entrepreneurship education.

Like youth social entrepreneurship, entrepreneurial education is also frequently seen as a response to the increasingly globalized, uncertain, and complex world we live in, requiring all people and organizations in society to be increasingly equipped with entrepreneurial competencies (Gibb, 2002).

To summarize, entrepreneurship education informs youth social entrepreneurship in vital ways. Despite the social change focus of social entrepreneurship, an understanding of and applications toward entrepreneurial activity are essential. As asserted by Martin and Osberg (2007): "Any definition of the term 'social entrepreneurship' must start with the word 'entrepreneurship.' The word 'social' simply modifies entrepreneurship. If entrepreneurship doesn't have a clear meaning, then modifying it with social won't accomplish much, either" (p. 30).

Design Thinking and Entrepreneurship

In the past decade, the concept of *design thinking* seems pervasive, crossing sectors as freely as air. Pinning down a meaning or approach is, not surprisingly, far from easy. Critical analyses demonstrate the splintered meaning within the discourse (Johansson-Sköldberg, Woodilla, & Çetinkaya, 2013). Explains one executive at IDEO, the best-known international design company: "Design thinking isn't one thing . . . but a bundle of mindsets and philosophies all wrapped up in one term, which obviously has the potential to lead to ambiguity and misunderstanding" (Lahey, 2017). At its essence, design thinking refers to a process for creative problem-solving. What distinguishes it from traditional problem-solving approaches, though, is its attention to human needs. Traditional processes are problem-focused, but design thinking is solution-focused and oriented to the future desirability of its effects on clients/customers. Design thinking relies on the designer's awareness and methodology to match people's needs with technologically feasible solutions and thereby create viable strategies. It has been contrasted to the traditional scientific method that seeks solutions through analysis, reducing problems to smaller parts. Instead, design thinking seeks solutions through synthesis, broadening the scope of the possible solutions to include both known and ambiguous aspects of the current situation, including human emotion, an oft-disregarded component in traditional approaches. In this way, design thinking is thought of as *human-centered design*. True design thinking begins, in fact, with empathy as a key tool for problem-solving. Says the president and CEO of IDEO: "Design thinking is a human-centered approach to innovation that draws from the designer's toolkit to integrate the needs of people, the possibilities of technology, and the requirements for business success" (www.ideou.com/pages/design-thinking).

Human-centered design has been adopted in multiple sectors, not limited to its business roots. Leaders in education and social services are applying intentional design thinking within their programming at increasing rates. True implementation of human-centered design aligns easily with the student-centered, client-centered methods already at play in these fields. Yet both the novelty of and creative license within the design thinking movement seems to be attracting attention, interest, and willing participants. An example in the field of Public Health demonstrates this process by using place-based, human-centered design principles to address maternal and child well-being (Vechakul, Shrimali, & Sandhu, 2015). Vechakul et al. conclude that their experience with human-centered design in public health can "enhance community engagement; expedite the timeframe for challenge identification, program design, and implementation; and create innovative programs that address complex challenges" (p. 2552). Of significance, they point out that human-centered design "encourages immersion in the community to deepen empathy" and that "reframing the challenge integrates insights into solutions" (p. 2554). In these ways, human-centered design is promising for its social impact, and it aligns well with the asset-focused, youth-centered, community-valued frameworks described here as youth social entrepreneurship.

Elements of design thinking and human-centered design are increasingly finding their way into K–12 schools, but not in all settings. Youth workers aiming to engage young people in innovative community solutions may be wise to include the language and processes of design thinking and human-centered design into their programs. The principles are familiar and thus easily transferred: "the key elements of design thinking will be familiar to any teacher well-versed in the basics of effective teaching: start with empathy, move ego to the side, and support students in the process of failing often and early on their way to learning" (Lahey, 2017).

Critics of using human-centered design within the public sector point to concerns. For example, Janzer and Weinstein (2014) argue that designers must be sensitive to a variety of complex social and cultural structures lest they contribute to neocolonialism. Therefore, any social applications of user-focused design can be deemed dangerous unless they account for larger, historic contexts. A burgeoning body of scholarship exists to explore and mediate these concerns (e.g., Sharma & Patil, 2017). The trajectory is to create "user participation" within a framework of "responsible decision-making" (p. 1025). Such a path appears to mirror the participatory values within research, evaluation, teaching, and youth work undertaken of late. While tensions exist in holding the social solutions to problems accountable to history and yet responsive to immediate needs, the movement toward human reaction, empathy, and interdependent systems appears to reflect a more robust, less reductionist future.

11

Economic Transformation

We prepare our students for jobs and careers,
but we don't teach them to think as individuals
about what kind of world they would create.

—MUHAMMAD YUNUS

Introduction

As youth social entrepreneurship precipitates social change at multiple levels—individual, community, and societal—economic change can act as one driver for impact. This chapter examines the mechanisms for improving young people's economic condition, usually via employment. Since many, though not all youth social entrepreneurship activities include youth acting within "a job," a more thorough investigation of the research supporting economic change for young people is well warranted and will equip the reader with frames within which to think about employment.

Furthermore, there is an expected effect on community assets through youth social entrepreneurship, because the community is often an additional economic asset within which an enterprise operates. What triggers and what limits such effects? In this chapter, the reader will encounter a systems perspective about school-to-work efforts that considers how the youth social entrepreneurship paradigm dovetails with this traditional body of practice and what lessons can be learned.

With an overall consideration of how human capital development impacts the broader social system, this chapter situates youth social entrepreneurship as one approach to changing communities through individual economic improvement and the creation of a future employment trajectory.

The aims of youth social entrepreneurship are broad, lofty, and complex: healthy, positive youth development (PYD) alone is not the final goal, and economic change at multiple levels is also targeted. Models of youth social entrepreneurship demonstrate this multilevel orientation as their program plans address the economic effects on the individual youth involved, the economic effects on the communities affected by their social enterprises, and the economic effects on the families and broader social systems.

An Economic Gap

Economic change through youth employment is a common approach within youth social entrepreneurship. That is to say, youth often begin their involvement in youth social entrepreneurship because they are seeking a job. The need for a paycheck, then, is a significant draw for youth to this model, and many programs leverage that desire by marketing their offerings as employment, first and foremost. This economic element differentiates youth social entrepreneurship from the more prolific youth development, out-of-school-time (OST) programs that promise other targets: physical health (e.g., athletics), leadership (e.g., student government), leisure (e.g., hiking club), and fine arts (e.g., youth orchestra). Commonly, youth OST experiences are in direct conflict with a paycheck, with many young people pressed to choose between a sports club and an after-school job. Youth social entrepreneurship programs aim to combine the youth development aspects of such extracurricular activities with employment and its financial benefits.

For youth from economically disadvantaged backgrounds, this "choice" is often nonexistent. The need to bring in a paycheck is even more significant as it may be for the benefit of the youth's family, or it may be the individual youth's only source of current and future financial security. Opportunities to access PYD via OST may be out of reach, then, due to priorities and time restrictions. When high-income peers are financially able to participate in OST and gain added skills and personal strengths (see Chapter 2 for discussion of developmental assets), but lower income youth are not, the gap in opportunities widens. The effects are far-reaching: from the impact on college enrollment (Gibbs, Erickson, Dufur, & Miles, 2015) to a decreased social network (Schaefer, Simpkins, Vest, & Price, 2011) to hindered emotional well-being (Ruvalcaba, Gallegos, Borges, & Gonzalez, 2017). The bottom line is that youth who must choose between a paycheck and youth development programs are likely to choose the income, at the cost of other, sometimes long-term outcomes. From this perspective, it may be seen as an act of equity to combine youth income with PYD as it decreases the necessity of a marginalized youth having to choose between the two.

The situation is exacerbated for jobless youth who may also be "disconnected youth," depending on school enrollment, with little employment prospects in their immediate or at least accessible neighborhoods. Employment opportunities for entry-level jobs tend to be more plentiful in higher income neighborhoods for obvious economic reasons—people who have money, spend money. Since joblessness is associated with higher rates of crime, the employment prospects of jobless youth are a critical concern (Wilson, 2016). The effects of community-based organizations on reducing youth joblessness through school-to-work efforts and increasing broader community economic development has been documented for decades (Fitzgerald, 1997).

"Learn and Earn"

Similarly, youth social entrepreneurship programs support youth in bridging their school-and-work or school-to-work experiences. The central idea is that involved youth can simultaneously "learn and earn"; that is, they can acquire new skills and experiences as part of their positive development while simultaneously accessing financial benefits such as a paycheck. Not all youth social entrepreneurship initiatives result in financial earnings for the youth involved, but many do. Of those that do, some offer an hourly pay-rate model for youth employment while others use a paid apprenticeship approach. Still others deploy a model of "earnings" that are not financial.

Paid Apprenticeship

The organization Urban Boatbuilders illustrates how a paid apprenticeship works with youth social entrepreneurship. Located in St. Paul, Minnesota, the program offers a "paid job training opportunity . . . to develop technical woodworking skills, social and emotional skills, and a connection to local waterways" (http://urbanboatbuilders.org/). They adhere to specific hiring guidelines, describing their employment recruits as "youth who qualify as low-income and/or have employment barriers." The youth employees/apprentices have the option to participate for 3 to 12 months, within which time they work alongside professional builders to learn "technical boat building skills while earning money." Youth aged 16–19 years at the time of application are eligible hires, and "low-income" is operationalized as those youth who receive free- or reduced-price lunches. Barriers to employment are defined as including, but not limited to, students with individualized education plans (IEPs) and those with limited English proficiency, juvenile offenders and youth in diversion programs, youth with chemical dependency issues, or youth who are parenting.

The products are handmade boats of a broad variety—skiffs, canoes, stand-up paddleboards, kayaks, and prams. Buyers choose from a stock of built boats or can commission a boat to fit their specifications.

In addition to the boatbuilding skills learned, youth apprentices participate in intentional social-emotional development activities and career readiness, including mock interviews, college visits, resume writing, and financial planning. Once they complete a boat, apprentices get to enjoy their hard work by launching and paddling the boat in nearby lakes.

Other Approaches to Earning

Bearings Bike Shop of Atlanta, Georgia, offers several ways for involved youth to learn and earn. Their Starting Point program provides points toward the "purchase" of a bicycle: every hour spent learning the skills of bike repair in the shop earns another point. When they have earned enough, they "make a withdrawal" and get their own bikes. All the bicycles are donated from around the local community, and each bike gets "a new life, and kids who might never own a bike get to do so, experiencing the joy of owning a bike of their own" (bearingsbikeshop.org). Youth in this program begin as young as age 6 years.

Their Skills for Life program includes leveled learning focused on bike mechanics as well as "character strengths." Successful completion of each higher level earns the youth opportunities to buy a bike and "earn fun perks like T-shirts, new locks, and special privileges in the shop."

Additionally, the teenaged youth at Bearings who have completed the highest levels of the Skills for Life program are eligible to apply for their Advanced Program. This offering gives them paid employment within the bike shop. In the summer, a small cohort of youth also participate in an Advanced Job Training program, working 20–25 hours each week; this program includes a weekly financial literacy program and visits to various workplaces throughout the city to see different careers and work environments. While in the shop, their primary responsibilities consisted of repairing and refurbishing bikes for resale, maintaining and preparing the shop space and supplies for the program, and serving as leaders of groups of kids during the shop's program hours.

Effects of (Un)employment

Understanding the effects of youth employment on the youth themselves as well as on their society is often seen through a negative lens. In other words, it is well established in the research that youth *un*employment has negative consequences on youth and their contexts (e.g., Heckman & Borjas, 1980). The inverse seems likely but is less substantiated that expected (then again, given the deficit focus of much youth research historically, perhaps this is not surprising).

Mroz and Savage (2006) assert findings that demonstrate the long-term negative impact of voluntary youth unemployment on later labor markets as well as on individual earnings 10 years later. The impact is significant for human capital: those who experience unemployment enter their next employment period with "a lower stock of human capital than otherwise identical individuals" (p. 260). This research supports the theoretical "dynamic human capital model" that suggests that people's behavioral tendency to seek out additional training is a "catch-up response." Unfortunately, this additional training is not usually enough, according to Mroz and Savage, since the long-term impact of youth unemployment is diminished future earnings. They write: "Forgone work experience may reverberate throughout a young person's life. Perhaps this is because one job leapfrogs into another, and early unemployment would delay some of the first jumps" (p. 292).

These findings suggest that the human capital dimensions of youth social entrepreneurship—such as training for customer service, the hospitality industry, or bicycle mechanics, among many others—are significantly less effective alone than alongside paid employment (i.e., a job). In this sense, the sum is potentially much greater than its parts. Knowing that "international evidence from evaluations of training programmes for disadvantaged youth is not encouraging," many experts warn against policies of "acquire skills first, work later" (Scarpetta, Sonnet, & Manfedi, 2010, p. 4).

In their report to the W. K. Kellogg Foundation, Belfield, Levin, and Rosen (2012) cite the impact of unemployment by explicating the societal economic burden of youth who are neither employed nor in school. They extrapolate income differences for unemployed youth over their lifetimes in contrast to employed peers. They found that the unemployed youth on average will accumulate $392,070 less in income than the average worker. Across the present-day cohort of 6.7 million opportunity youth, Belfield et al. (2012) say that society can expect this amount to total $2.6 trillion in lost money within the US economy, as well as upward of $325 billion in the costs of crime, poor health, and welfare.

The short-term, positive impact of paid employment for disconnected youth has been documented, in particular, through an evaluation conducted on the New York City Summer Youth Employment Program (SYEP) in the 2005–2008 (Gelber Isen, & Kessler, 2016). During this period, SYEP provided summer jobs to NYC youth aged 14-21, paid by the NYC government. This project finds that the SYEP significantly increased the average earnings and increased the probability of employment in the same year as program participation. Notably, they also found that SYEP participation was significantly associated with a decrease in the probability of incarceration and the probability of mortality, which has important and potentially pivotal implications for analyzing the net benefits of the program. However, their findings did not document a positive impact on future earnings after SYEP. Instead, they found a moderate decrease in average earnings for 3 years following the program.

While SYEP is not a youth social entrepreneurship venture, it shares common features: it often provides a "first job" for youth identified as having economic disadvantages; it offers a short-term employment when there might not be other options; and it provides training in financial literacy, job readiness, and career exploration alongside the paycheck. The results of the study on SYEP are worth keeping in mind for any practitioner involved in similar programming. First, the momentum that is created during the summer employment lasts into the next year but not beyond it. This suggests that sustained involvement of some form could help support the momentum from the beginning. Examples of this include programs that offer opportunities for advancement within the program as well as programs that keep "close ties" with their alumni, including them in events and following-up frequently for a top-off to the work they did together. Second, the effects of lower incarceration and mortality are profoundly important, given the disproportionality of incarceration and mortality among young people in the targeted population for these programs. Practitioners and policymakers would do well to note this decrease as itself a significant outcome of their employment offering and leverage similar programming to intervene in the incarceration and death patterns in other communities.

Economic Effects on Communities

Beyond the youth employment aspect of many youth social entrepreneurship programs are the aims of economic change for the communities to which the youth belong, both by the nature of having them employed versus unemployed and by including a social enterprise for others to encounter, often in the very neighborhoods where these youth live. In these ways, youth social entrepreneurship hopes to disrupt the economic depression of many communities, at least as much as possible. As noted in Chapter 4, some youth social entrepreneurship programs seek economic transformation more significantly in their program design than others, but all offer some economic-level impact when employment and/or enterprise with marginalized youth are involved.

Less attention has been given to research on the community-level effects of having youth social entrepreneurs active there. The economic effects that youth employment and/or enterprise have on their communities fall well within the systems concerns of macro-level social workers and social work researchers (Coyle, 2016). On the whole, entrepreneurship has received considerable attention as an inner-city economic development strategy. Others argue that social entrepreneurship is an important contributor to community economic development, being seen as "an effective socio-political and economic link between government and free market enterprise" (Wallace, 1999, p. 153). Taken alongside the established importance for so-called opportunity youth to be engaged in wage-earning roles and become connected to a healthy social network, youth social entrepreneurship models can help improve the community aspects impacted by both lack of entrepreneurship and by disconnected youth.

A telling connection exists in the school-to-work field, which provides an expansive body of research and practical examples. School-to-work programs have been supported extensively by both federal and local governments and touted as a solution for the transition between secondary school and the workplace. Through apprenticeships, mentorships, job shadowing, and internships, school-to-work programs have been designed to "(a) encourage all students to remain in school and achieve high standards of occupational and academic performance; (b) make education more relevant to students by integrating academic and occupational activities; and (c) enhance students' opportunities for employment or further postsecondary education by building effective partnerships among K–12 schools, postsecondary school, employers, community agencies, students and parents" (Collet-Klingenberg & Kenney, 2000, p. 53). US legislation in 1994 created the School-to-Work Opportunities Act to support a system that would prepare students for work after high school through the US Departments of Education and Labor (funding expired in 2001 and was not renewed). The enactment of the School-to-Work Opportunities Act of 1994 was intended to facilitate the education and career preparation of young people during their secondary school years, thus expanding pathways to postsecondary education, stable employment, and self-sufficiency. A number of lessons were learned by researchers during this funded effort. First, the positive outcomes included:

- improved attendance in school and a decreased likelihood that students participating in school-to-work programs would drop out;
- positive responses from teachers and employers involved in school-to-work programs;
- youth development goals, such as increased access to caring adults, enhanced motivation, and better planning for the future; and
- broadened career options for youth, including the option of college and other postsecondary enrollment, which is counter to the concerns voiced by critics that school-to-work might pigeonhole youth participants into narrow job options (Hughes, Bailey, & Mechur, 2001).

In short, effective School-to-Work programming is achievable if there is a strong partnership with businesses and a curriculum that trains and teaches students for the workforce. Documented challenges from the School-to-Work Act include fidelity to programming by schools, cost for both the school and the businesses to act as partners, unequal resources by geography, and inconsistent willingness from local businesses to be a partner (Kash, 2009). There are some lasting effects of the School-to-Work program as a national approach:

> [T]he movement had a substantial record of creativity and accomplishment. Among other things, it hastened the spread of career development activities for all students, strengthened ties between schools and local employers, and supported the creation of many innovative work-based education programs. By the end of the decade, however, the influence of the movement had begun to decline as other reform movements came to dominate the national educational landscape. (Stull & Sanders, 2003, p. 10)

Beyond Economic Growth Alone

The classical economists identified *land, labor, and physical capital* (i.e., tools and technology) as the three basic factors shaping economic growth. Later in the 1960s, neo-classical economists introduced the notion of *human capital*, arguing that a community's supply of job-ready workers ultimately determines how productively the economy will operate. The addition of *social capital* orients attention to the necessity of connection among workers if economic systems are to progress. To this end, human and social capital are complements: well-prepared workers are better able to organize, evaluate conflicting information, and express themselves to one another to improve both their own conditions and those of the larger economy. Woolcock (1998) explains:

> The latest equipment and most innovative ideas in the hands or mind of the brightest, fittest person, however, will amount to little unless that person also has access to others to inform, correct, improve and disseminate his or her work. Life at home, in the boardroom or on the shop floor is both more rewarding and productive when suppliers, colleagues and clients alike are able to combine their particular skills and resources in a spirit of cooperation and commitment to common objectives. In essence, where human capital resides in individuals, social capital resides in relationships. (p. 177)

12

Creating and Scaling Youth Social Entrepreneurship Programs

Rather, ten times, die in the surf, heralding the way to a new world, than stand idly on the shore.

—FLORENCE NIGHTINGALE, *FOUNDER OF MODERN NURSING, CONSIDERED AN EARLY SOCIAL ENTREPRENEUR*

Introduction

Youth social entrepreneurs and/or their adult partners may be curious about the nuts-and-bolts of creating social enterprises within their programs. This chapter aims to be a primer on the basic concepts that will help current and potential project developers shape their efforts. To this end, an overview of types of small businesses and social enterprises is included, along with conceptual resources for any venture.

Furthermore, this chapter explores the limits to and potential of growth for youth social entrepreneurship initiatives. Whether or not and how to "scale up" is a foremost concern for nonprofit and for-profit social enterprises. The reader will find here a discussion of perspectives and considerations to help drive forward such an essential programmatic decision.

Social Enterprises and Youth Social Entrepreneurship

As seen through the many case examples presented in this book, the structure of the youth social entrepreneurship model varies. Specifically, many programs create relatively social enterprises within larger nonprofits, while many others exist as independent entities whose sole purpose is social enterprise. There is no driving rule for this distinction: just as every social entrepreneur seeks to address observed needs based on the uniqueness of the need itself, so it is that both seemingly small and strikingly large social enterprises can be categorized together as branches on a common tree—the lemonade stand on the suburban street corner raising $100 for the local food shelf and TOMS shoes, which has resulted in donations of more than 60 million pairs of shoes worldwide, restoring sight to over 400,000 people, providing over 335,000 weeks of safe water and supporting birth services for more than 25,000 mothers, among other contributions (Mykoskie, 2012, p. 2). Both have a core social purpose and aim to meet it with an enterprise.

Because there is no reliable accounting for youth social entrepreneurship programs whatsoever, a sense of how many exist at any level of size is impossible. However, we are able to point to some of the largest organizations in the United States that fit the model, and we are able to detect how numerous some of the smaller ones truly are through their Internet presence and, in some cases, funders' counts. Internationally, the accounting is even more difficult, as youth social entrepreneurship is widespread in developed and developing countries alike (see Chapter 14 of this book).

Types of "Small" Enterprises

Youth social entrepreneurs who aim to create an enterprise with a social purpose sometimes find that the elements of business start-up are difficult to understand. The basic categories of small business can help sort through myriad enterprise entities. The common forms of small enterprise are:

1. *Small business*: Size varies greatly by the field but is defined consistently by being nondominant in their field and individually owned (no stockholders). Usually more than five employees are involved but fewer than 500.
2. *Micro-business*: Usually fewer than five employees, often on a part-time basis. These are typically run out of someone's home or another building that does not have the exclusive use of business. Average micro-businesses require very little start-up capital.
3. *Cottage business*: Operated from home with typically no more than two employees. Cottage businesses tend to be part-time in nature, but they do not have to be. The focus is often on manufacturing or production. Service-type businesses are not included in the cottage business model. Common products include clothing, baking, soaps, or decorative items. Most things produced in a cottage business tend to be labor-intensive because they are hand-made.

Stages of Enterprise Development

A lack of knowledge about the basics of enterprise development can be a hindrance to youth and/or to the adults who partner with them to implement youth social entrepreneurship programs. Fortunately, there are many resources available to guide the process in accessible ways. One such resource are the REDF workshops, a project of the Roberts Enterprise Development Fund (REDF; redf. org/who-we-are). With a unique focus as "venture philanthropy in the US that invests exclusively in the growth of social enterprises focused on employment," REDF provides several forms of support to social entrepreneurs: seed and growth capital to enterprises; advisory services; leadership in building the field; and growing the evidence base for social businesses. REDF's workshops offer Internet-based learning opportunities at no charge for people engaged in social entrepreneurship at all levels. The workshop website includes numerous case examples, webinars, tools, and articles geared to building and growing social enterprises. While there is not an established distinction made between social entrepreneurs who are involved youth versus adult entrepreneurs, the material included is relevant to social entrepreneurs regardless of age or experience. That is to say, youth who are at the helm of new or existing social enterprises can benefit from REDF's informative contents despite the organization's broad audience.

Not surprisingly, proper support during the process of creating and growing a social enterprise is crucial to its viability (Hines, 2005).

IDEA PHASE

The *vision* stage is simply ideation, that occurs when there is an idea for a social enterprise. Alternatively, an existing business or nonprofit seeks to form a social enterprise within its services or programming. The vision should include consideration of the needs of the community as well as of the potential users/clients/customers (e.g., human-centered design).

STARTUP PHASE

Startup enterprises are launched but are still working on developing their model and their business. Social entrepreneurs need to plan for the launch and survival of their venture. Such planning involves "translating the motivations into a collection of start-up actions which, upon execution, bring the organization into existence" (Katre & Salipante, 2012).

Perrini, Vurro, and Costanzo (2010) have outlined a social entrepreneurship conceptual process consisting of four main clusters of organizing activities: (1) opportunity evaluation for expected social and economic value; (2) innovation in products/services, methods, factors, and relations; (3) organization launching and functioning by developing necessary routines; and (4) enhancement of societal well-being through direct/indirect employment creation, access to information and knowledge, social cohesion, inclusion, and community and economic development. Specific behaviors associated with successful social enterprise start-up are:

- establishing a societal issue as the first activity,
- creating a business concept to bring about social change,
- carefully selecting products/services,
- acquiring skills,
- growing social contacts, and
- creating support for the social business.

GROWTH PHASE

After their operations are stabilized, enterprises in the *growth* stage are focused on continuing to grow the business and are starting to think about scale and replication. This may be seen as the "survival" phase, the time that essentially makes or breaks the venture. Key behaviors in this phase include "establishing a demand for the societal issue, mobilizing motivated volunteers, establishing an effective board of directors, diversifying the sources of funding, and establishing a track record of program delivery" (Katre & Salipante, 2012, p. 970).

"SCALING-UP" PHASE

Established enterprises have a proven model and a successful business, and they are ready to *replicate* and start up new enterprise or expand their services into new locations. Considerations central to this stage are described later in this chapter.

Funding the Social Enterprise

Given that social enterprises take in revenue, it may be tempting to wonder whether further funds are needed. The short answer is yes: social enterprises need funding beyond the income generated by their product or service, and they commonly seek that via grants. Social enterprises often strive to generate enough revenue to cover their costs, but there are many costs associated with their programming that go beyond business costs, known as "social costs" (REDFworkshops, 2017). Thus, even while a social enterprise is doing well financially and able to cover business costs, it's not unusual for it to still need additional grant support to cover its social costs.

Grant funding can come from a variety of sources: from the government, from public or private foundations, and from individual donors. The social enterprise's tax structure is an important variable in this process. Most of these funders are only able to give grants to nonprofit 501(c)3 organizations. (Note: In some cases, it is possible to access grant funding for a B-Corp or a for-profit organization, but typically these must first be funneled through a nonprofit sponsor.) Common funding streams for social enterprises are provided in Table 12.1.

TABLE 12.1

Types of funders

Type of funder	Description
Government	Grants from government agencies at federal, state, or local levels
Private foundation	Charitable organizations funded by private sources and legally required to distribute 5% of their income each year
Family foundation	A subset of private foundations, these typically involve the financial source (family members) in the grant decisions
Public foundation	Grant-making public charities, including faith-based organizations and hospitals (e.g., United Way)
Corporations	Grants are made through corporate-funded foundations or direct giving programs in the corporations
Intermediaries	Organizations that re-grant out the money they fundraise
Individuals	Individual donors such as friends and family

Summarized from the Roberts Enterprise Development Fund workshop on social enterprise grants: https://redfworkshop.org/learning-modules/capital-social-enterprises-grants/.

In-Kind Revenue

In-kind revenue is another common and often necessary source of income for all nonprofits and most social enterprises. Donations of goods as well as volunteer hours are significant sources of resource support. Solid relationships within the community for sustained in-kind revenue can be essential to a social enterprise's survival. Some organizations do this by forming an alliance or partnership to acquire a steady stream of in-kind resources. In-kind providers tend to appreciate the opportunity to support an organization's mission and programs without investing cash. Keeping a provider informed of what is done with their in-kind contribution encourages them to take on a greater role in programs and to continue donating.

Predicting the Success of a Social Enterprise

Popular wisdom about any so-called start-up, whether it is a social enterprise or a traditional, for-profit business, points to high failure probability. Indeed, risk is a factor in any entrepreneurial activity, by its very definition (see Chapter 1). This recognition begs the question of what factors might best help a venture to succeed while another fails. A study by Katre and Salipante (2012) engaged this central question in an interview study of a sample of North American social entrepreneurs. Their results reveal that entrepreneurs of successful social ventures "blend the organizing behaviors of both nonprofits and business ventures" (p. 968). Overall, they found that the organizing behaviors that are important to create and sustain a successful social enterprise shared characteristics of the behaviors applied in both nonprofit and business sectors. However, the significant differences found between successful versus struggling ventures were in *how* the activities were undertaken.

> For example, entrepreneurs of successful ventures employed behaviors to diversify and grow their knowledge and networks, whereas the founders of struggling ventures did not . . . this research provides insights as to which of the typical behaviors from the social sector may be combined with entrepreneurship for success. (p. 969)

Specific leadership behaviors can make or break the social enterprise. Namely, the difference between social enterprises that succeed and those that fail tends to be "intense personal involvement" by the founders to learn more and grow the venture, as well as to expand the social contacts of the enterprise. Ventures that flounder or fail tend to rely on virtual communication, delegation, and "restrictive, homogeneous social contacts" (Katre & Salipante, 2012, p. 976).

On the ground, Sisterhood Boutique staff has seen this reality. In an interview with the program's leadership, they named "the right team" as a crucial component to their success in sustaining the venture. Upon further probing, one staff member said that this means being able to "hold both the business and the youth development goals" at the same time. She shook her head and added, "it's not easy." Her colleagues went on to say that, in many ways, this is the most challenging aspect of their work: worrying simultaneously about the business's survival and the positive effects on their youth: "We're not just a business; we are both employers and mentors" (personal communication, June 2017).

As of 2017, Sisterhood Boutique seems to attack this challenge by shielding some of their younger staffers from the economic concerns of the enterprise, freeing them up to focus on leading the youth development and employment experiences. Structurally, this is possible given the social enterprise's connection to the larger entity, Pillsbury United Communities. This collective organizing nonprofit has broader capacity—approximately 180 staff, only a few of whom are directly involved with Sisterhood Boutique specifically. They operate in six neighboring locations with more than a dozen programs, resulting in organizational capacity that is large enough to help support the Sisterhood venture.

Staying Small?

Intuitively, there are a number of reasons that youth social entrepreneurship programs tend to include small—often micro- or cottage-size—businesses. Not the least important reason is that many have youth development as their primary focus and do not want to compromise that mission through business scaling. As pointed out in the business community: "Scaling a for-profit business is hard. So is scaling a philanthropic organization . . . the only way it all works is if one doesn't overshadow the other" (Buchanan, 2016).

Another important reason is limited capital to grow the enterprise. Increasingly, funds are available from social innovation-oriented philanthropic entities to help social entrepreneurs begin their enterprise. However, questions of what defines a "sustainable business model" prevent a ready flow of capital to continue funding for growth. A 2016 report by the Forum for Sustainable and Responsible Investment suggests this trend may be changing. "Sustainable, responsible and impact investing" opportunities seem to be expanding, offering new funding avenues for social enterprises, especially those registered as Benefit Corporations. Specifically, this biennial report found that "sustainable, responsible and impact" assets have expanded to $8.72 trillion in the United States in 2016, a 33% increase from 2014 (Field, 2017). The broadening landscape of investment, then, might translate into more growth potential for successful youth social enterprises . . . if they choose to "scale up." Many more variables must go into that decision than financing alone.

Kayser and Budinich (2015) outline the most common issues facing social entrepreneurs—youth or adults—in scaling up their programs. They point to the common belief that "small is beautiful" in social enterprises, due primarily to the pressure to stay nimble in programming. Growing in scale requires many more "standardized" approaches, for example, from staff member to staff member or from site location to new site location, to retain program quality.

Furthermore, in small enterprises and cottage industries, the founder or leader tends to be intimately attached to the work and can be reluctant give up the single-handed oversight that launched the project in the first place. In short, it is hard to "let go" for founders who see the enterprise as their baby (Kayser & Budinich, 2015, p. 112). These leaders ultimately become a bottleneck for growth, in what can be called the "founder syndrome."

Last, a lack of skills to scale a program or business is a predominant reason for stunted growth. Many social entrepreneurs are most passionate about the issue that they sought to address in the first place. The logistics of scaling their model is outside of their skill set and often, even, their interests. Most social entrepreneurs do not have "both innovator's and manager's skills" (p. 113). Hence, when and if program growth is needed to expand capacity, leadership must often recognize these limitations and be willing to seek resources to fill in the skill gaps.

A final issue to consider on the concern of scale: Is the measurement of a social enterprise's success more present in its size or in its influence? For many, the two are related—the more people engaged (size), the more extensive the impact (influence). But for others, extending size means "watering down" impactful, often highly personalized practices that have deep and lasting influence on a smaller number of people. While no single answer will fit every situation, and at its core it may be one for the ethicists, surfacing this question as a hinge point for decision-making can help move along decisions about scale.

Section IV

Focal Case Examples

Case 1: SOUL Sisters Leadership Collective

While none of the more traditional entrepreneurship education approaches is at play in SOUL Sisters Leadership Collaborative (SSLC), their Social Action Projects arguably incorporate human-centered design thinking. As previously described, once the young women in the SSLC program complete the first phase of foundational learning, they move to the more civically engaged, project-based Social Action Project phase. Working with the other youth in their cohort, they define a problem in the community and create an action to implement that addresses the problem, at least to some extent. The process of constructing solutions is creative and aspirational, imagining all possible modes. The young women consider both the systems and the lives of those involved, making it an empathic as well as analytic process.

Specifically, one SSLC Social Action Project in 2016 developed a social enterprise—creating and selling their own line of merchandise. The participants wanted to address a noted community problem of hate and lack of empathy and mutual care. Also, given the SSLC program's focus on healing and love, the young women used these concepts to formulate a proposed action. To this end, they integrated three separate program groups to contribute to a central, retail enterprise. They planned their creation to "Spread the Love." The key intention for the social enterprise project of SOUL Sisters, then is the youth development opportunities of leadership, learning, and community connecting versus a primary revenue-generating endeavor.

Staff facilitated the youth plan for creating retail products in several ways. First, they scaffolded the concept of social enterprise by dialoguing with the girls about youth entrepreneurship and youth social entrepreneurship. The participants themselves named the "social purpose" of their project as the distinguishing factor: creating t-shirts, they said, had more to do with fostering community change through messaging than it did with product creation and serving customers (Krieble, personal communication, 2015). The young women also described the importance of personal and communal identity within their enterprise, with the social justice aspects of SSLC reflected in the retail products.

Next, the adult staff helped the youth connect to outside resources; specifically, they helped broker a relationship with an adult partner from the New York City fashion industry. This local designer, Molly Shaheen, worked directly with the youth to create a line of leather handbags, high-fashion "elegant patent snake design folded over silky smooth plain black leather," styled in multiple colors. The Youth Leadership Board, located in both the NYC and Miami sites of SSLC, also designed clothing items independently of the trained designer. They collaborated "for weeks to imagine the design, execute the drawings, and create a product" (www.soulsistersleadership.org/product-page).The result is a collection of t-shirts and sweatshirts displaying a youth-created logo of "Love thyself." The back image reads: "Spread Love. It's the Brooklyn Way."

The younger participants created hand-designed notecards to add to the retail line. These 10- to 12-year-old participants in SOUL Sisters created designs around what love means to them. The greeting cards espouse statements such as "Love Is Key" and "Thank you for walking this road with me." All the cards were packaged under the product line "Spread the Love." Their work was supported by an adult partner, Emily Butera, in a greeting card small business, Sweet Domino Designs.

Last, the middle-schoolers created a tote bag espousing "Love Is Louder," with the image of a boombox blasting hearts from its speakers. Designed by a 12-year-old, the product helps to "rock the message that love is crucial for social change" (www.soulsistersleadership.org/shop).

At every stage, the youth "dictated the direction" of the enterprise, having first the idea, then making decisions about the products, then advertising and implementing professionalism as they brought their creation to market (Krieble, personal communication, 2015). Having established the context for their work together in the civic and political education phase of their program allowed the enterprise creation to happen "with some understanding of the systematic structures of power . . . with a deeper conversation and connection to their communities." For example, later, when the girls asked to produce a video commercial to advertise their retail products, they incorporated critical media literacy into the planning. That is to say, they could better consider the implications for their advertising because the effort would be framed by their recognition that messages affect people, identities, and systems. The result highlights the social responsibility of their partners and the impact on their opportunities (https://vimeo.com/171647165).

Case 2: Cookie Cart

Youth employment is at the center of Cookie Cart and is accompanied by many of the elements of traditional entrepreneurial capacity education, such as financial literacy and planning. Though the youth participants do not engage in the classically entrepreneurial actions of creating new products or processes, they do learn the business aspects of bakery operation and a skill set that is transferable to future entrepreneurial endeavors. Their focus on developing the human capital of the youth can be seen as crucial step within each young person's economic life trajectory. Most clearly, Cookie Cart's programming serves as an intervention to the unemployment costs described in Chapter 11. For many youth, this is their first paycheck, and learning to manage this new financial asset is a scaffolded part of the program.

Cookie Cart as an organization provides an illustrative example of a social enterprise challenged to scale-up. For years, they had a waiting list of youth that was twice as numerous as their capacity, with 200 youth asking to work there but the bakery could only take 100 per cohort. In 2010, the Cookie Cart board of directors and lead staff committed to expanding their capacity by tripling the number of youth. This was both "exciting and scary," recounts their director of development Marit Michels (personal communication, 2017). The hope was to "do better" by increasing how many young bakers they could have participate and hence grow their community impact. As a neighborhood-based organization, they saw two paths to expansion: increased capacity at their current location or opening a second location elsewhere. They decided to pursue both approaches.

This scaling decision was initially intended to happen simultaneously, but outside factors pressured the organization to complete one expansion approach at a time. The growth at the primary site would happen first and required a massive renovation of the building. Not only was the goal to include more young people and capacity that was limited by space, but also the building's age and condition warranted dramatic change. With significant fundraising and strong funding partners, Cookie Cart was able to invest $1.7 million to salvage the original building and have it stripped "down to the studs and rebuilt." This ultimately became an opportunity to consider what they really wanted in the space to best provide their programming. They conducted listening sessions with youth who contributed ideas for the renovation, some of which made it into the final plan, but not all. Some ideas are still in the works for the next phase of change, such as a separate homework area for youth.

One major change was moving the kitchen to the front of the building so the neighborhood can peer in through the windows, creating a much more communal element to their site, as described in the next section. The new building was opened in 2015.

The second leg of scaling up was the development of a second location. The new site was to be in St. Paul, Minnesota, across the Mississippi River from Cookie Cart's Minneapolis home. Because geographic neighborhood is an important aspect of programming for Cookie Cart, they began by carefully researching possible neighborhoods in the new urban location. Their decision was driven by clear criteria: the new bakery had to be near a high school so students could easily walk to it after classes were over, in a location that had households documented as low-income, and in a place where other employment and/or training options were sparse. Having identified options that fit this mission-driven criteria, they considered next their constraints: real estate availability, cost, and flexibility for partnerships, such as space-sharing. Next, Cookie Cart board and staff endeavored to get to know possible neighbors, residential and business, public and private, hoping to cultivate an identity for the new community to understand and welcome. A significant action in this realm was to run a pilot program in partnership with the high school nearest the new location. Having a strong recruitment partner is vital, says Michels.

This process of careful planning resulted in their significant growth: Cookie Cart's second bakery celebrated a grand opening in the spring of 2018, along with their capacity to engage a total of 300 youth shortly thereafter. Increasing capacity—scaling up—means a number of process adjustments. More staff will be needed, which requires hiring and training. They continue to adapt the organizational chart to meet the changing roles that will be asked of staff. This will be crucial if they are to become larger and yet stay nimble, a concern raised by most entrepreneurs when faced with scaling. Furthermore, maintaining a clear operations plan so that both sites implement good programming with fidelity was key. One step toward this has been formalizing elements of their curriculum which had not previously been captured. All of the steps are driven by the same "top priority—quality youth development" (Michels, personal communication, 2017) with the goal of impacting a larger social good, scaling up, and employing more youth.

Focal Cases Summary: Key Concepts from Section IV

While traditional entrepreneurship education has not been present within either SOUL Sisters or Cookie Cart programming, both have embraced entrepreneurial thinking within their youth programming. Employment is a facet for Cookie Cart youth, but not SOUL Sisters. Social enterprise is a common component for both: baking and selling at Cookie Cart and designing and selling retail items for SOUL Sisters. Both programs have experienced growth and change over the years of their existence; elements of scaling up processes have been experienced and managed. Funding and income generation continues to be an area of consideration for both programs, just as it is for all social enterprises. Balancing their enterprise income along with their programs is a central concern, one with lessons for all current and new youth social entrepreneurs: you must not lose the heart of your work in the growth of any one aspect.

SECTION V

Addressing the Larger Social Good

13

Community Transformation

> Neighborhoods and communities are complex organisms that will
> be resilient only if they are healthy along a number of interrelated
> dimensions, much as a human body cannot be healthy without
> adequate air, water, rest, and food.
>
> —BEN BERNECKE, *AMERICAN ECONOMIST*

Introduction

A systems perspective allows us to imagine and to interrogate the ways communities
are developed when the youth within them engage in social entrepreneurship.
Such community transformation, however small, stands as an act of social justice. The members of the community are inherently acting on the collective good,
which counters the competitive individualism and neoliberalism of contemporary times. Analyzing these effects takes some leaps of scholarly connecting, for
reasons of unmanageable variables: "This is no simple task, not the least of which
because 'community' as the unit of analysis is far less wieldy than a controlled
program design, but also because of the paucity of research examining the role of
deliberate community-wide effects on the health and well-being of youth" (Sesma,
Mannes, & Scales, 2013, p. 428).

In this chapter, a foundational overview of community development theory
is provided as fodder for connecting community change to youth social entrepreneurship. The chapter also includes special attention to elements of community
development, such as community asset-mapping and community social capital.
To round out the argument that youth social entrepreneurs effect community
change, the reader will consider research on youth organizing and activism, with
an eye to meaningful community engagement. Finally, the chapter attends to the
tricky but imperative issue of how community members (e.g., adults) can reciprocally support youth in their social change efforts. This dynamic form of engagement is referred to here as "youth–adult partnerships."

Community Development

Central to a productive definition of youth social entrepreneurship is the principle of community development; that is to say, not only are the youth involved health-fully impacted, but the programming happens in a way that ensues reciprocal community improvement as well. Many examples exist in which the community of the youth is disregarded in the entrepreneurial process, even though social change is the core ingredient of social enterprise! Many others, though, showcase effective inclusion of communities in their progress, and some of these programs are described in this chapter. A starting point, then, for youth social entrepreneurs who seek to include communities in their change models is a primer on community development theory.

Similar to the historical foundations of youth work theories, a deficit orien-tation of research on communities has produced a negative angle on community development theory. Decades of research investigating the causes of community problems has been helpful in raising awareness about the severity of the problems faced by poor neighborhoods, but this information does little to inform efforts to promote positive community change. In more recent years, scholars have begun to more systematically document the effectiveness of interventions that result in solutions to previously well-established problems.

For one example, *comprehensive community initiatives* (CCIs), started in the late 1980s and early 1990s, have promoted positive change in individual, family, and community circumstances in disadvantaged neighborhoods "by applying the principles of comprehensiveness and community building to improve physical, social, and economic conditions" (Fulbright-Anderson & Auspos, 2006, p. 10). Since then, extensive studies of this place-based, community-change approach have produced numerous lessons.

The concept of "community" has myriad meanings. Most of those can be categorized as either *community of place* or *community of interest* (Green & Haines, 2015). A geographic neighborhood is a community of place. Because neighborhoods have notable effects on youth development (Leventhal & Brooks-Gunn, 2000) and because neighborhoods are often the most tangible means for thinking about community, they are a frequently used proxy for a young person's community. Neighborhoods may be understood as "the spatial units in which face-to-face social interactions occur—the personal settings and situations where residents seek to realize common values, socialize youth, and maintain effective social control" (Schuck & Rosenbaum, 2006, p. 61). Research on communities bears out that social problems or assets "tend to be bundled together," known as the *neighborhood effect* (Green & Haines, 2015, p. 10). Pollution from local industry demonstrates an obvious example of a negative neighborhood effect, and city parks are an example of a positive neighborhood effect. There are positive neighbor-hood effects when public policy provides something which brings great benefits to most people. A growing body of literature on neighborhood effects suggests that these contextual factors may be even more influential on a person than individual characteristics (Green & Haines, 2015). Much research and practice related to community development relies on neighborhood-based strategies: changing neighborhood conditions by working within the neighborhood itself.

On the other hand, there is the philosophy of changing individual behavior in the hope of ultimately changing the neighborhood. One commonly applied approach is linking residents in low-income neighborhoods to employment and training services to improve neighborhood conditions as well as individual outcomes (Laprade & Auspos, 2006). This approach is expected to increase human capital at the individual level and produce better outcomes relating to employment, health, and so forth. Connecting residents of low-income housing to jobs, healthcare, and other needed supports and services is "also expected to increase their ability to meet rent payments and decrease incidences of major hospitalization or institutional care"(p. 159). At a sufficient scale, improved outcomes at the individual level could lead to improved economic and social outcomes at the neighborhood level.

Community Assets

The assets of a community include the people, physical structures, natural resources, institutions, businesses, or informal organizations of a defined neighborhood. Communities identify and assess their assets through a process known as *asset-based community development* (ABCD) and *asset mapping* (Kretzmann & McKnight, 1993). The ABCD process involves creating an inventory of assets and capacity, building relationships, developing a vision of the future, and leveraging internal and external resources to support actions toward that goal (Kerka, 2003). Asset mapping involves documenting the tangible and intangible resources of a community, viewing it as a place with assets to be preserved and enhanced, not deficits to be remedied. These approaches draw on several processes: appreciative inquiry; community social capital; participatory development, which is based on community empowerment and ownership; collaborative economic development models that place priority on making the best use of a community's resource base; and efforts to strengthen civil society by engaging people as citizens rather than clients (Mathie & Cunningham, 2002). In short, asset mapping is the process of identifying and providing information about a community's assets, or the status, condition, behavior, knowledge, or skills that a person, group, or entity possesses and that serves as a support, resource, or source of strength to one's self and others in the community.

Much work on community asset mapping and building happens through the Chicago-based Asset-Based Community Development Institute, which leverages "the skills of local residents, the power of local associations, and the supportive functions of local institutions [to] draw upon existing community strengths to

build stronger, more sustainable communities for the future" (https://resources.
depaul.edu/abcd-institute/Pages/default.aspx).

Youth social entrepreneurship intersects with community asset-building
and development in several different ways, depending in part on the type
of program one is examining (see Chapter 3). Not all endeavors use a
neighborhood-specific definition of community: many that engage youth seen
as "disconnected" often draw from multiple neighborhoods in a single city. In
this way, they comprise more of a community of interest than a community
of place.

Youth social entrepreneurship programs that are focused on employment—
and the economic growth of the young person—may subscribe to the community
development philosophy of improving from the individual up. That is, they see
that giving jobs to disconnected youth who might not otherwise have a job can enhance the human capital of the neighborhood. With enough youth involved, they
may reach a critical mass that can help sway a struggling community. Other youth
social entrepreneurship programs directly focus on the community itself. That is,
they aim to improve a place-based community, such as a geographic neighborhood, by setting up their enterprise to improve neighborhood-level conditions in
some way (Birkenmaier, 2016).

For example, Cycles for Change, located in both Minneapolis and St. Paul,
Minnesota, asserts a primary mission of community development. Specifically,
they strive "to build a diverse and empowered community of bicyclists" that
"transforms the streets and paths of the Twin Cities into places where everyone
feels safe and connected to their community" and lifts up "Black, Indigenous, and
people of color; immigrants and refugees; women, trans, femme, and gender-
nonconforming peoples; and youth" (cyclesforchange.org). Toward this mission,
they offer multiple programs, including youth apprenticeships. While Cycles for
Change acknowledges the economic opportunity for the youth in their program—
often a "first job" (cyclesforchange.org,)—their most important focus is on
leveraging the community assets to build a more equitable and empowered place
to live:

> Beyond providing basic job training, the Youth Apprenticeship trains the
> next generation of bicycle and community leaders. We believe in creating
> spaces that uplift young people to reach their full potential as leaders and be-
> come advocates for positive social change. Our young people are the carbon
> atom of a more socially just and equitable future. Bicycles are the catalysts
> for an equitable social and cultural shift. Traditionally the bicycle industry
> has not accurately represented the cultural and socio-economic diversity of
> our communities. This program creates spaces to honor the voices and power
> of presence that women, trans, femme and gender nonconforming peoples;
> black, Indigenous, and people of color; and youth have within the bicycle
> movement. (cyclesforchange.org/youth-apprenticeship-program/)

In practice, the community development mission produces youth development outcomes: "Last summer we had an apprentice that didn't know how to ride a bike, then she learned. . . . [The youth] have a bunch of caring adults, which is our staff team, who they can call family. If they have issues at school or issues in their family or issues here at work, there is someone that they can talk to. A lot of them have said before they started Cycles for Change, they didn't always use their voice or speak out when they saw something that made them uncomfortable. Their time here has really helped them find a voice and speak up more, which is incredible" (McCoy, 2017).

Participatory Asset Mapping

In *participatory asset mapping*, community members specifically identify their own community assets. They create a tangible display of the people, places, and experiences that make up their community and place them onto a map representing their community of place. By engaging community residents in a process of identifying both the existing and the missing community assets, community members achieve a clearer picture of the overall status of their neighborhood. Then, they are better able to organize around the cause of strengthening community resources, thus enhancing their empowerment capacity. Participatory asset mapping can also be used as a tool to raise community awareness and show the impact of these organizing efforts. The most common data-gathering techniques to map assets include focus groups of relevant community members, interviews with individual community members, written surveys, and community walks, where you walk through a neighborhood of interest to map out and collect information about that neighborhood's resources and dynamics. A small map can be used as a tool to directly record asset locations. Asset mappers can combine their walk with interviews of community members along the way to find out more about specific assets in detail. A community walk also offers the opportunity to take pictures and video of local assets, which can be placed on a map. Mapping software is available on the Internet through various sources and organizations (such as Healthy City, Google Maps, etc.) to help participatory asset mappers plot, map, and view their assets with just the click of a button. The results are a visual representation of community assets, "critical pictures of community knowledge and goals that can be used to achieve recognition of community strengths and implement place-based solutions" (Burns, Paul, & Silvia, 2012).

Community-Building Concepts

In one of the earliest empirically grounded studies of social capital in inner-city neighborhoods, Kenneth Temkin and William Rohe (1998) identified two dimensions of social capital relevant for community builders: *sociocultural milieu* and *institutional infrastructure*. Both can inform the practices of youth social entrepreneurs who are concerned about building communities. Sociocultural milieu refers to the observable behaviors of neighborhood residents and their attitudes about their neighborhood. It includes the sense of attachment and loyalty among neighbors, as well as the efficacy of residents for collective action. The second dimension, institutional infrastructure, refers to a neighborhood's organizational ability that allows them to act on their common interest. It encompasses both the existence of neighborhood groups and the connections that these groups have with the wider community.

Community builders consider the network of social ties found in the neighborhoods. Famously documented by sociologist Mark Granovetter in 1973, there are two types of social ties. *Strong ties* connect family members and friends to one another and are important sources of aid for survival and crisis management. *Weak ties*, which are found in acquaintanceship networks, are important sources of everyday assistance, job information, and access to other instrumental and social resources. Each serve significant roles; in particular, strong ties serve to bond people together, but weak ties serve as bridges for people. Weak ties are the bridging social capital needed for collective action and social mobility.

Community Social Capital

The effect of neighborhoods' collective efficacy and social cohesion on health also has been shown to have a strong effect on neighborhood health outcomes (Altschuler, Somkin, & Adler, 2004). Social networks form an important dimension of social capital at the neighborhood level because they are resources for individuals as well as for communities as a whole.

High levels of community social capital exhibit high levels of:

- Social and interracial trust
- Political participation in conventional and protest politics
- Civic leadership and involvement in groups, clubs, or local discussions about community problems
- Giving and volunteering to charities or special interest groups
- Faith-based engagement as members, participants, donors, and volunteers
- Equality of civic engagement across the community

When a group of neighbors informally keep an eye on one another's homes, that's social capital in action. When a tightly knit community of Hassidic Jews trade diamonds without having to test each gem for purity, that's social capital in action. Barn-raising on the frontier was social capital in action, and so too are e-mail exchanges among members of a cancer support group. Social capital can be found in friendship networks, neighborhoods, churches, schools, bridge clubs, civic associations, and even bars. The motto in *Cheers* "where everybody knows your name" captures one important aspect of social capital. (The Saguaro Seminar, 2012)

Communities that engage in active pursuit of their needs are considered to have higher levels of well-being. This type of *collective action* has long been understood as the tendency for groups with common interests to attempt to further those common interests. It is believed that a host of structural variables affect the likelihood of individuals engaged in collective action to overcome social challenges (Ostrom, 2009).

A key predictor of collective action has traditionally been socioeconomic status (Boardman & Robert, 2000, in Larsen et al., 2004). Residents with higher levels of socioeconomic status are more likely to believe in their ability to influence government decisions and are more likely to take collective action. One line of thinking for this inequality is that lower and moderate income neighborhoods face greater challenges in converting their bonding social capital into the more politically important bridging form of social capital. For example, Edin and Lein (1997) found that poor mothers living in public housing developments relied heavily on bonding social capital, such as money obtained from a network of family and friends, to make ends meet. While bonding capital allowed these mothers to cobble together enough resources to survive, their efforts never extended beyond their immediate network. That is, their bonding social capital did not become bridging social capital—connecting with individuals or organizations outside their network—that might have afforded them other forms of assistance.

There is a wealth of practical knowledge that strongly suggests that creating social capital is an important part of community builders' work (Anderson & Milligan, 2006), even when the empirical data are less robust than scholars wish.

Most obviously, community builders can create opportunities for residents to get to know each other informally to increase social cohesion and allow social ties to develop. For example, they can "organize community gardens, community celebrations, study circles, cleanup campaigns, block parties, rummage sales, block or building patrols, and other activities that require only a short-term commitment to help residents interact, get to know each other, and develop a sense of trust for each other" (Anderson & Milligan, 2006, p. 48).

Some forms of youth social entrepreneurship programs may fit this role well. The youth involved in the program can draw broader participation into their ventures than traditional enterprises or community nonprofits. Because the youths' strong ties—families and friends—tend to be committed to, or at least interested in, the success of the enterprise, they are more likely to congregate and connect to it as a shared social site. When and if the program then leverages that gathering of people, weak ties are created, thus extending the social capital of all involved.

Furthermore, since physical place is an important factors in the development of social networks, and therefore social capital, of a neighborhood, youth social enterprises often offer a space that draws in community members. The following example depicts a long-standing social enterprise that advances community development simultaneously with youth development.

The Food Project, located outside of Boston, Massachusetts, implements many of the previously stated community-building approaches. Their mission is "to create a thoughtful and productive community of youth and adults from diverse backgrounds who work together to build a sustainable food system" (http://thefoodproject.org/). They are well-known for their youth programs, in place since the 1990s to engage young people in personal and social change through sustainable agriculture. Through farming instruction, food distribution, food justice workshops, community gardens, and more, The Food Project employs 120 teenagers every year in their developmental programming. Recent third-party research on the community gardening aspect of this organization points to the impact on social capital of The Food Project participants. Studies of community gardening tend to focus on interactions within the space of the gardens (Alaimo, Beavers, Crawford, Snyder, & Litt, 2016). Participants in The Food Project also cite "sharing food" as an important part of their experience and a basis for building relationships with others (Shostak & Guscott, 2016). The researchers suggest that, "consequently. . . surplus produce from community gardens has spillover effects, not only for nutrition, but for social capital" (p. 12).

Community gardens often serve as sites for both cultural preservation and social integration for recent immigrants (Agustina & Beilin, 2012). The participants at The Food Project, who include many recent immigrants from the central Africa and Latin America, including the Caribbean, reported that cultivating vegetables and herbs "allows them to maintain important connections to their cultures of origin—including practices associated with farming, food and healing—and to find community in dense, but isolating, American cities" (p. 13). In this way, youth participants gain opportunities for enriching bonding social capital with family through reinforced homeland culture and adding bridging social capital through new connections. Because their community gardens are a shared space in which people from various backgrounds work side by side, the researchers found increased cross-cultural and intergenerational communication, newly established trusting relationships with vulnerable neighborhood residents, and documented organizing among gardeners to focus on issues of health and safety in their neighborhoods. Participants identify themselves as "gardeners," which they say allows them to make connections despite differences in their neighborhoods that "'bring down' barriers and allow for social interactions that cross cultures, generations, and languages" (p. 19). In these ways, The Food Project's community initiatives help build social capital for the gardening participants that lasts beyond the growing season.

Effects on Health and Well-Being

Safety, in all its forms, is a necessary precursor to healthy development. Developmental psychology grounds this belief in "Maslow's Hierarchy of Needs," which points to safety as the second foundational need after basic elements of survival. Maslow argued that safety needs are paramount in their influence on human growth (1954). He argued that in every individual there are two sets of forces: one that drives the individual to cling to safety out of fear (e.g., hanging on to the past; afraid to grow; afraid to take chances; afraid of independence, freedom, and separateness; forcing development to stagnate). The other set of forces propels the individual forward, toward wholeness of self and the full development of capabilities, towards self-confidence and fulfillment in the face of the external world. In this theory, unmet safety needs are what constrains human growth. People must first feel safe in their environment before they dare to move forward, take risks in decision-making, and ultimately actualize their human potential (Maslow, 1968).

The safety of a community, then, is a necessary condition for youth to experience positive growth. Neighborhood safety not only affects their likelihood of engaging in future crime and violence, but also affects a young person's problem-solving capabilities, academic achievement, family functioning, and employment prospects. Furthermore, by not allowing individuals to reach their full potential, neighborhood crime and violence—and the criminal justice system's current response to these problems—robs the neighborhood of important resources (Schuck & Rosenbaum, 2006).

The economic disadvantages of a neighborhood are associated with negative health outcomes, such as mental health problems and developmental differences (see Reiss, 2013, for a review). Research has established that stress from living in low-income neighborhoods takes a toll on children, adolescents, and adults alike, with documented main effects on aggression, delinquency, and anxious/depressed symptoms (Santiago, Wadsworth, & Stump, 2011). In this way, low-income neighborhoods are "key conduits for the transmission of risk for psychological problems" (Santiago et al., 2011, p. 229).

Advocating for neighborhood improvement initiatives, programs that encourage cohesion and investment in the community, and more resources for low-income families will be essential for ultimately breaking the cycle of poverty. The research findings stress the need for early childhood interventions to reduce mental health problems, as well as intervention programs in adolescence, especially for children who experience chronic poverty. Finally, the observed relationship between socioeconomic disparities and mental health problems in children and adolescents indicates that socioeconomic health disparities are not only the responsibility of individuals but of society as a whole.

Empowerment

Within development circles, policymakers and researchers alike have been particularly interested in using *empowerment*, at individual or community level, as a step on the road to poverty reduction. Much of the literature draws on ideas from political studies, philosophy, and sociology and has considered a range of issues including definitions of empowerment, empowerment from perspectives of social groupings (particularly by gender and race), and the methods by which empowerment can be promoted. Empowerment strategies include knowledge and critical consciousness; development of skills; honoring past history; highlighting values and beliefs; improving physical and mental health; combatting environmental barriers, hazards, poverty, and deprivation; enhancing family and peer support; increasing models and mentors; and expanding supportive policies and laws (Anand & Lea, 2011).

Youth Organizing and Community Engagement

Though community development and youth development are distinct fields of practice, their shared perspectives and approaches have great potential convergences. The interdisciplinary area of "youth organizing" synthesizes the asset-based approaches of community organizing and the strength-based work of positive youth development (PYD). There is burgeoning research on the processes and outcomes on which they overlap. To date, researchers have noted key elements youth organizing as including (1) relationship development, (2) popular education, (3) social action, and (4) participatory research and evaluation.

Youth organizing has been defined as "an innovative youth development and social justice strategy that trains young people in community organizing and advocacy, and assists them in employing these skills to alter power relations and create meaningful institutional change in their communities" (Funders Collaborative for Youth Organizing website, 2017). This definition highlights the intersection of four critical activities: social justice, youth development, community change, and community organizing. Youth organizing in relation to community organizing situates youth as leaders who set their own organizing agendas. Delgado and Staples (2008) describe this work as *youth-led community organizing*, which empowers marginalized young people to make substantive contributions to their communities. More broadly, youth activism refers to young people engaged in actions that "challenge the status quo and seek to reconfigure asymmetrical power relations" (Conner & Rosen, 2016, 2). Youth organizing can be seen as a particular form of youth activism, one that rose to prominence in the 1990s (Noguera, Ginwright, & Cammarota, 2006; Braxton, 2016). More recently, *youth participatory action research* evokes similar processes and outcomes as an "innovative, equity-focused approach to promote adolescent health and well-being that draws on the expertise of adolescents as they conduct research and improve conditions that support healthy development" (Ozer, 2017, p. 173).

Issues around which youth organize to engage youth activism commonly include social injustices in education, race, health, environment, gender, reproduction, immigrant rights, and LGBTQ issues (Christens & Kirshner, 2011). Succinctly, they are concerned about "quality of life and human rights issues" (Ginwright & Kirshner, 2012, p. 290). Youth organizers address areas of injustice by asserting their own assets, perspectives, and self-claimed political power. While specific approaches vary, four common elements are identified (Braxton, 2016):

1. They apply a foundational community-organizing process, recruiting support from a targeted constituency, identifying areas of concern, and creating campaigns for policy change to right the concerns.
2. They often include extensive education around power, helping young people see the systemic concerns at play in their local concern.
3. They include formal leadership development to support youth in necessary skills of public speaking, advocacy, and interacting with stakeholders, people in power, and often the media.
4. They incorporate social-emotional support for their members, either formally or informally, as well as academic and occupational support as relevant.

Youth organizing aims to make community-level impacts, such as new program implementation, changes to unjust policies, and/or the creation of new or more just institutions (Dolan, 2015). Youth organizing also aims to invigorate social changes such as shared power and intergenerational, multicultural collaboration (Christens & Dolan, 2011).

Documented increases in youth organizing seem to be an outgrowth of the influence PYD has had; that is, emphasizing that communities treat youth as capable of full, active participation in their society. This perspective has helped shape the work of out-of-school-time organizations, schools, nonprofits, universities, and foundations to include youth as central actors and, many times, to organize themselves for making change. At the opposite end of this inclusion spectrum, excluding youth from being full participants in many settings has been deemed a social injustice (Delgado & Staples, 2008).

Youth social entrepreneurship shares a number of characteristics with the established tradition of youth activism and organizing:

1. First, both hinge entirely on an asset focus that elevates personal and communal strengths as predominant to personal or communal

flaws. That is, even in the attempt to "fix" a problem, youth social entrepreneurship and youth organizing build on what exists rather than focusing on what is missing.

2. Second, both are concerned about adult–youth relations. Youth social entrepreneurship "lends itself to creation of youth–adult partnerships and interactions that historically have not been present in this society" (Delgado, 2004, p. 109). Likewise, youth activism has an "intergenerational nature of this work [where] youth and adults are able to reimagine the divisions between them, challenging our constructions of youth and the social roles we attribute to young people" (Conner & Rosen, 2016, p. 5).

3. Third, both rely on a dynamic interplay of the individual within a community context in which there is simultaneous benefit to both. Ozer (2017) points to the way YPAR, for example, enables young people to directly work to correct the conditions that influence their health and well-being and those of their peers. They are multidimensional in their concerns, the scope of their work, and the goals of their efforts.

An example of independent youth activism as an offshoot of youth social entrepreneurship occurred in the summer of 2017. Sisterhood Boutique, described in this book's Introduction, hosted "The Reality Gallery," an event described as "put together by youth from Sisterhood Boutique and Triple C Coffee Cart . . . to discuss and visualize the issues we face today in our community. . . . focusing on immigration and racism and the impact it has on US minorities." They advertised as well: "Free food, spoken word, coffee." Using an open mic format, the youth from these jointly managed enterprises hosted an event that raised the concerns so very present in their lives, one attended by other youth and adults alike. Such an event is an example of activism that raises awareness, connection to others, and empowerment through personal expression and voice.

Youth–Adult Partnerships

As the saying goes, behind every successful youth social entrepreneurship endeavor is an adult who knew when to get out of the way. This might not be a common maxim in society yet, but it is commonly believed among practitioners engaged in youth work. Youth–adult partnerships emphasize shared leadership, thus flattening the traditional hierarchy of power relationships. Establishing and sustaining healthy intergenerational working relationships—that is, youth–adult partnerships—is a difficult but essential element.

Christens, Powers, and Zeldin (2013) define youth–adult partnership as a five-part practice involving "a.) multiple youth and multiple adults deliberating and acting together; b.) in a collective [democratic] fashion; c.) over a sustained period of time; d.) through shared work; e.) intended to promote social justice, strengthen an organization and/or affirmatively address a community issue" (p. 182). At work are the principles of authentic decision-making, natural mentorship, reciprocity, and community connectedness. Many effective youth–adult partnerships rely on the adults' qualities as "empowerment agents" (Stanton-Salazar, 2011). They emanate and act on respect, care, and high expectations for the youth; a critical stance toward oppressive systems that affect youth; clear communication skills; shared culture, language, and lived experience; and local networks along with the capacity to help young people tap them to pursue their interests and needs (Erbstein, 2013).

Research suggests that while youth value the involvement of helpful adults in community organizing, young people need "tools to mitigate adults' power, and adults need to restrain their natural reflex to take control" (Blanchet-Cohon et al., 2012, p. 831). Key in the adults' role is giving "the right amount" of guidance and creating a space for youth to feel empowered to make decisions. Adults may feel challenged and unsure of how to take a back seat and be more patient in this role. To blame is a long history of disempowered youth and a culture that endorses "adultism." This prejudice is "the devaluing of the ideas and participation of young people that denies them voice and agency in the issues and institutions that shape their lives" (Warren & Kupscznk, 2016, p. 44). One need look no farther than most local high schools to find adultism at work: school rules, classroom policies, educational content, and assessment procedures that all apply to the young people in the school but are formed entirely by adults. This form of disenfranchisement is the norm, and its effects include school disengagement and a population of young people who are ill-prepared to take charge of their lives. A school may not be a democracy, but infusing democratic practices into the system where possible holds promise for the youth as well as for their relationships with adults and even with future civic participation (Kahne & Westheimer, 2003).

In summary, both research and practice underscore the importance for adults to "step back so youth can step up" as a way to foster authentic youth engagement and leadership. Simultaneously, though, adults are most effective when they apply their skills as agents of empowerment at the right times and in the right amounts.

The creation of an authentically power-sharing relationship is itself an act of social change. Asserts Delgado (2004, p. 109):

> The interconnectedness that results from social youth enterprises brings youth centrally into their own communities and does so in a manner that lends itself to creation of youth–adult partnerships and interactions that historically have not been present in this society.

14

The Global Context for Youth Social Entrepreneurship

Introduction

The scope of this book has intentionally remained within the boundaries of United States. While many of the theoretical influences discussed here are the same regardless of place, geographic context remains paramount for how people and communities engage social entrepreneurship. Recognizing the sociocultural bounds of youth development research and practices, the previous chapters have therefore focused entirely on American youth and their communities. This chapter turns our attention to a more inclusive view of youth social entrepreneurship. While the reader may suspect that this order of introduction—that is, the American setting first, the global setting second—reflects some preeminence of the American context within this field, this would be a patently false interpretation. Instead, examples of youth social entrepreneurship in developing countries offer a more robust structuring of this model than has been available in the United States to date. Furthermore, examples in Europe and Australia shed light on the long-standing approaches of youth social entrepreneurship as it is represented by myriad names. The mechanisms, though, are universal: young people making change in their communities at a variety of levels while simultaneously bettering their own outcomes, be those developmental, educational, economic, or all of those at once. Universally, they hinge on creative solutions, using innovations to persistent problems in the hands of individuals, rather than government leaders. In these ways, youth social entrepreneurship is a story that plays out every day in a multitude of ways and in an expanse of places, not confined to one place, one program, one theoretical paradigm.

The Global Context

OLD PRACTICE, NEW CONCEPT

Young people everywhere engage social entrepreneurship, whether or not they call it as such, and have for centuries in a variety of places. As it has been said of social enterprise in the Middle East: "old practice, new concept" (Doumit, 2017). One need only look to youth participation in informal economies around the globe to see vibrant examples of adolescents' creative money-making endeavors as a means of independence, family support, creative expression, and, in many cases, simple survival. Especially for youth in developing countries, the informal sector provides an ecosystem for entrepreneurial efforts as well as access to employment (World Bank, 2013). In addition, more formalized efforts to enrich the entrepreneurial and even social enterprising of youth has been under way in a variety of ways, as described in the following sections.

INFORMAL ECONOMY

The *informal economy* is generally understood to include economic activities that fall largely outside the purview of official regulation. The International Labour Organization (2015) defines it as "all jobs in unregistered and/or small-scale private unincorporated enterprises that produce goods or services meant for sale or barter." This includes a diverse set of revenue-generating activities: "from street vending to domestic service, from home-based enterprises to the informal employees of formal enterprises, and from waste picking to urban agriculture" (Brown & McGranahan, 2016, p. 98). Though individuals engaged in the informal economy are censured for not conforming to official regulations such as taxation, activities of the informal economy are not illegal and should not be confused with illegal goods and services.

Much debate exists in global economic circles about the role of the informal sector within developing countries. A prominent concern is often about taxation: "informality is almost always at or near the top of lists of tax challenges in developing countries" (Keen, 2015). Among development economists and policymakers, informal economies are often seen as associated with low productivity and poverty. Despite expectations that with increased development comes lower levels of activity in the informal sector, informal economies are "exceptionally persistent" (Keen, 2015). In many developing economies, job creation has mainly taken place in the informal economy, where around 60% of workers find income opportunities (Bacchetta, Ernst, & Bustamanta, 2009).

Young people (and women of all ages) make up a significant portion of the informal sector due to the systemic disenfranchisement that limits their participation in formal employment in developing countries. However, the informal economy is characterized by "less job security, lower incomes, an absence of access to a range of social benefits and fewer possibilities to participate in formal education and training programmes—in short, the absence of key ingredients of decent work opportunities" (Bacchetta et al, 2009, p. 9). Though considerations of formalizing the employment in this sector are complex and well beyond the scope of this book, it should be noted that connecting individuals in the informal economy to broader supports, such as training, micro-finance, and collaboration, has been found to positively impact the working conditions of those involved (World Bank, 2013). To this end, a number of international, nongovernmental agencies offer support to those starting or involved in informal economic employment, some particularly focused on youth. Examples of such support systems are included later in this chapter.

SOCIAL BUSINESS

While "social enterprise" is the terminology used in this book and is predominant in American and European discourse, a wider variety of terminology and definitions exist globally.

The related concept of "social business" or "social-purpose business" has more traction among developing countries. Efforts are afoot to better define these concepts as they exist regionally as well as globally, based on hope that a "distinct definition of social enterprise not only creates opportunity for policy dialogue that can eventually lead to the design of a useful legal framework, but also facilitates the development of adapted financing mechanisms and support services enterprises need to succeed" (Doumit, 2017, p. 1).

The term *social business* is attributable to the work of Muhammed Yunus (2011), which includes the practice of micro-loans to the poor but more broadly seeks to make a "fundamental change in the architecture of our capitalist economy . . . freeing it from basic flaws that lead to poverty and other social ills" (xiv). His Nobel prize–winning creation of Grameen Bank in the 1980s in Bangladesh set the stage for his ambitious vision of a "a world of three zeroes"— zero poverty, zero unemployment, and zero carbon emissions (Yunus, 2017). The individual- and village-level business-building efforts of Grameen Bank, in which "grameen" means "of the village bank" in the Bengali language, demonstrate investment in social causes versus potential profit. In a social business, by Yunus's definition, investors/owners gradually recoup the money invested, but do not take any dividend beyond that point. The potential for young people in Yunus's vision is significant. Having learned the social business model, youth can "develop business plans to address the most difficult social problems through social businesses" (2011, p. xxiv). Initiatives to help fund these ideas are becoming increasingly available and will be needed to continue to grow.

The idea of "social business" is gaining traction for development at the community and youth levels in a number of developing countries. It is increasingly being identified as an innovative approach not only to employment but to established youth development efforts and existing social sector strategies. The social business model fits well with social work professionals globally who are seeking methods to expand the scope of community development strategies and tap into the social capacities of youth. In a study looking at youth-focused social businesses, Magaiza and Crause (2014) conclude that

> social businesses are an asset-based approach representing a human face that social work can broker among communities, industry and policy makers, harnessing humanised free market capitalism to foster inclusion and expansion of livelihood options for young people. (p. 42)

Youth as Entrepreneurs and Social Entrepreneurs in Developing Countries

Developing countries may have an edge when it comes to innovation in that their populations are significantly younger than those in the developed world (Salkowitz, 2010). As technology becomes ubiquitous even in the poorest countries, the creative talent and ambitions of those young populations are finding expression through new businesses, new organizations, and new models of engagement.

EXAMPLES IN DEVELOPING COUNTRIES

Youth Business International (YBI) is a worldwide network of independent non-profit initiatives helping young people to start and grow their own businesses and create employment. Based in the United Kingdom, YBI operates in more than 40 countries. They function as a capacity-building, support network for young entrepreneurs in developing countries and are supported by well-endowed global corporations. Their social mission is to lift up the world's young adults aged 18–35 because they make up nearly 40% of the world's unemployed and yet "frequently lack the resources to start up their own business" despite a desire to do so, thus turning "job seekers into job creators" (https://www.youthbusiness.org/).

YBI hosts an annual "Global Youth Entrepreneur" summit, offers a "Young Entrepreneur" award, and a Global entrepreneurship week. Their reach is extensive: a 2015 report shows that YBI's members started 14,279 new businesses and helped 5,836 existing businesses to grow while providing practical skills based training to more than 52,000 people https://www.youthbusiness.org/resources/annual-reports/.

In 2005, Making Cents International launched as a global organization focused on "understanding how adolescents and young adults can reach their potential by gaining the life skills they need to get ahead economically" (Macaulay, 2016). Their target has been to increase the scale and sustainability of the worldwide youth economic opportunities sector. In the decade since its inception, it has created an annual conference to convene relevant stakeholders, coordinated like-minded funders, and honed terminology for the sector, such as "Youth Economic Opportunities" (http://www.makingcents.com/youth-development). Making Cents provides educational resources and communications about workforce and enterprise development for youth across continents. Gender, technology, and evaluation are of particular relevance to their current work.

The social change aspects of their mission are broad: "helping young people around the world fulfill their potential to become full-fledged members of their communities, socially as well as economically, to become players on a local, national or sometimes even global stage" and specific: "a dedicated track on adolescent girls that explored gender inclusivity—and often gender specificity—in programs" (Macauley, 2016). The services provided by Making Cents center on capacity-building, collaboration, program design, and strategic consulting to major corporations and foundations' contributing to youth employment and development. Youth development is one of their key practice areas:

> We promote positive youth development by providing young people with the knowledge and skills they need to fulfill their potential. We work with local partners to design asset-based interventions and deliver demand-driven products and services that increase young people's ability to obtain meaningful work, engage in value chains, access finance, and become leaders in their communities. (http://www.makingcents.com/youth-development)

Making Cents's efforts in PYD's intersection with economic opportunity (i.e., youth social entrepreneurship) takes many diverse manifestations. Examples include:

1. *Youth Agriculture in northern Uganda*: Training "26,250 at-risk, unemployed, or underemployed young people . . . in agricultural entrepreneurship" http://www.makingcents.com/youthempowermentthro ughagriculture.
2. *Rural Youth Economic Empowerment*: Youth living in Egypt, Morocco, Tunisia, and Yemen receive substantial financial and entrepreneurial support to start and grow their own businesses and find meaningful employment. By the end of the project, Making Cents International "provided savings or credit services to 20,543 youth, and non-financial supportive services to 14,252 youth" http://www.makingcents.com/ruralyo utheconomicempowermentprogram.
3. *Southeast Asian youth opportunities*: In collaboration with the US Embassy in Vietnam, Making Cents International engaged dozens of young people in business planning and facilitated their connections with mentors and networks to develop their ideas http://www.makingcents. com/youth social entrepreneurshipalivietnam.

EXAMPLES IN DEVELOPED COUNTRIES

Started in 1976, by Prince Charles, the Prince's Trust was created to address the needs of undereducated and un- or underemployed youth in England. In his words, "What struck me was that young people weren't being given the opportunities quickly enough. No one was putting the trust in them they needed" (https://www. princes-trust.org.uk/about-the-trust/history). Since then, the Trust's programs aim to support youth in accessing the education, training, and/or employment they seek in order to advance their lives through monetary awards, curriculum, skills training, and confidence-building, among others. To date, the Trust has reached more than 825,000 young people, with three in four achieving a positive outcome—moving into education, employment or, training. Their focus is on young people aged 11–30, "empowering them to get into jobs, education and training" (https://www.princes-trust.org.uk/). The slogan of this organization is "Youth Can Do It," suggesting an empowerment orientation despite structural inequalities or systemic limitations.

Also based in the UK, the Global Social Entrepreneurship Network serves as a hub for organizations engaged in social entrepreneurial endeavors. Among their stated values is a belief that "people in communities which face problems are part of the solution and they are most likely to create the most relevant solutions" (http:// www.gsen.global/about). Including social entrepreneurs of all sizes, their 2015 activities affected "2,600 social entrepreneurs worldwide." Their projects include one with a youth focus: the European Learning for Youth in Social Entrepreneurship (EL Youth Social Entrepreneurship) project has harnessed the knowledge of social entrepreneurship experts across Europe to create a toolkit that defines the best ways to support young social entrepreneurs. With ideas drawn from five countries, they have developed suggestions for best practices in their youth social entrepreneurship model, involving European young people aged 16–30 (http://www.gsen. global/projects/elyouth social entrepreneurship).

Housed at Georgetown University, the Global Social Enterprise Institute, supports their member organizations in more than 70 countries to develop their social enterprise plans. To date, the Global Social Enterprise Institute has engaged with more than 1,500 individuals and 300 social entrepreneurs throughout the world through programming, initiatives, lectures, workshops, presentations, coaching, business plan support, pro bono consulting, and technical assistance (http://www.gse.institute/our-impact/).

Youth Social Entrepreneurship "Training"

In the past decade, a number of training and/or conglomerate organizations have appeared with the purpose of advancing youth as change agents (i.e., youth social entrepreneurship but often without the socially critical lens). The following few will to give the reader a sense of the landscape.

WE Charity (formerly known as "Free the Children") offers support and events for adults and young people interested in global social impact. They focus mainly on young people in Canada, the United States, and the United Kingdom to promote service learning and active citizenship, with international development projects in Asia, Africa, and Latin America to improve education and child well-being.

Part of the "WE Movement," WE Day is the organization's flagship event. Beginning as a single location event 10 years ago, WE Day has evolved into a series of 19 stadium-sized events held across the United States, Canada, the United Kingdom, and the Caribbean. In 2016, approximately 200,000 students attended WE Day, which the organization refers to as the "Olympics for change-makers" (/ www.we.org/we-day/).

WE Schools is year-long service-learning program also offered through WE Charity. This program is delivered via educational partners in approximately 12,300 schools and groups in Canada, the United States, and the United Kingdom. The curricular focus is to "challenge young people to identify the local and global issues that spark their passion and empowers them with the tools to take action" (www.we.org/we-schools/). Provided are social action ideas and educational resources to help involved students learn the root causes of global issues like hunger, poverty, and reduced access to education. The program culminates in planning and carrying out at least one local and one global action that they identify in the aim to improve their communities and the world.

Based in the San Francisco and Oakland area, United Roots ("Youth Seed") strives to help create "an ecosystem of opportunities for young people" by offering multiple programs and fellowships to advance their social entrepreneurship. Many of the young people involved are older adolescents/young adults. United Roots addresses social issues "by empowering marginalized youth in socially innovative ways utilizing the following four strategies:

1. Civic Engagement: building coalitions between communities of color, decision makers, and employers to advocate for community change.
2. Personal Development: creating a safe, sustainable environment to heal and grow through community rituals, cultural healing practices, and wellness services.
3. Career and Workforce Mentorship: cultivating innovation and entrepreneurship through fellowships, mentorship, employment opportunities and business incubation.
4. Creative Arts Education: instilling confidence and developing talent through digital, technological and performing arts." (unitedrootsoakland.org)

Urban Roots also hosts an annual youth-led innovation event in Oakland, as 10 teams of youth social entrepreneurs present their proposals for social enterprises to create equity in low-income communities; the winner receives seed funding. An intensive fellowship program known as "Youth Impact Hub" also supports a small set of social entrepreneurs by developing their skills and helping to shape their enterprise idea (youthimpacthub.unitedrootsoakland. org).

Touted as a "new university model tailored for next generation innovators, leaders, and social entrepreneurs" (http://watson.lynn.edu/about/), Watson University provides options as extensive as a bachelor's degree or as short as a one-semester Incubator program. The degree-seeking offering is a bachelor's of science in social entrepreneurship. The Incubator offering engages a hand-selected group of scholars who are incubated through intensive mentorship, short workshops led by leading practitioners, award winning curriculum, and a powerful community of peers. There are tuition costs, although sliding scale and/or scholarship funding offers exist.

15

Youth Social Entrepreneurship Preparation, Education, and Advocacy

To ever gain real traction, we need the right language.

—PROGRAM OFFICER, *GRANT-MAKING FOUNDATION, OREGON*

Introduction

It is a common practice for books to end by paying attention to "what next?" This book is no exception. Having established the multidisciplinary case for the theory underlying youth social entrepreneurship, as well as having connected these theories to numerous examples from practice, the remaining concern is how to move forward. The need for empirical work on youth social entrepreneurship is described in Chapter 3; in this chapter, the need is to prepare the researchers and practitioners who will carry forward these ideas.

More specifically, this chapter explores the contexts and constituents most ripe for integrating youth social entrepreneurship terminology, concepts, and practical components, as well as for growing the field through strategic and feasible scaffolding efforts. Current, promising examples illustrate the means to this goal, while more general principles are offered in order to transcend time and place. The aim is to communicate both singular and specific opportunities for advancing this work, as well as the broad interconnectedness of education, professional development, philanthropy, and policy that can be unified toward youth social entrepreneurship advocacy.

The Need for Shared Terminology

While youth social entrepreneurship as an approach to youth development has a plurality of roots and branches through the world of nonprofits, schools, and community programming, much clarifying and unifying of the field remains unaccomplished. In particular, the need for definitional consistency about youth social entrepreneurship is evident. As a nascent field for inquiry but a long-standing approach for practice, a common language is essential for connecting committed individuals and groups.

When asked what is most needed to move the field forward, a program manager in youth social entrepreneurship philanthropy summed it up simply: "words" (P. Kramer, personal communication, October 15, 2016). What his brevity was emphasizing was the necessity for shared terminology to drive conversations about practice and to allow an examination of evidence that compares like processes to like processes. Continued assertion of a central definition and framework will solidify any evolving field and is particularly critical in one such as youth social entrepreneurship, which often resides in the grassroots and the local. Theoreticians of knowledge warn that defective or inadequate definitions of concepts can be dangerous (Hammersley, 2016), whereas well-formed and investigated definitions can unite participants and embolden action. Unifying and operational definitions across disciplines are often a minimal requirement to growing and sustaining a field of inquiry, practice, or both. To wit, the field of positive youth development (PYD) itself included a concentrated effort to clarify its definition throughout its evolution in order to extend its reach and cement its presence (Benson, Scales, Hamilton, & Sesma, 2007). In this example, scholars assert explanations of the roots of the interdisciplinary field along with meaningful frameworks and taxonomies for practitioners and researchers alike to take hold of. This common language has thus undergirded knowledge creation in that field in order to realize the "promise of [PYD] as both a scientific and applied field" (Benson et al., 2007, p. 115).

Theorizing and investigating definitions and common terminology for youth social entrepreneurship is just the beginning. Once formed, the language of the field must be transmitted and promulgated through many varied channels of discourse, including practitioner preparation, professional development, and the equipping of diverse advocates. Advocates in this field include especially those with the economic and political heft to impact society—philanthropic entities, policymakers, and lobbyists—but also average citizens and community members interested in supporting innovative approaches to the healthy development of youth.

The Need for Practitioner Preparation

In order for youth social entrepreneurship to fully take hold in the field of youth development, cohesive movement toward preparation of practitioners must occur. Currently, courses of study do not address youth social entrepreneurship directly. Even programs directed toward social entrepreneurship typically do not include youth-specific aspects of such a practice (per a review of curriculum at six institutions, 2016). Graduates interested in social change, youth development, and/or social entrepreneurship specialize in one area and make their own transfers of knowledge to another area in order to implement methods and applications. One anecdotal example likely tells the common story of others: a young man in

Chicago studied youth development leadership and exited academic life ready to put many approaches into practices. Upon realizing the need for an enterprise to sustain both the income and the interest of his students, as well as an astute understanding of the social change that could accompany such an enterprise, he embarked, on his own devices, on creating a program that resembles the youth social entrepreneurship described in this book. By piecemealing the elements of his graduate studies and field training together, he sought to create a new sort of program, essentially from scratch. Many current youth programs have been conceived in a similar way. While the grassroots origin is admirable and often most effective, "reinventing the wheel" should not be necessary. There can be, and perhaps should be, many ways to build the foundation of the youth social entrepreneurship approach. Embedding theoretical background and practical preparation into higher education is one such approach.

IN HIGHER EDUCATION

One obvious and targeted method to better equip current and future youth social entrepreneurship leaders is in their academic studies at the undergraduate or graduate levels. This can be done through coursework, research, field experience, or some combination of the three. Because many institutions of higher education include some form of "social justice" in their missions, a case for the inclusion of youth social entrepreneurship can be made as a means for creating more just communities and for contributing to the healthy development of youth.

Within undergraduate courses of study, youth social entrepreneurship is most sensibly taught to students of social sciences, many of whom will pursue an interest in community practice. University faculty can attend to the growing movement of youth social entrepreneurship initiatives through assigned readings and sample case studies. Because youth social entrepreneurship is inherently interdisciplinary, this approach to academic study can fit into programs of economics, sociology, youth development/psychology, education, geography, American studies, and more, depending on which focal lens an instructor offers to students. An economics course might examine the effects of social entrepreneurship on youth employment rates and on the affected economies of a community engaged in youth social entrepreneurship. A sociology course might investigate the social capital disparities that are addressed by youth social entrepreneurship and consider the ways in which a stratified society uniquely benefits from youth social entrepreneurship. Courses in youth development and/or developmental psychology will emphasize the healthy effects of youth leadership and empowerment offered by youth social entrepreneurship. Education curricula will benefit by highlighting the integrated nature of youth learning—inside and outside the school—and ways that youth social entrepreneurship can increase student achievement motivation and engagement. A course in geography might specifically examine the community transformations emblematic of youth social entrepreneurship, such as asset-mapping a neighborhood and building social enterprise most needed in that locale. American Studies courses might offer a close look at the historical and cultural systems that perpetuate disparities and identify opportunities for youth social entrepreneurship to dismantle current trends within the US context. Many other discipline-specific examples can be imagined; this list is meant to merely illustrate the broad reach of academic study that youth social entrepreneurship inherently offers. Incorporating attention to youth social entrepreneurship can both bolster the study of the targeted discipline as well as connect a new generation to youth social entrepreneurship as a model.

Within graduate studies, where a more specialized focus on research and/or practice is necessary, opportunities to understand youth social entrepreneurship are especially significant because they may yield leadership in developing and sustaining youth social entrepreneurship–focused organizations. What follows here is a far from exhaustive look at how graduate programs of study might do better at buoying the youth social entrepreneurship skills of their graduates to the benefit of youth and communities.

For one notable example, programs in Social Work often require a targeted specialty, such as public health, community engagement, children and families, or the like. The inherently interdisciplinary model of youth social entrepreneurship, though, does not fit squarely in any one specialized path and, hence, can be overlooked by students and faculty alike. A recent review of the course offerings at the University of Michigan's Masters of Social Work program, currently ranked as the top MSW school in the United States (US News & World report, 2016), demonstrates this reality. A student can specialize in community organizing (one facet of youth social entrepreneurship) or in community and social systems (another facet of youth social entrepreneurship) or in children and youth in families (another key facet of youth social entrepreneurship), but, importantly, the courses required of each do not include overlap (https://ssw.umich.edu/programs/msw/overview). Of course, there exist a number of introductory and foundation courses, as well as integrative upper level and field-based courses, where youth social entrepreneurship might be well incorporated. Yet missing is any assurance that a student would consider the multidimensional effects of well-implemented youth social entrepreneurship, as established in this text. Given the complexity of the disparities in current society, a similarly complex course of study would benefit all.

In another example area of study, a review of graduate schools' offerings in master's degree–level nonprofit management reveals that many similarities exist across curricula, such as leadership, strategic planning, budgets, and board governance. With a general orientation toward social change, many of these programs may include the creation and maintenance of social enterprises within their studies. The inclusion of PYD, however, is less likely. Without an included emphasis on the dynamic ways that youth and communities impact and are impacted by social enterprises, many initiatives led by these programs' graduates come up short in maximizing the positive outcomes for the involved youth, thus missing the chance to impact the opportunity gaps in their communities.

TENSIONS THAT PERSIST

An undercurrent of conflicting values exists in this work. Addressing it head-on must be included in any movement to grow youth social entrepreneurship as a model. In short form, the tension is thus: on the one hand, there is a belief that empowering individuals to create and pursue their own opportunities is a means to equality. This view is often aligned with supporters of capitalist economic models, with a core value being that anyone can and should participate in an open market. On the other hand, critics argue that entrepreneurial pursuits, including those of youth, can paint the problems of capitalism in broad relief—that some win and others fail. Philosophically there are scholars who name capitalism itself as the approach that undermines our society's ability to ever reach equity. How can youth social entrepreneurship successfully expand its reach without isolating either side of this value conflict?

Open discussions in higher education may be a beginning. Colleagues and I have personally experienced the heated exchanges that result when this topic is raised. Rather than shrink away from such contention, embracing it and facilitating its exploration is critical to progress. The cognitive conflict that results from a complex controversy, such as youth social entrepreneurship as capitalist contribution to inequity versus a potent solution to disparities, is precisely the fodder needed for intellectual gains to be made, based on the constructivist theory of education. Conceptual change is most likely when contradictions are present in meaningful ways to students, such as those motivationally related to their lived experience and prior knowledge and their own epistemological beliefs, values and attitudes, and reasoning strategies (Limón, 2001). Employing teaching strategies in relevant courses that allow students to grapple with cognitive conflict around youth social entrepreneurship may be both effective pedagogy, since it can lead to deep conceptual change, and also effective practitioner preparation, since it engages students in examining their own values as embodied by a specific youth development change model. An example of a teaching approach on this topic might be to read Article X on one side and Article Z on another, and then analyze each perspective's arguments in relation to a real youth social entrepreneurship case example, such as those offered in this volume. Putting human characteristics on the issues raised by mostly theoretical points of view can make the conflict most meaningful and the analysis most delicate.

IN K–12 SCHOOLS

While targeted youth social entrepreneurship inquiry may ultimately be a necessary element for well-rounded study in the disciplines described, a sensible home for an introduction to youth social entrepreneurship is in the earlier years of education. The intention is to familiarize students with the basic concepts relevant to social entrepreneurship, not to fully implement and activate social entrepreneurial efforts with every student (though some schools do). The benefit of introducing youth social entrepreneurship principles in K–12 would be twofold, at minimum: (1) eliminate starting from scratch with older youth and (2) alleviate the pressure on out-of-school-time entities to teach the relevant principles on their own. (See Chapter 10 of this volume for a more detailed analysis of how school-based entrepreneurship education differs from youth social entrepreneurship.)

Advocates for including social entrepreneurship in elementary school experiences point to the developmental potential of this curricular timing. Bornstein and Davis (2010) assert the importance of schools' teaching social change, which "should be integrated into education beginning in grade school" (p. 83) as a vital step in growing and deepening the field of social entrepreneurship. Developmental scholars such as Scales (2014) point more to the powerful contributions to youth internal assets, such as leadership and decision-making, which are fostered in the social entrepreneurship process. Further, and perhaps most importantly, educational equity leaders remind us that the authentic and meaningful experiences provided to youth engaged in social entrepreneurship can help fill many gaps. Pittman (2016) describes the expectation gaps that prevent youth from disenfranchised families and neighborhoods from full participation in healthy developmental activities. These expectation gaps occur both individually when youth ingest and internalize societal messages about what is expected from members of their social and/or economic groups, as well as externally, through the numerous expectation barriers present in their schools and communities, both implicitly and explicitly. Giving youth opportunities to make change in their immediate surroundings via social entrepreneurship—whether it's small-scale change in a classroom procedure or a larger scale enterprise that engages a neighborhood or beyond—results in an experience of genuine agency.

Marginalized youth benefit exponentially from experiences of agency due to the repeated, ongoing experiences of expectations gaps. Youth social entrepreneurship enables meaningful leadership and agency, such as is also developed through youth participatory action research (YPAR). YPAR is a growing movement in youth development and community change, emerging as a "a tool for increasing youth involvement in social movement organizing that can generate renewed enthusiasm for social change and create new opportunities for youth leadership" (Berg Powers & Allaman, 2012). YPAR has been shown to result in increased youth engagement and activism (Cammarota & Fine, 2008). An analogy can be drawn: putting youth in charge of something (research, enterprise, or change idea), supporting them and then getting out of their way can result in lasting outcomes. The more schools are able to participate in this process, the better, especially for youth without such opportunities elsewhere.

Changing school culture and curriculum is not a simple endeavor. Unfortunately, the pressures on schools serving low-income students make the incorporation of nontraditional or seemingly "nonacademic" approaches such as youth social entrepreneurship even harder. Such pressures include mandates for standardized test achievement, restricted financial resources, and overwhelmed staff focused on supporting survival needs of students and their families (Zeichner, 2009). The opportunity for social justice lies in breaking this cycle and finding innovative ways to give youth a chance to see themselves as powerful. In this way, incorporating youth social entrepreneurship into the school day itself requires its own social innovations.

One way this has been done is through partnerships with community-based organizations such as Girl Scouts and/or local businesses and colleges. For example, many schools and/or school districts have partnered with Ashoka's Youth Venture to include social entrepreneurship in their curricula since its inception in 1996. An illustrative, specific case example in this category is United Way/ Youth Venture (UW/YV) of Northern Central Massachusetts. Local districts have embedded the UW/YV's well-established version youth social entrepreneurship into their schools. While their model differs from the youth social entrepreneurship described in this text in that it does not exclusively focus on empowering youth who have been marginalized, many of the participants come from communities and families who are economically disenfranchised. Established in 2001, they have partnered with 20 middle and high schools, Mount Wachusett Community College, and two community-based organizations/after school programs and thousands of middle-school, high school, and community college students. The approach used by this organization is to begin each academic year with an annual "Fall Kick-Off" event at the local college which hosts the work. This event celebrates previous projects (called "Ventures") and teaches the students in attendance how to be even greater civic leaders in their community. Using centralized instruction, students participate in hands-on workshops during the annual fall event to help them with "understanding privilege, creating connections within the community, and understanding how to navigate government through their Ventures" (http://www.nvcoc.com/). Then, support is provided during the school year by UW/YV staff for students to work in teams to create their "Action Plans" and eventually their implementations. The criteria is that each Venture Idea offers positive social change for the targeted community and includes plans for sustainability. An example of successful Venture through in the UW/YV of Northern Central Massachusetts is the 2016 "Lift Up Foster Hearts," which provides foster children with toiletries and entertainment items. What differentiates this model is that each Venture team is supported *within* a school instead of from the community-based, out-of-school location of most youth social entrepreneurship programs (see previous chapter). Teachers and school staff are made aware of the plans, and many then become advocates for integrating the social entrepreneurial aspects into their academic curriculum. UW/YV of North Central Massachusetts "gives the power to those who wouldn't necessarily have a say in what's happening and gives them the chance to make an impact," said one high school participant (http://mwcc. edu/).

PROFESSIONAL DEVELOPMENT FOR PROGRAM DESIGNERS AND PRACTITIONERS

A persistent concern in the field of youth work is that "many frontline staff begin with little training, and develop their professional skills in isolation . . . with limited opportunity to reflect, read research, or learn from peers or expert practitioners" (Larson et al., 2015, p. 84). However, it is also well established that ongoing support through networks and training opportunities go a long way to sustained effectiveness for professionals in youth and/or community development. Given the sporadic attention paid to and disconnection within the field of youth social entrepreneurship, opportunities for focused networking and training are few and far between. Two types of support would be seen as most beneficial: professional development and program implementation. These are sometimes offered through funding agencies as part of a grant award.

Bornstein and Davis (2010) cite the improvement of collaboration as a "next major stage" for social entrepreneurship as a field (p. 115), and the benefits of collaboration are parallel for social entrepreneurs focused on youth development as well. While little documentation is available regarding existing, formal professional collaborations in youth social entrepreneurship, one significant example illustrates the potential for others. In 2013, the Sundance Family Foundation of St. Paul, Minnesota, created what they call the "youth social entrepreneurship Collaborative" as part of its concerted interest in advancing the youth social entrepreneurship model. This regionally based group includes youth and adult representatives from more than a dozen nonprofits in the Minneapolis-St. Paul area. Collaborative membership is open to any organization that sees its work as youth social entrepreneurship and is free of charge. Participation in the youth social entrepreneurship Collaborative has included periodic workshops hosted by the foundation, group meetings to focus on a central topic, and social media discussions and information sharing. Sample topics include measuring program outcomes, preparing grant proposals, and garnering community resources. Speakers have been invited to share current research on social-emotional learning, youth participatory research, and even on defining the field of youth social entrepreneurship.

In short, this approach offers a network into which a new program can connect its work to a community of other practitioners with common experiences. Such support is found to be helpful in the literature, as the recent decade has produced more systematic recommendations for professional development of youth workers. For example, Evans et al. (Evans, Sicafuse, Killian, Davidson, & Loesch-Griffin, 2009) documented how collaborative approaches to training and professional development can have significant impact and "may result in increased exposure to a broad range of professional development opportunities and significantly enhance the quality of youth programming" (p. 35).

Many youth social entrepreneurship–oriented programs may not have this regionally limited opportunity available to them. In such instances, a hosting agency could implement a new collaborative, given sufficient geographically local interest. Alternatively, a hosting agency might aim to create a virtual community for youth social entrepreneurship programs to connect with one another from afar and participate in online workshops or professional development sessions. This virtual community permits programmers to interact with like-minded peers in settings different from their own, which can illuminate new and unlikely approaches to extend an organization's practice. On the other hand, a lack of common geographic community can mean minimal common context for discussion, such as might occur with a program existing in a supportive city versus one that is without civic support.

There are benefits and challenges to be noted in any of collaborative efforts described. First, while the potential outcomes of interorganizational cooperation are many, three specific categories are described by Chen and Graddy (2010):

1. *Client goal achievement*: Collaborative participants gain resources to improve programming through sharing best practices and/or material goods.
2. *Enhanced interorganizational relationships*: The collaboration improves the "social capital in the community served" (p. 410).
3. *Organizational learning*: Collaborations have been found to primarily benefit the agency leading the partnership. Often, creating and leading a network improves the decision-making capacity of the convener.

Challenges to effective networks are also numerous. Competition in the public sector for similar funding often prohibits collaboration. The logistics for youth and adults to collaborate together often pose a difficulty, given the schedule clash of working and school commitments.

When, however, an appropriate opportunity for a collaborative network exists, such as one based on a common model like youth social entrepreneurship, the effects on the people involved can be notable: "People actively search for a common purpose. People compromise to forge a common process. People make decisions, and people do the work—with other people from other organizations" (McArthur et al., 2015, p. 110).

Advocating for Youth Social Entrepreneurship

ADVOCACY THROUGH FUNDING

A straightforward but often elusive method to growing the field of youth social entrepreneurship is through increasing the availability of funding opportunities.

By making it potentially attractive to funders, youth social entrepreneurship fits well into many of the key attributes sought by philanthropic agencies: (1) it engages multiple levels of constituents, (2) it offers some degree of sustainability if there is an income-generating enterprise, and (3) it potentially impacts several social systems at once. Furthermore, the inclusion of "social innovation" as a criteria for grant-making has increased notably in the past decade, so the entrepreneurial aspects of youth social entrepreneurship are well-aligned with current philanthropic interests.

Historically, a combination of government and philanthropic funding has fulfilled a significant portion of youth-focused programs (Eccles & Gootman, 2002). Youth social entrepreneurship initiatives typically follow this pattern, blending funding streams to establish and sustain operations. Similar to the need to advance collaborations among program practitioners, a current movement is under way to partner with like-minded foundations to better leverage financial and intellectual resources or to combine multiple funding sources under one governing organization.

Interviews with practitioners and funders yield a picture of often mismatched goals and pathways. Despite the sea change toward PYD during this millennium, a residual pressure toward deficit-focused youth work remains. This reality proves challenging for forward-thinking innovators of youth development, like those at Sisterhood Boutique. They describe the "disconnect" they experience in needing to secure funding that is deficit-focused despite their PYD model (Sajady, personal communication, 2017).

For funders, there are other concerns. One that has been raised is the lack of systems thinking among many constituents, programs, and collaborators who are "stuck in a linear world" and remain within their own silos of work (Hartley, personal communication, 2016). To reach the more impactful goals of complex solutions, there is a need for robust networking and a willingness for relational thinking to undergird proposed solutions.

An illustrative example is the Social Innovation Fund (SIF), a program of the Corporation for National and Community Service (CNCS) that combines public and private resources to grow the impact of innovative, community-based solutions that have compelling evidence of improving the lives of people in low-income communities throughout the United States (www.nationalservice.gov/programs/social-innovation-fund). Begun in 2009 with an original federal investment of $295 million, as of March 2016, their private-sector partners have leveraged matching-fund commitments valued at $627.5 million and awarded 43 grantees to act as grant intermediaries in 17 states and the District of Columbia, which funded approximately 450 nonprofit organizations.

A current challenge to the philanthropic sector's embrace of youth social entrepreneurship is the complexity of its model. A level of systems thinking is necessary to adequately address the interdependent factors and players of genuine youth social entrepreneurship initiatives. Some but not all institutions have this capacity—the ability to recognize the "linkages and interactions between the components" that comprise a larger entity (Tate, 2009, p. 115).

One such example is the Susan Crown Exchange, "a social investment organization with a fresh approach to catalyzing change through philanthropy" (http:// www.scefdn.org). They focus on initiatives that offer coordinated approaches to support young people versus fragmented models that focus on only one aspect of the youth experience. "The Readiness Project" by the Forum for Youth Investment (FYI) embodies exactly this value. FYI first reviewed "300 reports, studies, journal articles and books, ranging from neuroscience to systems thinking to future economic forecasts and workforce trends," then extracted "60 of the most credible standards and frameworks from each major youth-serving system" to result in a "comprehensive and systems-neutral science of readiness" (http://sparkaction. org/readiness). This complex, highly interdisciplinary approach to youth "readiness" reflects the systems thinking that comprehensive youth development seeks.

As more and more funders value complex, interconnected programming models, the horizon for youth social entrepreneurship initiatives to receive support brightens.

ADVOCACY THROUGH SUPPORTIVE POLICIES

Some public policy initiatives are better for enabling youth social entrepreneurship to reach youth than others, especially those with economic disadvantage. While always in flux, policies at the national and local levels are difficult to pin down. What can be identified, though, are the types of policies that are most supportive and examples of helpful approaches.

In general, many of the public policy conditions that benefit social entrepreneurship will also be beneficial to youth social entrepreneurship. Advocates of government's role in enabling social entrepreneurship cite several strategies. Katherine Hewson, Ontario Ministry of Economic Development Trade and Employment and the Ministry of Research and Innovation, for example, names three avenues: (1) the importance of a supportive tax environment for start-up social enterprises, (2) regulating for a strong financial marketplace, and (3) capacity-building to engage in the social sector (Doverall, 2014). Scholars of PYD programming often point to the need for comprehensive public policy to support their aims (Dixon-Román & Gordon, 2012). Thus, policies that both permit and support a full range of youth-led social entrepreneurial efforts can be seen as the most desirable. Policymakers, then, best foster the growth of youth social entrepreneurship when they allow connections among resources and capacity-builders who are committed to the youth social entrepreneurship model, such as through formal networks.

One example of an interconnected policy network can be seen through the Opportunity Youth Network (OYN). OYN was launched with key leaders from nearly 100 national organizations in March 2013, to capitalize on the momentum created by the White House Council on Community Solutions. This council elevated the nation's focus to the needs of the approximately 5.5 million "opportunity youth," aged 16–24 years, who are not in school and not working. OYN has sought to bring together high-level funders and corporations, as well as federal, state, and local government officials; nonprofits; and youth themselves to collaborate on the common goal of youth employment (aspencommunitysolutions. org).

ADVOCACY BY COMMUNITY MEMBERS

In the oft-cited words of cultural anthropologist Margaret Mead, "never doubt that a small group of thoughtful committed citizens can change the world. Indeed it's the only thing that ever has." The importance of support from the community at large for youth development initiatives, such as youth social entrepreneurship, cannot be underestimated. Here, "community" means any individuals who are connected in some way to the endeavors at hand. They may be leaders in the work or supporters and customers.

INDIVIDUALS

Critical to many of these programs is community participation through private donations and attendance at fundraising events. Because so many youth social entrepreneurship programs include an enterprise, community members can actively provide support as customers to these enterprises. For example, choosing to purchase reading material on-site or online through More than Words in Boston, Massachusetts, rather than through a national bookstore chain furnishes the consumer with both the desired product and an opportunity to contribute to More than Words' long-standing mission to "empower youth who are in the foster care system, court involved, homeless, or out of school to take charge of their lives by taking charge of a business" (www.mtwyouth.org).

OTHER SOCIAL ENTERPRISES AND COMMUNITY ORGANIZATIONS

A long-standing reality in the social service/nonprofit sector is that competition for limited funding dampens potential collaborations that would serve both organizations and their communities. However, both for-profit and nonprofit organizations are increasingly recognizing the value of connectedness with their so-called competitors (Hecht, 2013). This trend, known as "collective impact," stands to benefit social enterprises broadly and youth social entrepreneurial endeavors specifically.

A particular advantage to participation in a collective impact group is the provision of "backbone support" (Kania & Kramer, 2011). This is critical since "coordination takes time, and none of the participating organizations has any to spare.

The expectation that collaboration can occur without a supporting infrastructure is one of the most frequent reasons why it fails" (p. 1).

This can be especially necessary for youth-led social entrepreneurship in order to gain the needed structural support, ideas, data management, and more. For example, a collective impact group in Minneapolis, Minnesota, known as Pillsbury United Communities, hosts numerous programs and projects in its targeted geography to "create multidimensional solutions that move people to economic stability" (www.puc-mn.org). Several initiatives within this umbrella structure utilize youth social entrepreneurship approaches. Two specifically are the consignment shop, Sisterhood Boutique, started and run by East African young women, and the Triple C Coffee Cart, run by East African youth aged 14–21.

Pillsbury's infrastructure enables these youth social entrepreneurship programs to thrive because they have "focused on investing in organizational capacity in order to further its impact. It is a plan to disrupt our current thinking, to challenge convention and to establish even bolder goals that push us beyond our organizational comfort zone" (www.puc-mn.org).

CORPORATE SPONSORSHIP AS A COMMUNITY SUPPORT

A surge of attention and action has spawned myriad new collaborative efforts to address youth unemployment and especially for youth from marginalized communities. Most of these have some corporate backing. For example, the 100,000 Opportunities Initiative is a self-identified "coalition of leading companies" focused on disrupting patterns of unemployment for youth ("new sources of talent") from communities that "have not traditionally been included in our nation's prosperity" (100kopportunities.org). For another example, JP Morgan Chase's $75 million, 4-year New Skills For Youth initiative (January 2016) seeks to call attention to the issue of youth unemployment and draw other corporate funders into participation and support. Neither of these examples has yet included youth leadership for social change as an outcome; both identify job skills and access to first- and second-job opportunities as their primary mission. In this way, many US corporations interested in supporting disenfranchised youth in economic change do so through their own channels, not through approaches derived by youth themselves. While many economic experts may believe that turning this gear of unemployment will inevitably change the face of poverty and transform communities and thus promote PYD, many community and human developmental theorists warn that these structures risk perpetuating the disempowered identity of employee, not employer. Such approaches are then inherently not ones of change but of consistency in power structures. Still, the attention occurring in the corporate world toward identified "disconnected youth" aged 16–24 and not employed or in school (Belfield, Levin, & Rosen, 2012) has resulted in new collaborations throughout the business sector and across sectors. This movement potentially shifts action toward increasingly more complex and dynamic solutions, which is promising because simple, one-dimensional solutions are insufficient to solve the complex problems facing our marginalized communities. The continuing response must come from a multiplicity of fields committed to growing the academic preparation, professional training, funding, philanthropic leadership, and awareness of community members to energetically advance the field of youth social entrepreneurship and its intersectional, dynamic, and transformative practices.

Section V

Focal Case Examples

Case 1: SOUL Sisters Leadership Collective

COMMUNITY IMPACT

SOUL Sisters Leadership Collective (SSLC) impacts their larger communities in a number of ways. First, the youth-led Social Action Projects directly impact their communities, whether through the previously described "Spread the Love" retail enterprise, through planning and phone banking for the March for Black Women, or through youth-led spoken-word in the community.

Additionally and significantly, SSLC contributes professional development opportunities to the broader community. Part of the organization's model is to teach their "holistic model for all service providers that highlights positive youth development and expands that philosophy to include all staff of an organization" (www.soulsistersleadership.org/professional-development). This is accomplished through fee-for-service trainings, tailored to the needs of an individual or organization. Topics of training include Peacekeeping Circles & Restorative Justice Practices, the SOUL Model: Best-Practices for Gender-Specific Programming, trauma-informed care, positive youth development, and mindfulness and meditation in clinical practice. Outside of these planned training opportunities, partner agencies often ask SSLC to help them with the development of their social justice curriculum and/or present directly to their youth participants (Gibbs, personal communication, 2017).

Another way that SSLC impacts the broader community is just by doing what they do! Embodying "other ways of being with youth" for their partner agencies, many of whom have more traditional hierarchical practices, is a form of teaching and impact (Douglas, personal communication, 2017). Since their program goes to the partner sites rather than having youth come in to them, the SSLC staff are present in a wide variety of partner sites and bring with them their philosophy and practices in a sort of demonstration/show-and-tell. Though this is a difficult impact to conceptualize or measure, the program founders are keenly aware of its effects.

Finally, SSLC aims to have a policy impact, organizing at the local and national levels with other similarly minded organizations. For example, they are connected to the Young Women's Initiative, a multisector, national movement of gender-focused equity campaigns. In New York City, the initiative known as #SheWillBe aims to "identify the gaps in services for young women age 12–24, with a focus on women of color. The Young Women's Initiative brings together leaders and organizers who work with teens and young adults and advocate for them in all aspects of our society, with the goal of crafting policy recommendations that address racial, gender and other disparities. This is being done with young women at the center of the conversations—as active and consistent participants in discussions and through a multiplatform campaign to hear directly from them" (shewillbe.nyc/).

Case 2: Cookie Cart

In the arena of community development, Cookie Cart makes an ongoing, intentional effort to be a connected member of their neighborhood. First, the involved youth come from the neighborhood. They and their families make up the community in which Cookie Cart resides and operates.

Next, they foster relationships with neighborhood groups and institutions. For example, they commonly participate in the "Open Streets" events in their geographic community, bringing free cookies for community members. They also open their upstairs meeting space to community member for modest rental (a $50 purchase of cookies and coffee!). Neighboring community organizations take them up on this and host staff meetings and strategic planning sessions. Corporate partners also come to use the space for their smaller teams, sometimes in conjunction with a visit to the kitchen or volunteering time with the youth in scooping batter.

Most significantly, they moved their kitchen—the very site of their central youth development activities—to the front of their building during a recent, major renovation. The purpose for having the glass-windowed baking kitchen right at street level is simply to be engaging with the community. "At night, it glows," says Marit Michels, their Director of Development, drawing people's attention with a welcoming light.

Their programming is designed to elevate the human capital of their community and in turn enhance the community capital. In the careful decision-making around the location of their second site, their staff and board sought a neighborhood where employment and training opportunities were scarce and poverty was disproportionately high. By physically locating themselves in a geographic community with these characteristics of disparity, Cookie Cart poises its programming to transform at least some elements of the community. If nothing else, the added "first paycheck" employment for local youth nudges the opportunity gap a little smaller.

They have not measured the ways that their impact has affected the neighborhood specifically, but the investment in their building renovation alone ($1.7 million) is a real estate advantage. Furthermore, their connection to a number of Fortune 500 companies as sponsors, donors, and volunteers lends bridging capital to the neighborhood, pulling (adult) members of two communities of interest together who otherwise may seem miles apart.

Creating effective youth–adult partnerships at Cookie Cart is a feat of proper scaffolding. Because most of their involved youth enter the program between 15 and 17, they arrive with little to no experience in taking charge of their environments and making decisions to drive the organization. Their programming accommodates this by starting with less individual autonomy and gradually adding more responsibility. Youth can ultimately become "Cart Captains," who have a significant hand in the bakery operations and programming. In this way, there is significant movement from low-level youth agency to increased youth empowerment within the site. Such a shift is mimicked in the youth–adult partnerships: as youth move "up" in their time at Cookie Cart and potentially become Cart Captains, adult are able to become increasingly "hands-off" with them. To support this, the Cart Captain programming includes curriculum for leadership development, peer communication, and conflict resolution. Such skills are needed as the now-empowered youth leaders take on managerial tasks and lead their less experienced, often younger peers. They also naturally seem to exercise some of the leadership practices as well, such as "reminding" newer youth to "wear their nametags" or "pay attention when a guest speaker is here" (interview with Director of Development, Marit Michels, 2017).

Furthermore, staff say they are careful to retain a developmental appropriateness to their programming with youth. With their age "sweet spot" (Michels interview) at 15–17, and most participants beginning at 15, they see the slow maturing of these mid-teens. As developmental scientists concur, social relationships dominate the attention, interest, and energy of mid-adolescence. So it is not surprising, says Michels, that most of their youth in this stage name "meeting other kids" as their favorite part of being at Cookie Cart. To thrust entrepreneurship into their hands when they have come for a job, some training, and lots of new friends is arguably inappropriate for their stage of development, unless they are asking for that. In this way, again, the self-selected Cart Captains program places the social enterprise actions of youth into a more limited set of willing hands.

Perhaps the most developmentally appropriate part of their approach is "letting them make mistakes." It is an inevitable—and necessary—element of youth learning on the job, and staff would not want it any other way. They joke that they are "The world's most inefficient bakery" because they allow their bakers to make mistakes and grow from them. Putting them into leadership roles when they are not ready precludes this mistake-making process by raising the stakes on accuracy and intimidating the learner beyond his or her willingness to try.

Cookie Cart relies heavily on the melded expertise of their youth workers and their board of directors to help them adequately navigate the complex world of social enterprise. Because as a not-for-profit social enterprise they are inherently "part business/part nonprofit" (Michels, personal communication, 2017), the constituent contributions from the business/finance side and the human development programming side are often at odds in a necessary tension. Like any dialectical, they keep each other moving in the right proportions. Their funding model includes one-third of their revenue from cookies sales. This means that business aspects such as customer retention, quality of product, and efficiency need to be central. Yet the tension is that mistakes and slow growth are central to the youth development aspects of the bakery! This delicate dance, such that the tension is never resolved too much one way or the other, is necessary to keep all aspects in check. It is difficult, admits their director of development, but ultimately it is a needed balance to do what they do: empowering young people "one cookie at a time."

Conclusion of Focal Case Examples

The presentation of two main case examples through the progression of this book had multiple purposes. First, to provide the reader with field-based, practical applications to connect to the overarching topics of each section, thus breathing life into the theoretical discussions; second, to explore two quite different youth program models while still reflecting on their commonalities; and third, to model examples for other youth social entrepreneurs to consider and, perchance, embrace.

Notable differences between the two cases were likely identified easily by the reader. However, a brief analysis here aims to explicate their distinctions for the purposes of clarification and instruction. First, SOUL Sister is a relatively new program (less than 10 years), while Cookie Cart is long-standing (30 years). SOUL Sisters engages two regionally different settings, while Cookie Cart has deep roots in one metropolitan area. SOUL Sisters is led by its founders, who are also intimately involved in program design and hands-on youth facilitation, whereas Cookie Cart has an intricate, though nimble, organization structure with distinct staff roles. SOUL Sisters is gender-specific; Cookie Cart is not. SOUL Sisters serves a wide breadth of ages (8–18); Cookie Cart has a niche of only two teen years (15–17). SOUL Sisters embeds holistic health and emotional wellness within its programming; Cookie Cart follows a more limited and linear curriculum of economic and academic health. SOUL Sisters has included revenue-generating social enterprise via their retail line, but it is neither central nor sustainable; Cookie Cart upholds a strict model by which 33% of their funding comes from their product creation. SOUL Sisters operates on a smaller budget and smaller scale than Cookie Cart, which manages significant numbers of youth and budget resources (including annual donations of thousands of pounds of flour and butter!).

With so many differences, the reader may question the worth of studying them in juxtaposition. The intention is purposeful and can be best revealed by exploring their similarities, through which an emerging depiction of "youth social entrepreneurship" might be most identifiable.

SOUL Sisters and Cookie Cart are both highly asset-based in their work with youth. They do not see or treat young people as having deficits that need fixing; instead, youth have power that can be leveraged through targeted education and experience. Both organizations are cognizant of their geographic communities, connecting with great intention to other members of their social sector, the private sector, and neighbors at street level. They are both highly aware of the disparities in social capital that impede youth from accessing opportunities and social mobility, health, employment, and education. Beyond awareness, both programs do something to ameliorate these disparities as much as possible. Both SOUL Sisters and Cookie Cart value youth leadership and cultivate it with careful scaffolding. Both programs are designed for high-level youth engagement, focusing their youth work on hands-on, embodied activities. Both help youth make change by weaving positive youth development and community development approaches to advance social justice in their own lives and beyond.

APPENDIX

Youth Programs Cited in this Book

Bearings Bike Shop

Bearings Bike Shop is a youth development organization where kids in Atlanta can "earn and maintain a bicycle while developing the skills and character to succeed in adulthood." Bearings says: "We believe these young people are change makers. We believe they can repair broken chains—on bikes, as well as in their families and communities."

Location: 982 Murphy Avenue SW, Atlanta, Georgia 30310
Website: bearingsbikeshop.org

Cookie Cart

Cookie Cart is a 30-year-old organization that engages youth aged 15–18 with "lasting and meaningful work, life, leadership skills through experience and training in an urban nonprofit bakery." In addition to employment readiness, youth at Cookie Cart advance their interpersonal, leadership, and critical thinking skills.

Location: 1119 W. Broadway Avenue, Minneapolis, Minnesota 55411
Website: cookiecart.org

Cycles for Change

Cycles for Change is a nonprofit "working at the intersection of social justice and the bicycle movement." Their Youth Apprenticeship program works with high school-aged youth to "build the next generation of self-empowered community leaders and cyclists" through learning bike mechanics, running the shops, and contributing to "vibrant, equitable bicycling communities within the Twin Cities through paid positions."

Locations: 2010 26th Street, Minneapolis, Minnesota 55404; 712 University Avenue, St. Paul, Minnesota 55104
Website: cyclesforchange.org

The Food Project

Since 1991, The Food Project offers "a national model of engaging young people in personal and social change through sustainable agriculture" by farming 70 acres in multiple locations of eastern Massachusetts. Their program focus is on "identifying and transforming a new generation of leaders by placing teens in increasingly responsible roles, with deeply meaningful work."

Location: (main office) 10 Lewis Street, Lincoln, Massachusetts 01773
Website: thefoodproject.org

Good Life Organization

The Good Life Organization is a nonprofit that supports "the positive development of youth for the purposes of enhancing democratic participation and academic achievement." Their programming focuses on building the capacity of local leaders through speaking events, trainings, curriculum, and tools that "enable dialogue, critical reflection, and creative action." Their featured curriculum is "Fulfill the Dream," which emphasizes cultural relevance and social-emotional learning for youth leaders.

Location: 400 South Green St. Suite 205, Chicago, Illinois 60607
Website: goodlifealliance.org

Juma Ventures

Juma Ventures is a 25-year-old nonprofit that runs more than 20 social enterprise operations in nine cities—Atlanta, Dallas, Houston, New Orleans, Oakland, Sacramento, San Francisco, Santa Clara, and Seattle. Juma offers youth employment, financial capability, and academic services by partnering with major sports arenas and asset-building and educational partners across the country.

Location: (main office) 131 Steuart Street, Suite 201 San Francisco, California 94105
Website: juma.org

More Than Words Bookstore

More Than Words (MTW) is a nonprofit social enterprise that "empowers youth ages 16–21 who are in the foster care system, court involved, homeless, or out of school to take charge of their lives by taking charge of a business. MTW youth run two brick-and-mortar bookstores, a café and an online book-selling business as a vehicle to develop critical skills and experience. . . . They simultaneously have a second job, their 'YOU' job, through which they receive intensive case management to work towards measurable positive outcomes for education, work and life."

Locations: 56 Felton Street, Waltham, Massachusetts 02453; 242 East Berkeley St., 2nd Floor, Boston, Massachusetts 02118
Website: mtwyouth.org

Old Skool Café

Old Skool Café is a fully operational, youth-run restaurant in the supper-club tradition. The young people who work there "come to Old Skool Café from a variety of backgrounds, including those challenged by the conditions of poverty, domestic violence, street violence, drug use, gang life, incarceration, foster care, early parenting and more. Old Skool Café offers more than just employment [including] a supportive environment to help our youth receive job training skills and paid work experience in all aspects of the restaurant business. They are supported with other resources and a sense of family to help them succeed in all aspects of their lives."

Location: 1429 Mendell Street, San Francisco, California 94124
Website: oldskoolcafe.org/youth-run-supper-club

Sisterhood Boutique

"Sisterhood Boutique is a business venture designed and run by East African women, ages 14–23. Young women involved with the program are learning a variety of personal and professional skills from business development to event planning, while the colorful variety of clothing and accessories available at the shop provide affordable clothing options for residents of the neighborhood. Sisterhood Boutique carries a wide selection of gently used women's clothing, shoes, jewelry, accessories and scarves."

Location: 2200 Riverside Ave, Minneapolis, Minnesota 55454
Website: sisterhoodmn.org

SOUL Sisters Leadership Collective

SOUL Sisters offers programs that provide "a powerful community of mentors, activists, educators, and healers that support young women, femmes, and gender non-conforming/gender non-binary youth of color blossoming into leaders with political and self awareness, creative problem solving skills, and strong ethics. We are sensitive to the needs of youth in the foster care, juvenile legal, special education, shelter, and mental health systems."

Location: 6360 NE 4th Court, Miami, Florida 33138
Website: soulsistersleadership.org

South Atlanta Bike Shop

South Atlanta Bike Shop is a nonprofit youth development program in which young people aged 8–18 learn bike repair, job readiness, and leadership skills. They offer "earn-a-bike" in which youth can earn points by working in the bike shop and spend these to purchase bicycles, bicycle accessories, and replacement parts and pay for bike trip registration fees; they offer paid employment for teen participants as well.

Location: 1297 McDonough Blvd. SE, Suite 400, Atlanta, Georgia 30315
Website: southatlantabikeshop.org

Street Bean Coffee Roasters

Street Bean Coffee Roasters is a nonprofit organization whose mission is "to provide an opportunity for street-involved young people to discover and employ their gifts by serving coffee in our community [providing] . . . a catalyst to move onto successful future employment."

Locations: 2711 3rd Ave, Seattle, Washington 98109
5015 Roosevelt Way NE, Seattle, Washington 98109
Website: streetbean.org

Urban Boatbuilders

Launched more than 20 years ago, Urban Boatbuilders is a social enterprise that teaches youth the hands-on skill of woodworking with the aim to empower "their hands, heart, and mind to be engaged community members and environmental stewards." In this process, Urban Boatbuilders creates "a repertoire of light-weight, durable, and beautiful water-crafts which are sold to support our mission and the youth we serve."

Location: 2288 University Avenue West, St. Paul, Minnesota 55114
Website: urbanboatbuilders.org

YouthBuild

YouthBuild operates at 260 locations in 46 states of the United States and internationally in 15 countries. Their programs provide pathways to "education, jobs, entrepreneurship, and other opportunities leading to productive livelihoods and community leadership." In all locations, YouthBuild engages low-income youth aged 16–24 through classroom and hands-on construction projects that build or repair affordable housing, playgrounds, community centers, schools, clinics, parks, and the like. Their goal is to "rebuild their communities and their lives, breaking the cycle of poverty with a commitment to work, education, family, and community."

Location: (main office) 58 Day Street, Somerville, Massachusetts 02144
Website: youthbuild.org

REFERENCES

Aaronson, D. (2000). A note on the benefits of homeownership. *Journal of Urban Economics, 47*(3), 356–369.

Adolphs, R. (2009). The social brain: Neural basis of social knowledge. *Annual Review of Psychology, 60,* 693–716. doi.org/10.1146/annurev.psych.60.110707.163514

Agustina, I., & Beilin, R. (2012). Community gardens: Space for interactions and adaptations. *Social and Behavioral Sciences, 36*(0), 439–448.

Alaimo, K., Beavers, A. W., Crawford, C., Snyder, E. H., & Litt, J. S. (2016). Amplifying health through community gardens: A framework for advancing multicomponent, behaviorally based neighborhood interventions. *Current Environmental Health Reports, 3,* 302–312.

Allegretto, S., Doussard, M., Graham-Squire, D., Jacobs, K., Thompson, D., & Thompson, J. (2013). *Fast Food, Poverty Wages: The Public Cost of Low-Wage Jobs in the Fast-Food Industry.* Berkeley, CA: UC Berkley Labor Center.

Altschuler, A., Somkin, C. P., & Adler, N. E. (2004). Local services and amenities, neighborhood social capital, and health. *Social Science and Medicine, 59,* 1219–1229.

Anand, P., & Lea, S. (2011). The psychology and behavioural economics of poverty. *Journal of Economic Psychology, 32*(2), 284–293. doi.org/10.1016/j.joep.2010.11.004

Anderman, E., & Anderman, L. M. (2010). *Classroom Motivation* (2nd ed.). New York: Pearson Education.

Anderson, A., & Milligan, S. (2006). Social capital and community building. In K. Fulbright-Anderson & P. Auspos (Eds.), *Community Change: Theories, Practice, and Evidence* (pp. 21–62). Washington, DC: The Aspen Institute.

Ashoka. (2016). "All America" Manifesto. https://www.ashoka.org/en/country/united-states

The Aspen Institute Forum for Community Solutions. (n.d.). *Opportunity Youth Network.* Retrieved from https://aspencommunitysolutions.org/the-fund/opportunity-youth-network/

Bacchetta, M., Ernst, E., & Bustamanta, J. (2009). *Globalization and Informal Jobs in Developing Countries: A Joint Study of the International Labour Office and the Secretariat of the World Trade Organization.* Geneva: World Trade Organization Publications.

Bandura, A. (1973). *Aggression: A Social Learning Analysis.* Englewood Cliffs, NJ: Prentice-Hall.

Belfield, C. R., Levin, H. M., & Rosen, R. (2012). *The Economic Value of Opportunity Youth.* Retrieved from https://www.serve.gov/new-images/council/pdf/econ_value_opportunity_youth.pdf

Ben-Eliyahu, A., Rhodes, J. E., & Scales, P. C. (2014). The interest-driven pursuits of 15-year-olds: "Sparks" and their association with caring relationships and developmental outcomes. *Applied Developmental Science, 18,* 76–89.

Benson, P. L. (1990). *The troubled journey: A portrait of 6th–12th grade youth*. Minneapolis, MN: Search Institute and Lutheran Brotherhood; and unpublished Search Institute data from student surveys during the 2014–2015 school year.

Benson, P. (1997). All kids are our kids. *Adolescence, 32*, 147–168.

Benson, P. L. (2008). *Sparks: How Parents Can Ignite the Hidden Strengths of Teenagers*. San Francisco, CA: Jossey-Bass.

Benson, P. L., Scales, P. C., Hamilton, S. F., & Sesma, A. (2007). Positive youth development: Theory, research, and applications. *Handbook of Child Psychology*, (16). doi: 10.1002/9780470147658.chpsy0116

Berg Powers, C., & Allaman, E. (2014). *How Participatory Action Research Can Promote Social Change and Help Youth Development*. A report from the Born This Way Foundation, the Berkman Center for Internet & Society at Harvard University, and the John D., & Catherine T. MacArthur Foundation. Retrieved from Harvard University website: http://cyber.harvard.edu/sites/cyber.harvard.edu/files/KBWParticipatoryAct ionResearch2012.pdf

Beverly, S. G. (2013). Asset building for and by young people. *Economics of Education Review, 33*, 52–57.

Beverly, S., & McBride, A., & Schreiner, M. (2003). A Framework of asset-accumulation stages and strategies. *Journal of Family and Economic Issues, 24*, 143–156. doi:10.1023/A:1023662823816.

Beyond the Bell. (2015). *Supporting Social and Emotional Development Through Quality Afterschool Programs*. American Institutes for Research. Chicago, IL. Retrieved from www.beyondthebell.org.

Birkenmaier, J. (2016). Financial capability and asset building: Building evidence for community practice. *Journal of Community Practice, 24*(4), 357.

Birkenmaier, J., Curley, J., & Sherraden, M. (Eds.). (2013). *Financial Education and Capability: Research, Education, Policy, and Practice*. New York: Oxford University Press.

Blakemore, S. J. (2008). The social brain in adolescence. *Nature Reviews Neuroscience, 9*, 267–277. doi:10.1038/nrn2353

Blanchet-Cohen, N., Manolson, S., & Shaw, K. (2012). Youth-led decision making in community development grants. *Youth & Society, 46*(6), 819–834. doi: 10.1177/0044118X12455024

Bordas, J. (2016). Leadership lessons from communities of color: Stewardship and collective action. *New Directions for Student Leadership, 2016*(152), 61–74. doi:10.1002/yd.20209.

Bornstein, D., & Davis, S. (2010). *Social Entrepreneurship: What Everyone Needs to Know*. New York: Oxford University Press.

Bourdieu P. (1985). The forms of capital. In J. G. Richardson (Ed.), *Handbook of Theory and Research for the Sociology of Education* (pp. 241–258). New York: Greenwood.

Bourke, B. (2014). Positionality: Reflecting on the research process. *The Qualitative Report, 19*(33), 1–9. Retrieved from http://nsuworks.nova.edu/tqr/vol19/iss33/3

Boyle, T. (2012). 21st century knowledge, skills, and abilities and entrepreneurial competencies: A model for undergraduate entrepreneurship education. *Journal of Entrepreneurship Education, 15*, 41–56.

Bracher, M., Santow, G., Morgan, S., & Trussell, J. (1993). Marriage dissolution in Australia: Models and explanations. *Population Studies, 47*(3), 403–425.

Braxton, E. (2016). Youth leadership for social justice: Past and present. In J. Osberg & S. M. Rosen (Eds.), *Contemporary Youth Activism: Advancing Social Justice in the United States: Advancing Social Justice in the United States*. Santa Barbara, California: Praeger.

Bronfenbrenner, U. (1979). *The Ecology of Human Development: Experiments by Nature and Design*. Cambridge, MA: Harvard University Press.

Brown, D., & McGranahan, G. (2016). The urban informal economy, local inclusion and achieving a global green transformation. *Habitat International, 53*, 97–105. doi.org/10.1016/j.habitatint.2015.11.002

Brown, T. M., & Rodríguez, L. F. (2009). Issue editors' notes. *New Directions for Youth Development*, (123), 1–9.

Buchanan, L. (2016). What's next for TOMS, the $400 million for-profit built on karmic capital. *Inc. Magazine*, May 2016. Retrieved from https://www.inc.com/magazine/201605/leigh-buchanan/toms-founder-blake-mycoskie-social-entrepreneurship.html

Bulloch, G. (November 6, 2014). The rise of a fourth sector skill set. *Stanford Social Innovation Review*. Retrieved from ssir.org/articles/entry/the_rise_of_a_fourth_sector_skills_set

Burke, B., & Harrison, P. (2002). Anti-oppressive practice. In R. Adams, L. Dominelli, & M. Mayne (Eds.), *Anti-Oppressive Practice* (pp. 227–236). Basingstoke: Palgrave MacMillan.

Burns, J. C., Paul, D. P., & Silvia, R. P. (2012). *Participatory Asset Mapping: A Community Research Lab Toolkit*. Advancement Project's Urban Peace Institute. Retrieved from http://www.communityscience.com/knowledge4equity/AssetMappingToolkit.pdf

Cammarota, J., & Fine, M. (Eds.). (2008). *Revolutionizing Education: Youth Participatory Action Research in Motion*. New York: Routledge Taylor & Francis Group.

Cammarota, J., & Romero, A. (2009). A social justice epistemology and pedagogy for latina/o students: Transforming public education with participatory action research. *New Directions for Youth Development, 2009*(123), 53–65. doi:10.1002/yd.314

Camangian, P. (2017). From coping to hoping: Teaching students to thrive through social trauma. Presentation at Macalester College, November 7.

Card, D. (1998). *The Causal Effect of Education on Earnings*. Berkeley: Center for Labor Economics, University of California at Berkeley.

Carnevale, A. P, Smith, N., & Strohl, J. (2013). *Recovery: Job Growth and Education Requirements Through 2020*. Washington, DC: Georgetown Center for Education and the Workforce. Retrieved from https://cew.georgetown.edu/wp-content/uploads/2014/11/Recovery2020.FR_.Web_.pdf

Carnochan, S., Samples, M., Myers, M., & Austin, M. J. (2013). Performance measurement challenges in nonprofit human service organizations. *Nonprofit and Voluntary Sector Quarterly*, 1–19. doi: 10.1177/0899764013508009

Carr, D. (2005). *Professionalism and Ethics in Teaching*. New York: Routledge Publishing.

Carter, P. L., Welner, K. G., & Ladson-Billings, G. (2013). *Closing the Opportunity Gap: What America Must Do to Give Every Child an Even Chance.*Oxford: Oxford University Press.

Castagno, A., & Brayboy, B. (2008). Culturally responsive schooling for indigenous youth: A review of the literature. *Review of Educational Research, 78*(4), 941–993. doi:10.3102/0034654308323036

Castiglione, D., Van Deth, J. W., & Wolleb, G. (Eds.). (2008). *The Handbook of Social Capital*. New York: Oxford University Press.

Chambers, S. (July 7, 2015). Does it pay to train people to set up their own business? *Financial Times*. Retrieved from https://www.ft.com/content/3f9e8ffe-1f0b-11e5-ab0f-6bb9974f25d0

Chen, B., & Graddy, E. A. (2010). The effectiveness of nonprofit lead-organization networks for social service delivery. *Nonprofit Management & Leadership, 20*(4), 405–422. doi:10.1002/nml.20002

Chhabra, E. (Januay 31, 2015). Social enterprise versus non-profits: Is there really a difference? *Forbes*. Retrieved from www.forbes.com/sites/eshachhabra/2015/01/31/social-enterprise-vs-non-profits-is-there-really-a-difference/47954b5f628e

Child Trends. (2015). *High School Dropout Rates: Indicators of Child and Youth Well-Being*. Retieved from https://www.childtrends.org/indicators/high-school-dropout-rates/

Christens, B., & Dolan,T. (2011). Interweaving youth development, community development, and social change through youth organizing. *Youth and Society, 43*(2), 528–548.

Christens, B., & Kirschner, C. (2011). Taking stock of youth organizing: An interdisciplinary perspective. *New Directions for Child and Adolescent Development, 134*, 28–41.

Christens, B., Powers, J., & Zeldin, S. (2013). The psychology and practice of youth-adult partnership: Bridging generations for youth development and community change. *American Journal Community Psychology, 51*, 385–397.

Coles, R. (Ed.) (2001). *The Erik Erikson Reader*. New York, NY: Norton & Company.

Collet-Klingenberg, L., & Kenney, L. (2000). Manufacturing and production technician youth apprenticeship program: A partnership. *Peabody Journal of Education, 75*(3), 51–63. doi: 10.1207/ S15327930PJE7503_4

Collier, D., Laporte, J., & Seawright, J. (2008). Typologies: Forming concepts and creating categorical variables. In J. M. Box-Steffensmeier, H. E. Brady, & D. Collier (Eds.), *The Oxford Handbook of Political Methodology*. Oxford Handbook Online. doi: 10.1093/oxfordhb/9780199286546.003.0007

Conner, J., & Rosen, S. M. (Eds.). (2016). *Contemporary Youth Activism: Advancing Social Justice in the United States*. Santa Barbara, CA: Praeger.

Cookie Cart. (2016). *2016 Community Report*. Retrieved from http://cookiecart.org/annualreport/

Copeland, W. E., Keeler G., Angold, A., & Costello, E. J. (2007). Traumatic events and posttraumatic stress in childhood. *Archives of General Psychiatry, 64*(5), 577–584. doi:10.1001/archpsyc.64.5.577

Coyle, S. (March/April 2016). Trends in macro social work education. *Social Work Today, 16*(2), 16. Retrieved from http://www.socialworktoday.com/archive/032216p16.shtml

Damon, W. (2008). *The path to purpose*. New York, NY: The Free Press.

Dees, G. (1998). Enterprising nonprofits. *Harvard Business Review, 76*(1), 54–67.

Delgado, M. (2004). *Social youth entrepreneurship: The potential for youth and community transformation*. Westport, Conn: Praeger.

Delgado, M., & Staples, L. (2008). *Youth-Led Community Organizing: Theory and Action*. New York: Oxford University Press.

Didienne, A. (March 3, 2016). Social enterprises: The fourth sector. *Triple Pundit: People, Planet, Profit*. Retrieved from www.triplepundit.com/2016/03/social-enterprises-fourth-sector

Dixon-Román, E., & Gordon, E. W. (2012). *Thinking Comprehensively About Education: Spaces of Educative Possibility and Their Implications for Public Policy*. New York: Routledge.

Dolan, T. (2015). Combining youth organizing and youth participatory action research to strengthen student voice in education reform. *Teachers College Record, 117*(13), 153–170.

Doumit, G. (2017). Social entrepreneurship in the Middle East: Old practice, new concept. *Stanford Innovation Review*. Retrieved from https://ssir.org/articles/entry/social_entrepreneurship_in_the_middle_east_old_practice_new_concept

Doverall, M. (2014). Three things public policy must do for social enterprise to thrive in 2023. *Social Enterprise World Forum*. Retrieved from https://tricofoundation.ca/three-things-public-policy-needs-to-do-for-social-enterprise-to-thrive-in-2023/

Durlak, J. A., Domitrovich, C. E., Weissberg, R. P., & Gullotta, T. P. (Eds.). (2015). *The Handbook of Social and Emotional Learning: Research and Practice*. New York: Guilford Press.

Durlak, J. A., Weissberg, R. P., & Pachan, M. (2010). A meta-analysis of afterschool programs that seek to promote personal and social skills in children and adolescents. *American Journal of Community Psychology, 45*, 294–309.

Dweck, C. (2006). *Mindset: the new psychology of success*. New York, NY: Ballantine Books.

Eccles, J., Barber, B., Stone, M., & Hunt, J. (2003). Extracurricular activities and adolescent development. *Journal of Social Issues, 59*(4), 865–889.

Eccles, J., & Gootman, J. (Eds.). (2002). *Community Programs to Promote Youth Development*. Washington, DC: National Academies Press.

Eccles, J. S., & Templeton, J. (2002). Extracurricular and other after-school activities for youth. *Review of Research in Education, 26*(1), 113–180. doi:10.3102/0091732X026001113

Economic Policy Institute. (May 27, 2015). *The Class of 2015: Despite a Rising Economy, Young Grads Still Face an Uphill Climb*. Retrieved from http://www.epi.org/publication/the-class-of-2015/

Edin, K., & Lein, L. (1997). *Making Ends Meet: How Single Mothers Survive Welfare and Low-Wage Work*. New York: Russell Sage Foundation.

Elert, N., Andersson, F., & Wennberg, K. (2015). The impact of entrepreneurship education in high school on long-term entrepreneurial performance. *Journal of Economic Behavior & Organization, 111*, 209–223.

Erbstein, N. (2013). Engaging underrepresented youth populations in community youth development: Tapping social capital as a critical resource. *New Directions for Youth Development, 2013*(138), 109–124. doi:10.1002/yd.20061

Evans, W. P., Sicafuse, L. L., Killian, E. S., Davidson, L. A., & Loesch-Griffin, D. (2009). Youth worker professional development participation, preferences, and agency support. *Child & Youth Services, 31*(1/2), 35–52. doi:10.1080/01459350903505579

Feldman, A., & Matjasko, J. (2005). The role of school-Based extracurricular activities in adolescent development: A comprehensive review and future directions. *Review of Educational Research, 75*(2), 159–210.

Field, A. (January 31, 2017). More evidence of impact investing growth—and what it means for social entrepreneurs. *Forbes*. Retrieved from https://www.forbes.com/sites/annefield/2017/01/31/more-evidence-impact-investing-growth-and-what-it-means-for-social-entrepeneurs/6d36641c7b7f

Fine, M. (2012). Youth participatory action research. In N. Lesko & S. Talburt (Eds.), *Keywords in Youth Studies: Tracing Affects, Movements, Knowledges* (pp. 333–348). NY: Taylor & Francis.

Fisher, S., Graham, M., & Compeau, M. (2008). Starting from scratch: Understanding the learning outcomes of undergraduate entrepreneurship education. In R. T. Harrison &

C. Leitch (Eds.), *Entrepreneurial Learning: Conceptual Frameworks and Applications* (pp. 321–356). New York: Routledge.

Fitzgerald, J. (1997). Linking school-to-work to community economic development in urban schools. *Urban Education*, 32, 489–511.

Flores, A. (2007). Examining disparities in mathematics education: Achievement gap or opportunity gap? *The High School Journal*, 91(1), 29–42.

Fox, M., Mediratta, K., Ruglis, J., Stoudt, B., Shah, S., & Fine, M. (2010). Critical youth engagement: Participatory action research and organizing. In L. Sherrod, J. Torney Puta, & C. Flanagan (Eds.), *Handbook of Research and Policy on Civic Engagement with Youth* (pp. 621–650). Wiley Press.

Frantz, G. (2014). Individual and collective trauma. *Psychological Perspectives*, 57(3), 243–245. doi:10.1080/00332925.2014.936214

Fredricks, J. A., Blumenfeld, P. C., & Paris, A. H. (2004). School engagement: Potential of the concept, state of the evidence. *Review of Educational Research*, 74, 59–109.

Freire, P. (1970). *Pedagogy of the Oppressed*. New York: The Continuum International Publishing Group.

Freire, P. (1973). *Education for Critical Consciousness*. New York: Seabury Press.

Freire P. (2005). The banking concept of education. In D. Bartholomae & A. Petrosky (Eds.), *Ways of Reading* (7th ed., pp. 255–267). New York: St. Martin's Press.

Fulbright-Anderson, K., & Auspos, P. (2006). *Community Change: theories, practice and evidence*. Queenstown, MD: Aspen Institute. Retrieved from https://assets.aspeninstitute.org/content/uploads/files/content/docs/rcc/COMMUNITYCHANGE-FINAL.PDF.

Gay, G. (2010). *Culturally Responsive Teaching* (2nd ed). New York: Teachers College Press.

Gelber, A., Isen, A., & Kessler, J. B. (2016). The effects of youth employment: Evidence from New York City lotteries. *The Quarterly Journal of Economics*, 131(1), 423–460.

Geldhof, G. J., Porter, T., Weiner, M. B, Malin, H., Bronk, K. C., Agans, J. P., . . . Lerner, R. M. (2012). Fostering youth entrepreneurship: Preliminary findings from the Young Entrepreneurs Study. *Journal of Research in Adolescence*, 24(3), 431–446. doi-org.ezproxy.macalester.edu/10.1111/jora.12086

Geldhof, G. J., Weiner, M., Agans, J. P., Mueller, M. K., & Lerner, R. M. (2014). Understanding entrepreneurial intent in late adolescence: The role of intentional self-regulation and innovation. *Journal of Youth and Adolescence*, 43(1), 81–91. doi: 10.1007/s10964- 013-9930-8.

Gibb, A. (2002), In pursuit of a new 'enterprise' and 'entrepreneurship' paradigm for learning: creative destruction, new values, new ways of doing things and new combinations of knowledge. *International Journal of Management Reviews*, 4, 233–269. doi:10.1111/1468-2370.00086

Gibbs, B. G., Erickson, L. D., Dufur, M. J., & Miles, A. (2015). Extracurricular associations and college enrollment. *Social Science Research*, 50, 367–381. doi:10.1016/j.ssresearch.2014.08.013

Ginwright, S. (2010). *Black Youth Rising: Activism and Radical Healing in Urban America*. New York: Teachers College Press.

Ginwright, S. (2011). Hope, healing and care: Pushing the boundaries of civic engagement for African-American youth. *Liberal Education*, 97(2), 34–39.

Ginwright, S. (2016). *Hope and Healing in Urban Education: How Urban Activists and Teachers Are Reclaiming Matters of the Heart*. New York: Routledge.

Ginwright, S., & Cammarota, J. (2007). Youth activism in the urban community: Learning critical civic praxis within community organizations. *International Journal of Qualitative Studies in Education,* (20) 693–710. doi: 10.1080/09518390701630833

Ginwright, S., & Kirshner, B. (2012). Youth organizing as a developmental context for African American and Latino adolescents. *Child Development Perspectives, 6*(3), 288–294. doi.org/10.1111/j.1750-8606.2012.00243.x

Giroux, H. (2010). *Youth in a Suspect Society: Democracy or Disposability?* Basingstoke, Hampshire, England: Palgrave Macmillan.

Giroux, H. A. (2013). *America's Education Deficit and the War on Youth.* New York: Monthly Review Press.

Green, G. P., & Haines, A. (2015). *Asset Building and Community Development.* Thousand Oaks, CA: Sage.

Green, R. K., & White, M. J. (1997). Measuring the benefits of homeowning: Effects on children. *Journal of Urban Economics, 41,* 441–461.

Guthrie, K. L., Bertrand Jones, T., Osteen, L., & Hu, S. (2013). *Cultivating Leader Identity and Capacity in Students from Diverse Backgrounds: ASHE Higher Education Report, 39:4.* San Francisco, CA: Jossey-Bass.

Halpern, D. (2005). *Social Capital.* Boston, MA: Polity Press.

Hamilton, S. F., Hamilton, M. A., & Pittman, K. (2004). Principles for youth development. In S. F. Hamilton & M. A. Hamilton (Eds.), *The Youth Development Handbook: Coming of Age in American Communities* (pp. 3–22). Thousand Oaks: Sage Publications, Inc.

Hamilton, S. F., & Hamilton, M. A. (Eds.). (2004). *The Youth Development Handbook: Coming of Age in American Communities.* Thousand Oaks, CA: Sage Publications.

Hammersley, M. (2016). Glossing inadequacies: Problems with definitions of key concepts in some methodology texts. *International Journal Of Social Research Methodology, 19*(6), 731–737.

Hardaway, C. R., & McLoyd, V. C. (2009). Escaping poverty and securing middle class status: How race and socioeconomic status shape mobility prospects for African Americans during the transition to adulthood. *Journal of Youth & Adolescence, 38,* 242. doi:10.1007/s10964-008-9354-z

Harpine, E. C. (2013). *After-School Prevention Programs for At-Risk Students: Promoting Engagement and Academic Success.* New York: Springer.

Hartman, E. (2016). Decentering self in leadership: Putting community at the center in leadership studies. *New Directions for Student Leadership, 2016*(150), 73–83. doi:10.1002/yd.20172

Heck, K. E., & Subramaniam, A. (2009). Youth development frameworks (University of California 4-H Center for Youth Development Monograph). Davis: University of California.

Hecht, B. (January 10, 2013). Collaboration is the new competition. *Harvard Business Review.* Retrieved from https://hbr.org/2013/01/collaboration-is-the-new-compe

Heckman, J., & Borjas, G. (1980). Does unemployment cause future unemployment? Definitions, questions and answers from a continuous time model of heterogeneity and state dependence. *Economica, 47*(187), 247–283. doi:10.2307/2553150

Hess, F. (Ed.). (2006). *Educational Entrepreneurship: Realities, Challenges, Possibilities.* Cambridge, MA: Harvard Education Press.

Hines, F. (2005). Viable social enterprise: An evaluation of business support to social enterprises. *Social Enterprise Journal, 1*(1), 13–28. https://doi.org/10.1108/17508610580000704

Hutchins, E. (1995). *Cognition in the wild.* MIT Press: Cambridge, MA.

Hughes, K. L., Bailey, T. R., & Mechur, M. J. (2001). *School-to-Work: Making a Difference in Education. A Research Report to America.* New York: Institute on Education and the Economy (IEE), Teachers College, Columbia University. Retrieved from http://www.tc.columbia.edu/iee/PAPERS/Stw.pdf

International Labour Organization. (2015). KILM 8: Employment in the informal economy. Retrieved from http://www.ilo.org/wcmsp5/groups/public/---dgreports/---stat/documents/publication/wcms_422437.pdf

Irby, M., Ferber, T., & Pittman, K. (2001). *Youth Action: Youth Contributing to Communities, Communities Supporting Youth.* Washington, DC: The Forum for Youth Investment, Impact Strategies, Inc.

Janzer, C., & Weinstein, L. (2014). Social design and neocolonialism. *Design and Culture, 6*(3), 327–343. doi:10.2752/175613114X14105155617429

Johansen, V., & Schanke, T. (2013). Entrepreneurship education in secondary education and training. *Scandinavian Journal of Educational Research, 57*(4), 357–368. doi:10.1080/00313831.2012.656280

Johansson-Sköldberg, U., Woodilla, J., & Çetinkaya, M. (2013). Design thinking: Past, present and possible futures. *Creativity & Innovation Management, 22*(2), 121–146. doi:10.1111/caim.12023

Jones, T. B., Guthrie, K. L., & Osteen, L. (2016). Critical domains of culturally relevant leadership learning: A call to transform leadership programs. *New Directions for Student Leadership, 2016*(152), 9–21. doi:10.1002/yd.20205

Jumpstart Coalition for Personal Financial Literacy. (2015). *National standards in K-12 personal finance education.* Retrieved from www.jumpstart.org/what-we-do/support-financial-education/standards/.

Junior Achievement Scope & Sequence: High school programs. (2017). Retrieved from https://www.juniorachievement.org/documents/20009/63782/JA+Scope+and+Sequence+High.pdf

Kahne, J., & Westheimer, J. (2003). Teaching democracy: What schools need to do. *Phi Delta Kappan, 85*(1), 34–66.

Kania, J., & Kramer, M. (Winter, 2011). Collective impact. *Stanford Social Innovation Review, 9*(1), 36–41. ssir.org/articles/entry/collective_impact

Kash, K. M. (2009). School-to-work programs effectiveness. *Online Journal of Workforce Education and Development, III*(4),1–9.

Katre, A., & Salipante, P. (2012). Start-up social ventures: Blending fine-grained behaviors from two institutions for entrepreneurial success. *Entrepreneurship: Theory & Practice, 36*(5), 967–994. doi:10.1111/j.1540-6520.2012.00536.x

Kauffman Center for Entrepreneurial Leadership Staff. (2001). *The Growth and Advancement of Entrepreneurship in Higher Education: An Environmental Scan of College Initiatives.* Kansas City, MO: Ewing Marion Kauffman Foundation.

Kayser, O., & Budinich, V. (2015). *Scaling Up Business Solutions to Social Problems: A Practical Guide for Social and Corporate Entrepreneurs.* Basingstoke, Hampshire, England: Palgrave Macmillan.

Kearns, L. (2013). The construction of "illiterate" and "literate" youth: The effects of high-stakes standardized literacy testing. *Race, Ethnicity & Education, 1*, 121–140. Retrieved from http://dx.doi.org/10.1080/13613324.2013.843520

Keen, M. (June 8, 2015). Why we need to rethink the informal economy. *World Economic Forum* website. Retrieved from https://www.weforum.org/agenda/2015/06/why-we-need-to-rethink-the-informal-economy

Kellner, D., & Share, J. (2005). Toward critical media literacy: Core concepts, debates, organizations, and policy. *Discourse: Studies in the Cultural Politics of Education, 26*(3), 369–386. doi: 10.1080/01596300500200169

Kerka, S. (2003). Community asset mapping: trends and issues alert 47. *Trends and Issues Alert*. Ohio: The Ohio State University.

Kirshner, B. (2007). Introduction: Youth activism as a context for learning and development. *American Behavioral Scientist, 51*(3), 367–379. doi:10.1177/0002764207306065

Ko, S. J., Brymer M. J., Layne C. M., Ford J. D., Kassam-Adams N., Berkowitz S. J., . . . Wong M. (2008). Creating trauma-informed systems: Child welfare, education, first responders, health care, juvenile justice. *Professional Psychology: Research and Practice, 39*(4), 396–404. doi:10.1037/0735-7028.39.4.396

Komives, S. R., Dugan, J., Owen, J., Slack, C., & Wagner, W. (2011). *The Handbook for Student Leadership Development, 2nd ed*. Indianapolis, IN: Jossey-Bass.

Komives, S. R., & Guthrie, K. L. (2015). Series editors' notes. *New Directions for Student Leadership, 2015*(145), 1–3. doi:10.1002/yd.20118

Kourilsky, M. L., & Walstad, W. B. (2007). *The Entrepreneur in Youth: An Untapped Resource for Economic Growth, Social Entrepreneurship, and Education*. Northampton, MA: Edward Elgar Press.

Krathwohl, D. R. (1993). *Methods of Educational and Social Science Research: An Integrated Approach*. New York: Longman.

Kretzmann, J. P., & McKnight, J. L. (1993). *Building Communities from the Inside Out: A Path Toward Finding and Mobilizing a Community's Assets*. Chicago, IL: ACTA Publications.

Krueger N. F. (2003). The Cognitive psychology of entrepreneurship. In Z. J. Acs & D. B. Audretsch (Eds.), Handbook of Entrepreneurship Research. *International Handbook Series on Entrepreneurship*, vol. 1. Springer, Boston, MA.

Kruse, T. P., Marcus, P., & Kim, J. (November 2014). *More Than a Job: Youth Social Entrepreneurship*. Presented at the National Association of Multicultural Education annual conference, Tucson, AZ.

Lackéus, M. (2015). *Entrepreneurship in Education: What, Why, When, How*. Organisation for Economic Co-operation and Development. Retrieved from www.oecd.org/cfe/leed/BGP_Entrepreneurship-in-Education.pdf

Lackéus, M., & Williams-Middleton, K. (2014). Venture creation programs: Bridging entrepreneurship education and technology transfer. *Education and Training, 56*(7). doi:10.1108/ET-02-2013-0013

Ladson-Billings, G. (1994). *The Dreamkeepers: Successful Teachers of African American Children*. San Francisco, CA: Jossey-Bass Publishing.

Ladson-Billings, G. (1995). Toward a theory of culturally relevant pedagogy. *American Research Journal, 32*(3), 465–491.

Lahey, J. (January 4, 2017). How design thinking became a buzzword at school. *The Atlantic*. Retrieved from: https://www.theatlantic.com/education/archive/2017/01/how-design-thinking-became-a-buzzword-at-school/512150/

Langford, B., & Badeau, S. H. (2015). Investing to improve the wellbeing of vulnerable youth and young adults: Recommendations for policy and practice.Youth Transition Funders Group website. Retrieved from http://www.ytfg.org

Laprade, M., & Auspos, P. (2006). Increasing a neighborhood's residential environment: pathways to physical and social change. In K. Fulbright-Anderson & P. Auspos (Eds.), *Community Change: theories, practice and evidence.* Queenstown, MD: Aspen Institute.

Larsen, L., Harlan, S., Bolin, B., Hackett, E., Hope, D., Kirby, A., & Wolf, S. (2004). Bonding and bridging: Understanding the relationship between social capital and civic action. *Journal of Planning Education and Research, 24*(1), 64–77. doi: 10.1177/0739456X04267181

Larson, R. (2000). Toward a psychology of positive youth development. *American Psychologist, 55*(1), 170–183. doi: 10.1037//0003-066X,55.1.170

Larson, R. W., Walker, K. C., Rusk, N., & Diaz, L. B. (2015). Understanding youth development from the practitioner's point of view: A call for research on effective practice. *Applied Developmental Science, 19*(2), 74–86. doi:10.1080/10888691.2014.972558

Lerner, J. V., Phelps, E., Forman, Y., & Bowers, E. P. (2009). Positive youth development. In R. M. Lerner & L. Steinberg (Eds.), *Handbook of Adolescent Psychology: Vol. 1. Individual Bases of Adolescent Development* (3rd ed., pp. 524–558). Hoboken, NJ: John Wiley.

Lerner, R., & Overton, W. (2008). Exemplifying the integrations of the relational developmental system: Synthesizing theory, research, and application to promote positive development and social justice. *Journal of Adolescent Research, 23*(3), 245–255. doi: 10.1177/0743558408314385

Lerner, R. M. (2007). *The Good Teen: Rescuing Adolescence from the Myth of Storm and Stress.* New York, NY: Random House.

Lerner, R. M., Johnson, S. K., & Buckingham, M. H. (2015). Relational developmental systems-based theories and the study of children and families: Lerner and Spanier (1978) revisited. *Journal of Family Theory, 7*, 83–104. doi:10.1111/jftr.12067

Lerner, R. M., Lerner, J. V., Almerigi, J., Theokas, C., Phelps, E., Gestsdottir, S. (2005). Positive youth development, participation in community youth development programs, and community contributions of fifth grade adolescents: Findings from the first wave of the 4-H Study of Positive Youth Development. *Journal of Early Adolescence, 25*(1), 17–71. doi: 10.1177/0272431604272461

Lerner, R. M., Lerner, J. V., Lewin-Bizan, S., Bowers, E. P., Boyd, M., Mueller, M., Schmid, K. L., & Napolitano, C. M. (2011). Positive youth development: Processes, programs, and problematics. *Journal of Youth Development, 6*(3), 40–64.

Lesko, N., & Talburt, S. (Eds.). (2012). *Keywords in Youth Studies: Tracing Affects, Movements, Knowledges.* New York: Taylor & Francis.

Leventhal, T., & Brooks-Gunn, J. (2000). The neighborhoods they live in: The effects of neighborhood residence on child and adolescent outcomes. *Psychological Bulletin, 126*(2), 309–337. http://dx.doi.org/10.1037/0033-2909.126.2.309

Light, P. (2011). *Driving Social Change: How to Solve the World's Toughest Problems.* Hoboken, NJ: John Wiley & Sons.

Limón, M. (2001). On the cognitive conflict as an instructional strategy for conceptual change: A critical appraisal. *Learning and Instruction, 11*(4), 357–380.

Lin, N. (2002). *Social Capital: A Theory of Social Structure and Action.* Cambridge, UK: Cambridge University Press.

Lin, N., Cook, K., & Burt, R. S. (Eds.). (2008). *Social Capital: Theory & Research.* New Brunswick, NJ: Transaction Publishers.

Lindau, S., Vickery, K., Choi, H., Makelarski, J., Matthews, A., & Davis, M. (2016). A community-Powered, asset-Based approach to intersectoral urban health system planning in chicago. *American Journal of Public Health, 106*(10), 1872–1878. doi:10.2105/AJPH.2016.303302

Little, T., Walls, T., & Malmberg, L. E. (2009). Agency. In S. J. Lopez (Ed.), *The Encyclopedia of Positive Psychology.* Chichester, England: Wiley-Blackwell Publishers.

Loke, V., Watts, J. L., & Kakoti, S. (2013). Financial capabilities of service providers in the asset-building field. In J. Birkenmaier, J. Curley, & M. Sherraden (Eds.), *Financial Education and Capability: Research, Education, Policy, and Practice* (pp. 298–322). New York: Oxford University Press.

Luter, D. G., Mitchell, A. M., & Taylor, H. L. (2017). Critical consciousness and schooling: the impact of the community as a classroom program on academic indicators. *Education Sciences, 7*(1), 25; https://doi.org/10.3390/educsci7010025

Mahoney, J., & Cairns, R. (1997). Do extracurricular activities protect against early school dropout? *Developmental Psychology, 33*(2), 241–253.

Magaiza, G., & Crause, E. (2014). Social businesses as a tool and approach for youth development in sub-Saharan Africa. *South African Journal of Social Work and Social Development, 26*(1), 42–54.

Mandel, L., & Qazilbash, J. (2005). Youth voices as change agents: Moving beyond the medical model in school-based health center practice. *The Journal of School Health, 75*(7), 239–242.

Maran, M. (2003). *Changing Lives, Changing Times: The First Decade of Juma Ventures.* Retrieved from http://www.surdna.org/images/stories/content_img/docs/pubs/juma_ventures_changing_lives_changing_times.pdf

Martin, J. (2011). Impact of *Assets and the Poor* grows 20 years after its release. *The Source.* Retrieved from source.wustl.edu/2011/12/impact-of-assets-and-the-poor-grows-20-years-after-its-release/

Martin, R. L., & Osberg, S. (Spring 2007). Social entrepreneurship: The case for definition. *Stanford Social Innovation Review. 5*(28), 29–39. ssir.org/articles/entry/social_entrepreneurship_the_case_for_definition

Maslow, A. H. (1954). *Motivation and Personality.* New York: Harper.

Maslow, A. H. (1968). *Toward a Psychology of Being* (2nd ed). New York: D. Van Nostrand Company.

Mathie, A., & Cunningham, G. (2003). From Clients to Citizens: Asset-Based Community Development as a Strategy For Community-Driven Development. *Development in Practice, 13*(5), 474–486.

Mayer, J. D., Salovey, P., & Caruso, D. R. (2008). Emotional intelligence: New ability or eclectic traits? *American Psychologist, 63*(6), 503–517. doi:10.1037/0003-055x.63.6.503

McArthur, J. C., Betts, W. D., Bregón, N. R., Chamberlain, F. M., Katsos, G. E., Kelly, M. C., & Stockton, P. N. (2015). Interorganizational cooperation. *JFQ: Joint Force Quarterly*, *4*(79), 106–112.

McCauley, F. (March 15, 2016). The pivot to yes: Positive youth development and our agricultural program in Liberia. *Making Cents International blog*. Retrieved from http://www.makingcents.com/single-post/2016/03/15/The-Pivot-to-Yes-Positive-Youth-Development-and-Our-Agriculture-Program-in-Liberia

McClelland, D. C. (1961). *The Achieving Society*. Princeton, NJ: Van Nostrand.

McCoy, S. (May 8, 2017). Youthprise visits Cycles for Change. *Youthprise.org*. Retrieved from https://youthprise.org/blog/youthprise-visits-cycles-for-change/

McEwen, C., & McEwen, B. (2017). Social structure, adversity, toxic stress, and intergenerational poverty: An early childhood model. *Annual Review of Sociology*, *43*(1), 445–472. doi:10.1146/annurev-soc-060116-053252

McKernan, S. M., & Ratcliffe, D. (2009). Asset building for today's stability and tomorrow's security. *New England Community Development*. Federal Reserve Bank of Boston, Issue 2.

Moberg, K., Stenberg, E., & Vestergaard, L. (2012). *Impact of entrepreneurship education in Denmark—2012*. Odense, Denmark: The Danish Foundation for Entrepreneurship—Young Enterprise.

Modecki, K. L., Zimmer-Gembeck, M. J., & Guerra, N. (2017). Emotion regulation, coping, and decision making: Three linked skills for preventing externalizing problems in adolescence. *Child Development*, *88*, 417–426. doi:10.1111/cdev.12734

Moll, L., Amanti, C., Neff, D., & Gonzalez, N. (1992). Funds of knowledge for teaching: Using a qualitative approach to connect homes and classrooms. *Theory Into Practice*, *31*(2), 132–141.

Morris, A. S., Criss, M. M., Silk, J. S., & Houltberg, B. J. (2017). The impact of parenting on emotion regulation during childhood and adolescence. *Child Development Perspectives*. doi:10.1111/cdep.12238

Mroz, T., & Savage, T. (2006). The long-term effects of youth unemployment. *Human Resources*, *XLI*(2), 259–293. doi: 10.3368/jhr.XLI.2.259J

Murphy, R., & Sachs, D. (May 2, 2013). The rise of social entrepreneurship suggests a possible future for global capitalism. *Forbes*. Retrieved from https://www.forbes.com/sites/skollworldforum/2013/05/02/the-rise-of-social-entrepreneurship-suggests-a-possible-future-for-global-capitalism/2aece567348c

Mycoskie, B. (2012). *Start Something that Matters*. New York, NY: Spiegel & Grau.

Nasir, N., & Kirshner, B. (2003). The cultural construction of moral and civic identities. *Applied Developmental Science*, *7*, 138–147.

Nichols, S., & Berliner, D. (2007). *Collateral Damage: How High-Stakes Testing Corrupts America's Schools*. Boston, MA: Harvard Education Press.

Noguera, P., Ginwright, S., & Cammarota, J. (2006). *Beyond Resistance! Youth Activism and Community Change: New Democratic Possibilities for Practice and Policy for America's Youth*. New York: Routledge.

Obschonka, M., Silbereisen, R. K., & Schmitt-Rodermund, E. (2011). Successful entrepreneurship as developmental outcome: A path model from a lifespan perspective of human development. *European Psychologist*, *16*(3), 174–186. doi:/10.1027/1016-9040/a000075

O'Connell, M. E., Boat T., & Warner K. E. (Eds.). (2009). *Preventing Mental, Emotional, and Behavioral Disorders Among Young People: Progress and Possibilities*. Washington, DC: National Academies Press.

Ostrom, E. (2009). Collective action theory. In C. Boix, & S. Stokes (Eds.), *The Oxford Handbook of Comparative Politics*. Oxford, England: Oxford University Press. doi: 10.1093/oxfordhb/9780199566020.003.0008

Osgerby, B. (2004). *Youth Media*. London: Routeledge.

Otto, A. (2013). Saving in childhood and adolescence: Insights from developmental psychology. *Economics of Education Review, 33*, 8–18. doi: 10.1016/j.econedurev.2012.09.005

Overton, W. F. (2015). Process and relational developmental systems. In W. F. Overton & P. C. Molenaar (Eds.), *Theory and Method: Vol. 1. Handbook of Child Psychology and Developmental Science* (7th ed., pp. 9–62). Hoboken, NJ: Wiley.

Ozer, E. (2017). Youth-led participatory action research: Overview and potential for enhancing adolescent development. *Child Development Perspectives, 11*(3), 173–177. doi. org/10.1111/cdep.12228

Parsa, H. G., Self, J. T., Njite, D., & King, T. (2005). Why restaurants fail. *Management, 46*(3), 304–322. doi: 10.1177/0010880405275598

Perrini, F., & Vurro, C., & Costanzo, L. (2010). A process-based view of social entrepreneurship: from opportunity identification to scaling-up social change in the case of San Patrignano. *Entrepreneurship & Regional Development, 22*, 515–534. doi:10.1080/08985626.2010.488402.

Pinderhughes, H., Davis, R., & Williams, M. (2015). *Adverse Community Experiences and Resilience: A Framework for Addressing and Preventing Community Trauma*. Oakland, CA: Prevention Institute.

Pittaway, L., & Cope, J. (2007). Entrepreneurship education. *International Small Business Journal, 25*(5), 479–510. doi:10.1177/0266242607080656

Pittman, K. (1999). The Power of Engagement. *The Forum for Youth Investment*. Retrieved from http://forumfyi.org/content/youth-today-power-enga

Pittman, K., Irby, M., Tolman, J., Yohalem, N., & Ferber, T. (2003). Preventing problems, promoting development, encouraging engagement. *The Forum for Youth Investment*. Retrieved from http://citeseerx.ist.psu.edu/viewdoc/download?doi=10.1.1.471.1224&rep=rep1&type=pdf

Pittman, K. (March 29, 2016). Getting to readiness, by design. *The Forum for Youth Investment*. Retrieved from http://sparkaction.org/content/getting-readiness-design

Plumly, L. W., Marshall, L. L., Eastman, J., Iyer, R., Stanley, K. L., & Boatwright, J. (2008). Developing entrepreneurial competencies: A student business. *Journal of Entrepreneurship Education, 11*, 17–28.

Pokrasso, R. S. (January 5, 2016). Nonprofit vs. for-profit: Which is better for social entrepreneurs? *Conscious Company Media*. Retrieved from https://consciouscompanymedia.com/social-entrepreneurship/nonprofit-vs-for-profit-which-is-better-for-social-entrepreneurs/

Portes, A. (2000). The two meanings of social capital. *Sociological Forum, 15*, 1–12.

Pritchard, M. E., Myers, B. K., & Cassidy, D. J. (1989). Factors associated with adolescent saving and spending patterns. *Adolescence, 4*(95), 711–723.

Pugh, K. J., & Phillips, M. (2011). Helping students develop an appreciation for school content. *Theory Into Practice, 50*(4), 285–292. doi: 10.1080/00405841.2011.60738

Putnam, R. (1995). "Bowling alone: America's declining social capital." *Journal of Democracy*, 65–78.

Putnam, R. (2000). *Bowling Alone: The Collapse and Revival of American Community*. New York: Simon & Schuster.

Reeves, R. (2017). *Dream Hoarders: How the American Upper Middle Class Is Leaving Everyone Else in the Dust, Why that Is a Problem, and What to Do About It*. Washington, DC: Brookings Institution Press.

Ravitch, D. (2010). *The Death and Life of the Great American School System: How Testing and Choice Are Undermining Education*. New York: Basic Books.

REDFWorkshops. (2017). Allocating social costs in different organizational structures. *Roberts Enterprise Development Fund*. Retrieved from redfworkshop.org/learn/organizational-structures

Reiss, F. (2013). Socioeconomic inequalities and mental health problems in children and adolescents: A systematic review. *Social Science & Medicine*, 90, 24–31. https://doi.org/10.1016/j.socscimed.2013.04.026

Rosen, M. L., Sheridan, M. A., & Sambrook, K. A. (2017). Salience network response to changes in emotional expressions of others is heightened during early adolescence: Relevance for social functioning. *Developmental Science*. doi:10.1111/desc.12571

Roth, J. L., & Brooks-Gunn, J. (2003). What exactly is a youth development program? Answers from research and practice. *Applied Developmental Science*, 7, 94–111. http://dx.doi.org/10.1207/S1532480XADS0702_6

Rumberger, R. (2011). *Dropping Out: Why Students Drop Out of High School and What Can Be Done About It*. Cambridge, MA: Harvard University Press.

Ruvalcaba, N. A., Gallegos, J., Borges, A., & Gonzalez, N. (2017). Extracurricular activities and group belonging as a protective factor in adolescence. *Psicologia Educativa*, 23(1), 45–51. doi:10.1016/j.pse.2016.09.001

Substance Abuse and Mental Health Services Administration (SAMSHA). (2014). *Trauma-informed approach and trauma-specific interactions*. Retrieved from: www.samhsa.gov/nctic/trauma-interventions.

Sabeti, H. (2011). The for-benefit enterprise. *Harvard Business Review*, 89(11), 98–104.

The Saguaro Seminar: Civic Engagement in America. (2012). Harvard Kennedy School of Government website. Retrieved from https://sites.hks.harvard.edu/saguaro/

Sakamoto, I. (2007). An anti-oppressive approach to cultural competence. *Canadian Social Work Review/Revue Canadienne De Service Social*, 24(1), 105–114.

Salasuo, M., & Hoikkala, T. (2012). Culture. In N. Lesko & S. Talburt (Eds.), *Keywords in Youth Studies: Tracing Affects, Movements, Knowledges* (pp. 247–252). New York: Taylor & Francis.

Salkind, N. J. (2008). *Encyclopedia of Educational Psychology*. Thousand Oaks, California: Sage.

Salkowitz, R. (2010). *Young World Rising: How Youth, Technology and Entrepreneurship are Changing the World from the Bottom Up*. Hoboken, NJ: John Wiley & Sons.

Salovey, P., & Mayer, J. D. (1990). Emotional intelligence. *Imagination, Cognition, and Personality*, 9, 185–211. doi:0.2190/DUGG-P24E-52WK-6CDG

Santiago, C. D., Wadsworth, M. E., & Stump, J. (2011). Socioeconomic status, neighborhood disadvantage, and poverty-related stress: Prospective effects on psychological syndromes among diverse low-income families. *Journal of Economic Psychology, 32*, 218–230. https://doi.org/10.1016/j.joep.2009.10.008

Scales, P. C. (2014). Developmental assets and the promotion of well-being in middle childhood. In A. Ben-Arieh, F. Casas, I. Frones, & J. E. Korbin (Eds.), *Handbook of Child Well-Being. Theories, Methods and Policies in Global Perspective* (pp. 1649–1678). Dordrecht, Netherlands: Springer.

Scales, P. C., Benson, P. L., & Roehlkepartain, E. C. (2011). Adolescent thriving: The role of sparks, relationships, and empowerment. *Journal of Youth and Adolescence, 40*, 263–277.

Scarpetta, S., Sonnet, A., & Manfredi, T. (2010). Rising youth unemployment during the crisis: How to prevent negative long-term consequences on a generation? *OECD Social, Employment and Migration Working Papers*, No. 106. OECD Publishing, Paris. http://dx.doi.org/10.1787/5kmh79zb2mmv-en

Schaefer, D. R., Simpkins, S. D., Vest, A. E., & Price, C. D. (2011). The contribution of extracurricular activities to adolescent friendships: New insights through social network analysis. *Developmental Psychology, 47*(4), 1141–1152. doi:10.1037/a002409

Schuck, A., & Rosenbaum, D. (2006). Promoting safe and healthy neighborhoods: What the research tells us. In K. Fulbright-Anderson & P. Auspos (Eds.), *Community Change: Theories, Practice, and Evidence* (pp. 61–140). Washington, DC: The Aspen Institute.

Search Institute. (n.d.). *40 Developmental Assets for Adolescents*. Retrieved from http://www.search-institute.org/content/40-developmental-assets-adolescents-ages-12-18

Seligman, M., & Csikszentmihalyi, M. (2000). Positive Psychology: An Introduction. *The American Psychologist, 55*, 5–14. doi:10.1037/0003-066X.55.1.5

Sesma, A., Mannes, M., & Scales, P. (2013). Positive adaptation, resilience and the developmental assets framework. In S. Goldsten & R. B. Brooks (Eds.), *Handbook of Resilience in Children* (pp. 427–442). Boston, MA: Springer. doi:10.1007/978-1-4614-3661-4_25.

Sharma, S., & Patil, K. (2017). Past, present and future of collaborative design: From user centric to user driven design. In A. Chakrabarti & D. Chakrabarti (Eds.), *Research into Design for Communities: Vol. 1. Proceedings of iCoRD 2017* (pp. 1025–1036). Singapore: Springer. doi:10.1007/978-981-10-3518-0_87

Shelton, C. (2011). Helping first-generation college students succeed. *Journal of Psychological Issues in Organizational Culture, 1*(4), 63–75. doi:10.1002/jpoc.20041

Sherraden, M. (1991). *Assets and the Poor: A New American Welfare Policy*. Armonk, NY: M. E. Sharpe.

Sherraden, M. (1992). *Assets & the Poor*. New York: Routledge.

Sherraden, M. (2001). Assets and the Poor: Implications for Individual Accounts and Social Security. Invited Testimony to the President's Commission on Social Security, Washington, DC. Retrieved from http://govinfo.library.unt.edu/csss/meetings/Sherraden_Testimony

Shoemaker, S. (2014). The "Y" in YSE: Six interviews with YSE youth. Report to the Chuck Green Fellowship committee, Macalester College, St. Paul, MN.

Shostak, S., & Guscott, N. (2016). Grounded in the neighborhood, grounded in community: Social capital and health in community gardens. In S. Shostak (Ed.), *Food Systems and Health Advances in Medical Sociology* (pp.199–222). Bingley, UK: Emerald Publishing.

Silverman, S. K. (2011). Cultural Deficit Perspective. In S. Goldstein& J. A. Naglieri (Eds.), *Encyclopedia of Child Behavior and Development.* Springer, Boston, MA.

Siegel, D. (2013). *Brainstorm: the power and purpose of the teenage brain.* New York, NY: Tarcherperigee.

Slaten, C., Rivera, R., Shemwell, D., & Elison, Z. (2016). Fulfilling their dreams: Marginalized urban youths' perspectives on a culturally sensitive social and emotional learning program. *Journal of Education for Students Placed at Risk (jespar),* 21(2), 129–142. doi:10.1080/10824669.2015.1134331

Smilor, R. W. (1997). Entrepreneurship: Reflections on a subversive activity. *Journal of Business Venturing,* 12(5), 341–346.

Stairs, A. J., Donnell, K. A., & Dunn, A. H. (2012). *Urban teaching in America: Theory, research, and practice in K-12 classrooms.* SAGE Publications Inc. doi:10.4135/9781452244013

Stanton-Salazar, R. D. (2011). A social capital framework for the study of institutional agents and their role in the empowerment of low-status students and youth. *Youth and Society,* 43, 1066–1109.

Steele, W., & Malchiodi, C. (2015). *Trauma-Informed Practices with Children and Adolescents.* New York: Routledge.

Stronks, K., van de Mheen, H., van de Bos, J., & Mackenbach, J. (1997). The interrelationship between income, health, and employment status. *International Journal of Epidemiology,* 26(3), 592–600.

Stull, W. J., & Sanders, N. M. (2003). *The School-to-Work Movement: Origins and Destinations.* Westport, CT: Greenwood Publishing Group.

Substance Abuse and Mental Health Services Administration. (2014). *SAMHSA's Concept of Trauma and Guidance for a Trauma-Informed Approach.* HHS Publication No. (SMA) 14-4884. Rockville, MD: Author.

Summer Youth Labor Force News Release. (2017). Employment and unemployment among youth—summer 2016. *Bureau of Labor Statistics.* Retrieved from https://www.bls.gov/news.release/archives/youth_08172016.htm

Surowidjojo, A. (2015). What is restorative justice? *Reclaiming Futures.* October 26, 2015. Retrieved from reclaimingfutures.org/blog/2015/10/26/watch-this-webinar-what-is-restorative-justice/

Swaringen, N. (2017). Two interconnecting puzzle pieces: Trauma-informed practice and restorative justice. *Youth Today.* Retrieved from https://youthtoday.org/2017/05/the-time-is-right-for-collaboration-between-trauma-informed-education-and-restorative-justice/

Talburt, S., & Lesko, N. (2012). A history of the present of youth studies. In N. Lesko, & S. Talburt (Eds.), *Keywords in Youth Studies: Tracing Affects, Movements, Knowledges* (pp. 1–15). New York: Taylor & Francis.

Tate, W. (2009). *The Search for Leadership: An Organisational Perspective.* Devon, UK: Triarchy Press.

Temkin, K., & Rohe, W. (1998). Social capital and neighborhood stability: An empirical investigation. *Housing Policy Debate,* 9(1) 61–88.

Tompkins-Bergh, C., & Miller, A. (2015). *Entrepreneurship Education and Training: What Works?* Kansas City, MO: Ewing Marion Kauffman Foundation.

Tuck, E. (2009). Suspending damage: An open letter to communities. *Harvard Educational Review, 79*(3), 409–427.

University of Calgary. (Winter 2012). *Intervention to Address Intergenerational Trauma and Aboriginal Youth.* Retrieved from www.ucalgary.ca/wethurston/files/wethurston/Report_InterventionToAddressIntergenerationalTrauma.pdf.

Underwood, M., Satterthwait, L., & Bartlett, H. (2010). Reflexivity and minimization of the impact of age-cohort differences between researcher and research participants. *Qualitative Health Research, 20*(11), 1585–1595. doi: 10.1177/1049732310371102

Unreasonable Institute. (August 13, 2013). From dope dealer to hope dealer: One man's quest to reimagine education. Retrieved from https://unreasonable.is/from-dope-dealer-to-hope-dealer.

U.S. Department of Labor. (June 2016). *Workforce Innovation and Opportunity Act (WIOA): Overview.* Retrieved from https://www.doleta.gov/WIOA/Overview.cfm.

US News & World Report. (2016). Best grad schools rankings. Retrieved from http://grad-schools.usnews.rankingsandreviews.com/best-graduate-schools/top-health-schools/social-work-rankings

Vanevenhoven, J. (2013). Advances and challenges in entrepreneurship education. *Journal of Small Business Management, 51*(3), 466–470. doi:10.1111/jsbm.12043

Vanevenhoven, J., & Liguori, E. (2013). The impact of entrepreneurship education: Introducing the entrepreneurship education project. *Journal of Small Business Management, 51*(3), 315–328. doi:10.1111/jsbm.12026

Valentine, G., Skelton, T., & Chambers, D. (1998). Cool places: an introduction to youth and youth cultures. In T. Skelton & G. Valentine (Eds.), *Cool Places: Geographies of Youth Cultures.* London: Routledge.

Valencia, R. R. (1997). *The Evolution of Deficit Thinking: Educational thought and practice.* Ney York, NY: Routledge Psychology press.

Vechakul, J., Shrimali, B., & Sandhu, J. (2015). Human-centered design as an approach for place-based innovation in public health: A case study from Oakland, California. *Maternal & Child Health Journal, 19*(12), 2552–2559. doi:10.1007/s10995-015-1787-x

Volk, D., & Long, S. (2005). Challenging myths of the deficit perspective: Honoring children's literacy resources. *Young Children, 60*(6), 12–19.

Wagner, W., & Mathison, P. (2015). Connecting to communities: Powerful pedagogies for leading for social change. *New Directions for Student Leadership, 2015*(145), 85–96. doi:10.1002/yd.20126

Wallace, S. L. (1999). Social entrepreneurship: The role of social purpose enterprises in facilitating community economic development. *Journal of Developmental Entrepreneurship, 4*(2), 153–174.

Wallsjasper, J. (December 8, 2014). Sisterhood is powerful: Young Somali women find experience, community in startup boutique. MinnPOST. Retrieved from www.minnpost.com/business/2014/12

Wanchel, E. (August 3, 2016). Teens ask for summer jobs after gangs try to recruit them. *Huffington Post.* Retrieved from: http://www.huffingtonpost.com/entry/teen-boys-get-job-to-avoid-gangs-georgia_us_579f943ae4b08a8e8b5edd3b)

Warland, C., Applegate, D., Schnur, C., & Jones, J. (2015). Providing true opportunity for opportunity youth: Promising practices and principles for helping youth facing barriers to employment. Chicago, IL: Heartland Alliance's National Initiatives on Poverty & Economic Opportunity.

Warren, M. R., & Kupscznk, L. (2014, April). The emergence of a youth justice movement in the United States. Paper presented at the annual meeting of the American Educational Research Association, Philadelphia, PA.

Webley, P., & Nyhus, E. (2013). Economic socialization, saving and assets in European young adults. *Economics of Education Review, 33*, 19–30. doi: 10.1016/j.econedurev.2012.09.001

Weick, K. E. (1995). *Sensemaking in organizations.* Thousand Oaks, CA: Sage Publications.

Weiss, H. E. (2012). The intergenerational transmission of social capital: A developmental approach to adolescent social capital formation. *Sociological Inquiry, 82,* 212–235. doi:10.1111/j.1475-682X.2012.00414.x

Whitman, J. (2007). *Reaching and Serving Teen Victims: A Practical Handbook.* Washington, DC: National Center for Victims of Crime and the National Crime Prevention Council. http://www.ncpc.org/resources/files/pdf/violent-crime/ teen%20victims.pdf

Wilder Research. (2016). Developing preliminary-evidence of metro area YSE program. Prepared for the Sundance Family Foundation. Retrieved from http://www. sundancefamilyfoundation.org/who-we-are-2/mission-and-vision/

Williams, J. P. (2007). Youth-subcultural studies: Sociological traditions and core concepts. *Sociology Compass, 1*(2), 572–593. doi: 10.1111/j.1751-9020.2007.00043.x

Wilson, W. J. (2016). Black youths, joblessness, and the other side of "Black Lives Matter." *Ethnic & Racial Studies, 39*(8), 1450–1457. doi:10.1080/01419870.2016.1153689

Woolcock, M. (1998). Social capital and economic development: Toward a theoretical synthesis and policy framework. *Theory and Society, 27*(2), 151–208. doi: http://www.jstor. org/stable/657866

Woolcock, M. (2001). The place of social capital in understanding social and economic outcomes. *Canadian Journal of Policy Research, 2*(1), 11–17. Retrieved from www.oecd. org/innovation/research/1824913.pdf

Woolcock, M., & Narayan, D. (2000). Social capital: Implications for development theory, research, and policy. *The World Bank Research Observer, 15*(2), 225–249. doi: http:// www.jstor.org/stable/3986417

World Bank. (2013). *World Development Report 2014: Risk and Opportunity—Managing Risk for Development.* Washington, DC: World Bank. https://openknowledge.worldbank. org/handle/10986/16092

Wyn, J., & White, R. (1997). *Rethinking Youth.* London: Sage.

Xiong, C. (2016). Obituary: Sister Jean Thuerauf left North Side Legacy with Cookie Cart. Minneapolis *Star Tribune.* Retreived from http://www.startribune.com/obituary-sister-jean-thuerauf-left-north-side-legacy-with-cookie-cart/383714221/

Yosso, T. J. (2006). Whose culture has capital? A critical race theory discussion of community cultural wealth. *Race, Ethnicity, and Education,* (1), 69–91. doi:10.1080/ 1361332052000341006

Yunus, M. (2011). *Building Social Business: The New Kind of Capitalism that Serves Humanity's Most Pressing Needs.* New York: PublicAffairs Press.

Yunus, M. (2017). *A World of Three Zeros: The New Economics of Zero Poverty, Zero Unemployment, and Zero Carbon Emissions.* New York, NY: Perseus Books.

Zehr, H. (2002, 2014). *The Little Book of Restorative Justice*. New York, NY: Good Books.

Zeichner, K. (2009). *Teacher Education and the Struggle for Social Justice*. New York: Routledge.

Zeldin, S. (2004). Youth as agents of adult and community development. *Applied Developmental Science, 8*(2), 75–90.

INDEX